D0961403

KANSAS

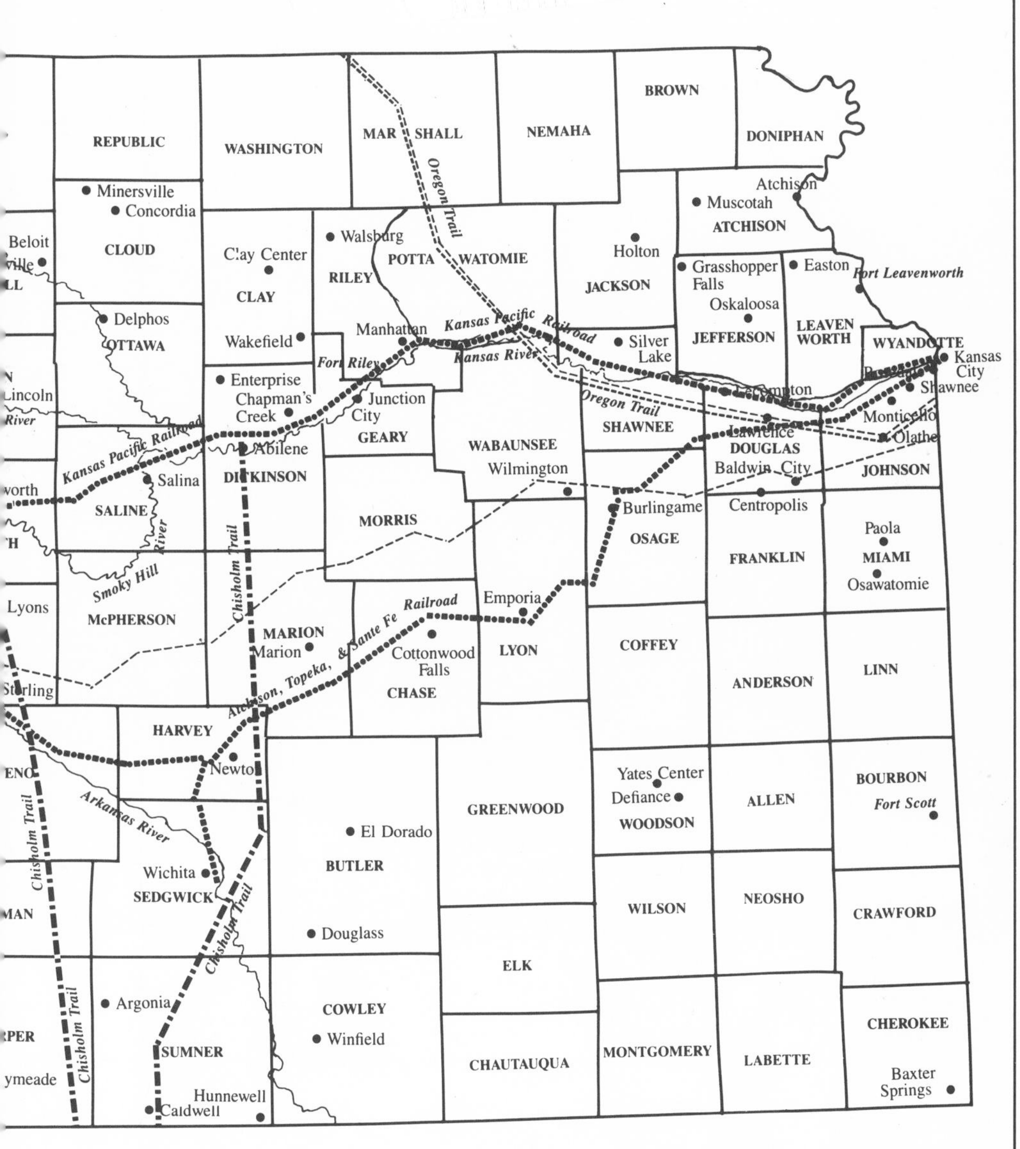
REPUBLIC
WASHINGTON
MAR SHALL
NEMAHA
BROWN
DONIPHAN
Oregon Trail
Minersville
Concordia
CLOUD
Beloit
Clay Center
CLAY
Walsburg
RILEY
POTTA WATOMIE
Holton
JACKSON
Atchison
Muscotah
ATCHISON
Grasshopper Falls
Oskaloosa
JEFFERSON
Easton
LEAVEN WORTH
Fort Leavenworth
Delphos
OTTAWA
Wakefield
Manhattan
Kansas Pacific Railroad
Kansas River
Fort Riley
Silver Lake
WYANDOTTE
Kansas City
Shawnee
Monticello
Olathe
Lincoln
River
Enterprise
Chapman's Creek
Junction City
GEARY
Oregon Trail
SHAWNEE
Lawrence
DOUGLAS
Baldwin City
JOHNSON
Kansas Pacific Railroad
Abilene
DICKINSON
WABAUNSEE
Wilmington
Salina
SALINE
Smoky Hill River
MORRIS
Burlingame
OSAGE
Centropolis
FRANKLIN
Paola
MIAMI
Osawatomie
Chisholm Trail
Lyons
McPHERSON
MARION
Marion
Atchison, Topeka, & Sante Fe Railroad
Cottonwood Falls
CHASE
Emporia
LYON
COFFEY
ANDERSON
LINN
Sterling
HARVEY
Newton
Arkansas River
Chisholm Trail
Yates Center
Defiance
WOODSON
ALLEN
BOURBON
Fort Scott
GREENWOOD
El Dorado
BUTLER
Wichita
SEDGWICK
Chisholm Trail
WILSON
NEOSHO
CRAWFORD
Douglass
ELK
Argonia
COWLEY
Winfield
SUMNER
Hunnewell
Caldwell
CHAUTAUQUA
MONTGOMERY
LABETTE
CHEROKEE
Baxter Springs
Kansas Pacific Railroad
Chisholm Trail
Western Trail

PIONEER WOMEN

Voices from the Kansas Frontier

JOANNA L. STRATTON

Introduction by

ARTHUR M. SCHLESINGER, JR.

SIMON AND SCHUSTER NEW YORK

The photographs and illustrations in *Pioneer Women* are used by permission of the Kansas State Historical Society. The exceptions are the photographs used by courtesy of the author and so identified.

Published by Simon and Schuster
A Division of Gulf & Western Corporation
Simon & Schuster Building
Rockefeller Center
1230 Avenue of the Americas
New York, New York 10020

Designed by Elizabeth Woll
Manufactured in the United States of America

Library of Congress Cataloging in Publication Data

Stratton, Joanna L.
Pioneer women.

Bibliography: p.
Includes index.
1. Women—Kansas—History. 2. Pioneers—Kansas—History. 3. Frontier and pioneer life—Kansas. I. Title.
HQ1438.K2S77 305.4'2'09781 80-15960
ISBN 0-671-22611-8

Acknowledgments

After nearly five years of reading and editing the remembrances of others, it is now my turn to do the reminiscing. All told, these have been the most challenging years of my life. My work on this book has been no less than a labor of love. These pioneer memoirs have enthralled me, these stoic lives have fascinated me, these proud women have inspired me. First and foremost, I thus applaud the eight hundred women who were willing so many years ago to share their experiences and record their recollections.

But I am also indebted to the many others who have contributed their ideas, their help and their encouragement to this book. First of all, I owe special gratitude to the three daughters of Lilla Day Monroe. It was Lenore Monroe Stratton who was responsible for the preservation of these papers. Devoting years of her own life to the project her mother had left unfinished, she alone took on the enormous task of typing, indexing and annotating each of these narratives. Throughout the writing of this book, her assistance has been invaluable to me. I am thankful for her intimate knowledge of Kansas history, for her insight into historical research and for her appreciation of literary style.

Her sisters, Day Monroe and Cynthia L. Monroe, also deserve recognition. I am grateful to Day Monroe for her deep and abiding interest in the creation of this book and in my progress as a writer. Over the years, our long conversations about her mother and the early

Kansas feminists have made the past and my roots especially meaningful. I am also indebted to Cynthia L. Monroe for her unremitting enthusiasm for my undertaking. In the months preceding her death in 1976, she wrote me several times of her mother's hopes and dreams for this women's history. In my most trying hours, it was to her letters that I often turned for encouragement and inspiration.

Academically, I owe special thanks to my two advisers at Harvard. Frank Freidel, Charles Warren Professor of American History, provided me with the initial support for my project. His insight into the frontier period and his critical analysis of these pioneer writings were particularly valuable. Michael F. Jimenez, a history graduate student at the time, contributed greatly to the early development of this book. I am grateful for his perceptive analysis of the historical process, for his unending encouragement of my work, and most of all, for his enduring friendship.

Other individuals made important contributions to the publication of this book. I am grateful to Dena Kleiman of *The New York Times*, who helped to bring these pioneer memoirs out from the obscurity of fifty years. I am also indebted to Lynn Nesbit, my agent, who worked to make my publishing dream a reality. My editor, Nan A. Talese, has been a guiding force and a patient friend throughout the writing of this book. It has been a pleasure and a privilege to work with her. I am grateful to Catherine Shaw for her editorial advice and assistance with this book. In addition, I owe sincere thanks to Nancy Sherbert and the staff of the Kansas State Historical Society, who so generously shared their photographs with me.

Finally, my deepest appreciation goes to my family and the many friends who have shared with me the joys and the frustrations of writing. Among others, I am especially grateful to Patricia Zincke for her sensible advice and steady good humor, to Grady M. Hughes for his empathy and candor, and to Lydia G. Stratton for her infectious enthusiasm.

> "I can no other answer make but thanks,
> And thanks, and ever thanks."*

JOANNA L. STRATTON

* *Twelfth Night*, Act III, Scene 3, lines 14–15.

To my great-grandmother for her independence.
To my grandmother for her wisdom.
To my mother for her strength.

Contents

PART FOUR

PART FIVE

Photo sections follow pages 160 and 256

Introduction

HISTORY IS LIVED in the main by the unknown and forgotten. But historians perforce concentrate on the happy few who leave records, give speeches, write books, make fortunes, hold offices, win or lose battles and thrones. The historical profession is by no means insensitive to this discrepancy, nor complacent about the way the mass of humanity had been consigned forever to the shadows. Modern social historians devise brave new techniques, quantitative and other, to achieve what Emmanuel Le Roy Ladurie has called "the silent, mathematical resurrection of a total past."

Then occasionally voices ring out of the darkness—voices that historians never expected to hear, whose existence they had almost forgotten. This remarkable book is the product of such testimony delivered across the years. General readers too, anyone interested in a deeply human story, stand in debt to Lilla Day Monroe for her enterprise in eliciting these recollections by Kansas pioneer women; to Joanna Stratton for the skill and devotion with which she completed her great-grandmother's work; and, most of all, to the eight hundred women who so many years after recorded their memories, at once fragrant and melancholy, of life on the old frontier.

It is notable that this is a chronicle of women. For women have constituted the most spectacular casualty of traditional history. They have made up at least half the human race; but you could never tell that by looking at the books historians write. The forgotten man is nothing to the forgotten woman. As my father dryly observed sixty years ago in *New Viewpoints in American History*, "All of our great historians have been men and were likely therefore to be influenced by a *sex* interpretation of history all the more potent because unconscious." In recent times the women's-liberation movement has begun to raise the consciousness even of male historians. The result is the belated recognition that women have been around, too, and that life could not have gone on without them. *Pioneer Women* illustrates how poignant such truisms are in a specific context.

Something must be said about the context. In the late twentieth century, after Kansas has lost its early identity and subsided into comfortable desuetude, it is hard to remember that half a century ago the historian Carl Becker could still describe it as "no mere geographical expression, but a 'state of mind,' a religion, and a philosophy in one." It was all these things because the experience of inventing Kansas had been so desperate that only those of purest faith and mightiest will could survive. Kansans had been subject, as Becker pointed out, not just to the normal hazards of the frontier but to an almost unparalleled succession of special calamities—border wars in the 1850s, guerrilla raids in the Civil War, Indian raids thereafter; hot winds, droughts, prairie fires, torrential rains, blizzards, cyclones; locusts, rattlesnakes, gray wolves; the persecutions of nature accompanied by the scourge of man in the form of outlaws, horse thieves, "mortgage fiends" and a contracting currency. "Until 1895, the whole history of the state was a series of disasters," Becker wrote, "and always something new, extreme, bizarre, until the name Kansas became a byword, a synonym for the impossible and the ridiculous." "In God we trusted, in Kansas we busted" was the sardonic farewell of retreating pioneers. After the drought of 1860 Kansas lost nearly a third of its white population. As late as 1896, William Allen White of Emporia wrote, "Kansas has apparently been a plague spot and, in the very garden of the world, has lost population by ten thousands every year."

Those who stuck it out became Kansans, a mystic community set apart by ordeal and survival. "They endured all that even Kansas could inflict," as Becker put it. ". . . Having conquered Kansas, [the Kansan] knows well that there are no worse worlds to conquer." In subsequent years the male Kansan received his share of commemoration. The women were, as usual, forgotten. So the voices in this book are fresh and new—voices of the marvelous women who survived the bushwhackers and the redskins (and the Kansas men), the blistering sun and the angry wind, pursuing the daily round in quiet heroism without ostentation or complaint. They found compensation in watching their families and their homesteads grow, in possessing and subduing the majestic prairie, in the blaze of spring flowers, the dying glories of the autumn sun, the utter silence of the winter snow, in the responsibility indomitable women stoically assumed in the isolation and solitude of the wilderness. And how well they remembered it for Lilla Day Monroe half a century later, and how well they wrote about it, with such vividness, precision and unforced eloquence!

Kansas life had such compensations, but it remained a harsh life for a long time. Recall one of the most familiar passages in American literature:

> When Dorothy stood in the doorway and looked around, she could see nothing but the great gray prairie on every side. Not a tree nor a house broke the broad sweep of flat country that reached the edge of the sky in all directions. The sun had baked the plowed land in a great mass, with little cracks running through it. Even the grass was not green for the sun had burned the tops of the long blades until they were the same gray color to be seen everywhere. Once the house had been painted, but the sun had blistered the paint and the rains washed it away, and now the house was as dull and gray as everything else. When Aunt Em came there to live she was a young pretty wife. The sun and wind had changed her, too. They had taken the sparkle from her eyes and left them a sober gray; they had taken the red from her cheeks and lips, and they were gray also. She was thin and gaunt, and never smiled, now. . . . Uncle Henry never laughed. He worked hard from morning till night, and did not know what joy was. He was gray also, from his long beard to his rough boots, and he looked stern and solemn, and rarely spoke.

The cyclone whirled Dorothy away to follow the golden road to the Emerald City. The contemporaries of Aunt Em and Uncle Henry, lacking so charming an escape, turned to defiance and action. They had put up with the worst that nature could do to them; there was nothing to be done about that; but they saw no reason to put up with misfortunes imposed by man and society.

Once again, as *Pioneer Women* reminds us, the women of Kansas played their role. Mary Ellen Lease called on Kansas farmers to raise less corn and more hell; Carry Nation invaded Kansas saloons with an ax. The Kansas Woman's Christian Temperance Union produced in 1880 the first state prohibition amendment. A woman-suffrage amendment, despite the personal intervention of Susan B. Anthony and Elizabeth Cady Stanton, was less successful. Nonetheless, Kansas had sixteen women mayors by 1900. Lilla Day Monroe, herself the first woman admitted to practice before the Kansas Supreme Court, continued the fight, in time successful, for the suffrage amendment. In the same fervent conviction about the importance of women to history, she collected the testimonies that form the basis for her great-granddaughter's book.

The cumulating social resentments poured into the great Populist revolt and surged behind Bryan in 1896. "What's The Matter With Kansas?" William Allen White of Emporia asked in a famous editorial that year. "Go east and you hear them laugh at Kansas; go west and they sneer at her; go south and they 'cuss' her; go north and they have forgotten her. . . . She has traded places with Arkansas and Timbuctoo."

He continued:

> What's the matter with Kansas? We all know; yet here we are at it again. We have an old mossback Jacksonian who snorts and howls because there is a bathtub in the State House; we are running that old jay for Governor. We have another shabby, wild-eyed, rattle-brained fanatic who has said openly in a dozen speeches that "the rights of the use are paramount to the rights of the owner"; we are running him for Chief Justice, so that capital will come tumbling over itself to get into the state. We have raked the old ash heap of failure in the state and found an old human hoop skirt who has failed as a businessman, who has failed as an editor, who has failed as a preacher, and we are going to run him for Congressman-at-Large. . . . Then, for fear some hint that the state had become respectable might percolate through the civilized portions of the nation, we have decided to send three or four harpies out lecturing, telling the people that Kansas is raising hell and letting the corn go to weed.

This suggests the spirit of the old rambunctious Kansas—though Bill White himself, of course, quickly repented his ferocious words and became in the end the most genial and almost the last (along with his friend Alf M. Landon) exponent of Kansas progressivism. The women of Kansas made their vital contribution to that defiant spirit, and, as this book shows, they had abundantly earned their right to do so. Today we sing songs about being as corny as Kansas in August, but this is another and smugger age. Joanna Stratton's splendid book evokes the Kansas of the pioneers, of the rebels and above all of the Kansas breed of dauntless and independent women.

ARTHUR M. SCHLESINGER, JR.

Foreword

EVER SINCE THE EARLY DAYS of my childhood, my grandmother's spacious Victorian home had been a source of endless fascination for me. Built in 1887 on one of the elm-shaded brick streets of Potwin, Topeka's historic district, the stately frame house offered a quiet link with the past. With its high ceilings, elaborate woodwork and tiled fireplaces, the house possessed a warm and graceful grandeur. Downstairs, the family parlor was comfortably furnished with a Victorian loveseat, old wing chairs and inlaid tables. The elegant library, with its well-worn books and its handsome corner secretary, was a relaxing spot for afternoon reading or evening card games. On hot summer nights, the screened veranda, with its swinging gliders, was a favorite place for family talk. A curving walnut staircase rose to the airy bedrooms above.

But my favorite place of all was the expansive third-floor attic of the house. Tightly crammed with an assortment of family heirlooms and forgotten mementos, the upper rooms had always been a storehouse of surprises. As a child, I spent countless hours there, exploring the trunks of antique gowns and feathered hats and the collection of old campaign buttons. As I grew older, I was enthralled with the shelves of old books and magazines, the boxes of family correspondence and the packets of faded daguerreotypes.

In fact, it was my continuing curiosity about the attic's hidden treasures which led me, during one particular visit, to the filing cabinets wedged beneath the eaves. It was the winter of 1975, and I was visiting my grandmother during a semester break from Harvard. Making my annual pilgrimage to the quiet upper sanctuary, I decided to explore the corner cabinets. Rummaging through the files of family letters and business correspondence, I came upon several drawers filled with old yellowing folders. Carefully labeled and arranged alphabetically, they contained the personal memoirs of eight hundred Kansas women. There lay the collection of pioneer reminiscences which had been a part of my family since the 1920s when Great-Grandmother Monroe set out to record the legacy of frontier women.

It was an exhilarating moment of discovery for me. As I sat poring over the carefully penned writings, a human pageantry came alive before my eyes. There were stories of pioneer mothers and Indian squaws, schoolmarms and circuit riders, cowboys and horse thieves. There were tales about coyotes and grasshoppers, blizzards and cyclones, surprise parties and suffrage campaigns. Some accounts bemoaned the trials of homesteading and the loneliness of pioneer life; others recaptured the excitement of frontier towns and the joys of prairie childhoods. As I read on, I was gripped by the candor of these women. They did not attempt to glorify their accomplishments or minimize their struggles. They did not ask for praise or present self-eulogies. Instead, their writings were filled with the simple details of their day-to-day lives. They described their families, their homes and their communities; they wrote about their fears, their hopes and their dreams.

I paused that morning at the words of Katherine Elspeth Oliver:

> I have been thinking as I wrote of how mother would demur at this autobiographical enterprise: "Writing about me? Oh, there is nothing to be said about me of importance to Kansas—nothing thrilling or momentous about my pioneering days." That is what they will all be saying—these modest pioneer women.
>
> No, they didn't do anything "outstanding"—many of them. There were very few heroines with a capital *H* in the story of Kansas. Their service was their valor; valor to "carry on" . . . in dugout or shack, in tent or "room 'n' lean-to," with the same industry, persistence and cheerfulness as in the comfortable homes "back east"; to carry on and to bring forth with heroism strong sons and daughters for the new Commonwealth.

Inspired by the warmth and grit of these women, I decided to retrieve the treasured narratives from their attic repository. Returning to Harvard with the manuscripts in hand, I set out to rediscover the brave but forgotten lives of a generation of women who had the determination and tenacity to conquer loneliness, withstand privations and overcome long odds.

It was my great-grandmother Lilla Day Monroe who first envisioned this book. Born and raised in rural Indiana, she first came to Kansas in 1884 as the frontier period was drawing to a close. Settling in Wakeeney on the barren western plains, she was an early witness to both the hardships and the pleasures of pioneer life. As she watched Wakeeney develop from a quiet outpost into a lively community, she was continually struck by the strength and resilience of the pioneer women she encountered there. It was her early memory of them which led her, forty years later, to work to record their lives and to preserve their legacy.

In her own lifetime, Lilla Day Monroe was widely acknowledged as one of the most dynamic and influential women in Kansas. Shortly after her arrival in Wakeeney, she met and married a promising young attorney, Lee Monroe. In addition to caring for their four children, she studied the law and worked as a clerk in her husband's law office. Eventually, she gained the legal expertise required to pass the bar examination and, in May of 1895, was admitted to practice before the Kansas Supreme Court, the first woman ever permitted to do so.

When her family moved to Topeka in 1902, Lilla Day Monroe became active in the struggle for woman suffrage. In seeking to establish an effective lobbying organization for the cause, she founded and presided over the Good Government Club. At the same time, she edited her own magazine, *The Club Member*, to better inform women about the suffrage campaign, pending legislation and current events. Likewise, she assumed a prominent role in the Kansas State Suffrage Association, serving as its president for a number of years. When the suffrage amendment was eventually submitted to the Kansas electorate in 1912, she managed the statewide campaign for its final acceptance.

Her lobbying efforts, however, did not end with the passage of the amendment. With the support of women's clubs across the state, she continued to strive for progressive welfare, labor and property laws to protect the well-being of women and children alike. Among her many interests, she lobbied vigorously for equal property rights, minimum-wage standards, improved working conditions, child-hygiene regulations and state primaries.

In later years, Lilla Day Monroe saw the need for a publication that would help women become intelligent voters and informed citizens. In December of 1921, she initiated her second newspaper, *The Kansas Woman's Journal.* Published monthly, this journal served as a statewide forum where women could freely express their views concerning pending legislation, women's rights, welfare issues and current political events.

It was during the 1920s that Lilla Day Monroe launched her effort to chronicle the history of Kansas pioneer women and began to seek out the survivors of the frontier period. Initially, she intended to collect only a limited number of remembrances for a lengthy magazine article. As more women heard of her undertaking, however, the collection began to grow rapidly. By 1925, her efforts had expanded into a full-time project. With the assistance of the Woman's Kansas Day Club, she wrote countless letters to women across the state, urging them to write about their daily lives and experiences as early settlers. In addition, she solicited further contributions through her own *Kansas Woman's Journal*, where a number of the reminiscences were eventually published.

Intending to compile an anthology of these memoirs, she observed:

> Of making books there is no end. Therefore it seems another book ought to carry with it a good and sufficient reason for its being, not merely an excuse but a reason. The reason which seemed to me not only good but most inspirational was the fact that no history, not even the archives of our State Historical Society, with which I soon became connected after coming to Kansas in 1884, carried a good portrayal of the pioneer housewife, and no history of the part women played in the early struggles to make Kansas, a state unique in its cultural ideas, an empire of hard-headed settlers who loved peace enough to fight for it and who brought their children up to love Kansas soil with a passion of patriotism.
>
> From a family of pioneer women, women who had pioneered in Ohio and Indiana, my sympathies were with the Kansas pioneers. Their troubles were so close at hand, their sacrifices cut to the quick, their surroundings were so drab and disheartening that it always brought a lump to one's throat to think of the old days. But

> the women were so brave. They were such valiant soldiers that it seemed to me in some way they should be immortalized in Kansas history. The government had idealized and almost deified the Indian, he was in bronze and plaster. The cowboy had been immortalized in song and story and even the buffalo was used to adorn a government coin withal.
>
> These stories are the record of the woman side of pioneer life. They picture the deprivations, the cruel hardships, the sacrifices, the dangers as no other history ever has done or could do. Histories have to do with the political, the official governmental side of civilization. History chronicles the large and glorious deeds of the standard bearers, but tells little of the men on whose shoulders they are borne to victory, and they tell nothing at all of the courageous women who keep the business of the house going. The world has never seen such hardihood, such perseverance, such devotion, nor such ingenuity in making the best of everything as was displayed by America's pioneer women. Their like has never been known.

As a further testimonial to pioneer women, Lilla Day Monroe initiated a project to have a commemorative statue erected on the grounds of the State Capitol in Topeka. In order to raise funds and publicity for it, she organized the Kansas Pioneer Women's Memorial Association. This organization carried out a statewide funding drive over several years and eventually commissioned a native sculptor, Merrill Gage, to design and create the statuary.

As she explained in her own memoirs:

> The Kansas Pioneer Woman's Memorial Association was organized and chartered for the sole purpose of honoring the pioneer women who helped to lay the foundation of our commonwealth. There was no desire on the part of the organizers to slight father, but simply a wish to bring father's pioneer wife up to his shoulders in the appreciation of hardships. . . . Some here asked why a piece of statuary? Why not a building, something useful? Buildings will always be built as needed. Since buildings require constant care and upkeep, our organization could never go out of business, as we're prone to do when the memorial is done. Besides, a thing of beauty is a joy forever and we want to beautify our State House Square.

Due to her deteriorating health, Lilla Day Monroe eventually gave up her publication of the *Kansas Woman's Journal* in order to devote all of her time and energy to the completion of her pioneer projects. Her work on the memorial statue culminated with the dedication of the site in 1928, but the burdensome task of soliciting and editing the memoirs continued. By 1927 she had already assembled more than six hundred writings from all parts of the state. Yet the arduous work of collecting was far from complete. "Ill health has grievously delayed and hindered my work," she lamented. "On an average, each story requires about ten letters. That does not mean that I wrote ten times for each story, but it means that in gathering these sketches more than six thousand letters went out from my office."

Despite the heavy work load, however, she continued to give her ebbing strength to the project. "It has been my most satisfying piece of public service," she maintained. "I have discovered some of the finest spirits in the whole world. My mail is never uninteresting, no day is hopelessly dull while working upon this history, which is purely a labor of love and appreciation of women."

In the end, however, death intervened before Lilla Day Monroe could complete her self-appointed goal. At her passing in 1929, Lenore Monroe Stratton, my grandmother, assumed the reins of the project. Anxious to fulfill her mother's dream, she devoted her own time and energy over a number of years to this voluminous work, carefully typing, indexing and annotating each of the eight hundred pioneer stories. Eventually, her own family responsibilities and community activities kept her from completing her work on the collection. In time, the narratives were filed away in attic cabinets, the women's words remaining unpublished and their lives quietly forgotten.

In the main, the history of Kansas pioneer women did not begin with the building of family dugouts or the breaking of the tough prairie sod. It did not originate with the crowded railroad cars or the ox-drawn prairie schooners which streamed across the Kansas borders. Instead, it dated back long before to a restive spirit nurtured in the small towns of Indiana, in the clapboard houses of New England and on the stately plantations of the South. It began with a nation determined to expand forever westward and a people thirsting for fresh opportunities. It is a history which spanned four decades and which saw a nation endure the pains of civil war and the turbulence of industrialization.

The women represented in this collection of memoirs came to Kansas primarily in three waves of emigration. Approximately one quarter of them arrived during the territorial years of Kansas history, dating from 1854 until 1861. For the nation at large, this was a period of intense political polarization and sectional animosity. The slavery controversy was at the core of the country's turmoil, with abolitionists pitted against slaveholders and the Northern states at bitter odds with those of the South. During these years, as the country slowly moved toward civil war, Kansas became the first battleground over slavery. While emigrants from the North fought to make Kansas a free state, Southern partisans surged westward with the hope of creating yet another slave state.

It was not until 1865, after four long years of war, that the second major wave of emigration to Kansas began. It was in the decade that followed that nearly half of the women in this collection moved westward with their families. For the United States, this was a pivotal period of change. Not only was the nation trying to rebuild its economy and reunite its people after the ravages of the war, but it was undergoing the rapid and unprecedented process of industrialization. This was the great "Gilded Age," an era which witnessed the emergence of large corporations and wealthy industrialists, of huge factories and long assembly lines. Applauding the "rags-to-riches" heroes of the day, Americans renewed their dedication to hard work, individual effort and national progress. While the East prospered with its factories, its companies and its banks, the West was being populated by homesteaders eager to build homes, develop communities and start new lives.

The remaining twenty-five percent of the women in this anthology came to Kansas during the years 1875 to 1890, the final period of emigration. For many Americans, these were years of increasing dissatisfaction and unrest. Although industrialization brought with it substantial material benefits, it was also accompanied by underlying problems not easily solved. In the burgeoning cities of the Northeast, the new class of industrial laborers often found themselves faced with impersonal working conditions, long shifts, labor strikes and crowded living conditions. In the rural areas of the West and the South, struggling farmers were often encumbered by the vicissitudes of perpetual personal debt, unstable agricultural prices and soaring railroad rates.

Who were these pioneer women? Where did they come from and what were their backgrounds? Why did they leave their homes and what did they hope to find in Kansas?

In a profile of the eight hundred women in this collection, several general characteristics emerge. In the main, these women were from families of average background and modest means. They embarked on their journey to Kansas in quest of greater economic opportunities than had been available to them elsewhere. Most of them were literate women who had received their fundamental educations in country schoolhouses or women's seminaries back home. Predominantly Protestant by religion, they maintained an unwavering faith in God and in the future. Primarily wives and mothers, they lived lives that revolved around the home. With a firm dedication to the welfare of their families, they ultimately set out to civilize the frontier itself.

In geographic background, the majority of these women came from the nearby Midwestern states. Of the women who discussed their former homes, approximately sixty percent came from the states of Illinois, Ohio, Indiana, Iowa and Wisconsin. A quarter of the number were equally divided between the Northeastern states and those of the South. Finally, a small proportion of these women were European immigrants from such countries as Sweden, England, Russia and Germany.

For some of the women, the move to the Kansas frontier was the last stop in a gradual migration westward. Originally from towns and cities in the Eastern coastal states, they had moved continually westward in intermediate steps as new states and territories were opened to white settlement. "I have pioneered all my life, and that's a long time," proclaimed Elizabeth Hobart Woods, whose family had followed a path from Boston through New York to Ohio, Illinois and finally to Kansas. Although pioneer life was more grueling on the barren Kansas plains than it had been in the lusher wooded regions of the East, these seasoned settlers often adjusted more readily to the separation from former homes, friends and kindred.

Most of the women, however, were unfamiliar with and unprepared for the ongoing rigors of pioneer life that lay ahead. Despite the excitement and anticipation shared by most and the sense of high adventure stirring in some, they all were faced with the prospect of leaving the familiar for the unknown. In the end, there was the likelihood of no return. These women were to experience not only the initial pains of separation, but the later pangs of loneliness and isolation that often pierced their quiet hours.

This book is not a chronicle of the political events or economic developments of the frontier period. It is not a history based upon the recollections of statesmen or the interpretations of annalists. Rather, it is a personal account of the pioneer experience, described by those for whom "history" was nothing more than daily life. It is an intimate look inside the dugouts and the soddies, the schools and the barnyards, the stores and the churches of early Kansas. It is an examination of families and friendships, communities and congregations, sewing circles and temperance unions. It is a history written through loneliness and deprivation, but guided by courage and stamina.

This is an unusual history of the frontier, for it is written through the eyes and the words of the women who lived it. Nevertheless, by focusing only on the memoirs of eight hundred particular women, it is ultimately limited in scope and in depth. It is restricted in part by the authors themselves. In soliciting these papers, Lilla Day Monroe gathered only the memoirs of white homesteading women. Although the collection certainly entails a representative cross section of Kansas pioneer women, the voices of the marginal women—the indigent working classes, the barmaids and the prostitutes, the black women and the native Americans—remain unrecorded. Furthermore, of the white women themselves, this group includes only the survivors of the pioneer period. This collection of memoirs does not concern those pioneers who tried and failed; it does not tell of the thousands of other women who gave up hope and retreated to the East.

Topically, this history is confined to the subjects and experiences which these women considered appropriate for publication. Although the authors were frank about the trials and hardships of homesteading, they often avoided discussing the more private and uncomfortable facets of their everyday lives. In their reminiscences, surprisingly few women discussed the anguish of departure or the discomfort of the journey to Kansas. Intimate topics such as pregnancy, childbirth and death were addressed only in the euphemisms of the time, while love and sex were avoided altogether. If schoolteaching brought trials beyond primitive teaching quarters, the women did not mention them. If the bonds of friendship between neighbors gave way to eventual animosities, they did not reveal them. If the strains of pioneering caused disharmony in their families or unhappiness in their marriages, these women were unwilling to record them for posterity.

The manuscripts in this collection are limited not only by the topics they cover but by their genre as well. These writings are personal reminiscences written several decades after the actual events and experiences occurred. They are neither diaries nor letters; they are memoirs. Many of the authors wrote childhood recollections, some composed tributes to their pioneer mothers, others submitted biographies of friends or relatives long since dead. In many instances, memory and retrospection surely led some women to paint romanticized accounts of their lives and experiences. Yet for most women, the lapse of time between the events and their recording did not blur the detail of descriptions. Instead, the intervening years served to deepen the insight and heighten the perspective of the writers. As one author explained: "I find that as the flying years close all vision of the future, my mind, like that of all old people, . . . feeds more on the events of the past, as it must feed on something. I really do now think more of the early events of my life, than those of a later date."

Due to the common experience of everyday living, there is an inevitable repetition of subject matter and writing styles in a collection of this magnitude. As a result, only a portion of the eight hundred pioneer reminiscences have been included in this book. I selected these excerpts for a variety of reasons: historical interest, topical diversity, graphic detail, personal candor and humorous appeal. At best, the editorial process was a difficult and subjective one, and it was often with much regret that I chose to omit particular stories. The remaining unpublished narratives certainly deserve equal recognition, but they cannot be encompassed within the limits of this book alone. An index to the entire Lilla Day Monroe Collection is included as an appendix to this book.

In the course of the years I shared with these remarkable women, they became a part of my own life. I came to know them intimately as individuals and ultimately as friends. Their grit and their determination had conquered hopeless odds, but their patience and their wit lightened and warmed their bleak hours. I lived in their homes and met their neighbors. I worried with them through their darkest nights and exalted in their small triumphs. I understood when they wept and was cheered when they laughed.

Through these memoirs, I found that I had left my own world to travel across Kansas with Carrie Stearns Smith in a jolting Democrat stage. I shivered with Emma Brown in her rain-soaked soddy. I watched Hannah Hoisington defend a neighbor's cabin against a pack of wolves and marveled as Jennie Marcy confronted a stampede of Texas longhorns. I celebrated Christmas Day with little Harriet Adams and joined in a polka with lighthearted Catherine Cavender. I saw Anna Morgan held hostage by the Cheyenne. I witnessed Mrs. Lecleve endure childbirth alone in her cabin. I sang hymns with Lydia Murphy Toothaker and campaigned for woman suffrage with the Reverend Olympia Brown.

These were yesterday's pioneer women whose proud heritage yet has meaning on today's frontier.

JOANNA L. STRATTON

Ad Astra per Aspera
To the Stars Through the Wilderness

—Kansas state motto

PART ONE

CHAPTER ONE

To the Stars Through the Wilderness

The Journey

> *"Pioneering is really a wilderness experience. We all need the wisdom of the wilderness—Moses did, Jesus did, and Paul did. The wilderness is the place to find God, and the city is the place to study the multitude; a knowledge of both makes master builders for the state and nation."*
>
> —Lulu Fuhr

THEY CALLED IT "the Great American Desert." In the eyes of early explorers, Kansas appeared to be little more than an arid wasteland, unfit for cultivation and unsuitable for habitation. As a result, the Kansas wilderness remained relatively unknown until the middle of the nineteenth century. Originally a part of the Louisiana Purchase, it had been strictly maintained by the government as an Indian territory and as such was officially closed to any white settlement. Only a trickle of missionaries, soldiers, and surveyors were allowed to penetrate this barren, unfamiliar landscape.

But by 1850 an ever-increasing population and a growing economy focused attention on the country's need for new land. Expansive and promising, the Great Plains seemed to answer the call of a nation, and in May 1854 Congress, after considerable debate, passed the Kansas-Nebraska Act. With Kansas and Nebraska now open to settlement, a homesteading fever swept across the country. In Kansas alone, there were nearly fifty million acres of virgin grassland for the taking. People of all backgrounds and nationalities, rich or poor, were entitled to stake their claims and own a share of these untried plains.

Within months, settlers from the East, the South, the Midwest and even foreign countries streamed into the prairie heartland. Excited by the cheap land and the new opportunities to be found there, they bravely said goodbye to friends and family and abandoned every routine and comfort of their old lives.

"How our friends crowded around us at parting," wrote Lillie Marcks about her family's departure from Tiffin, Ohio, in May 1869. "Some cried and talked of Indians and bears. I was seven years old, had been staying with friends in Tiffin three weeks and they felt so badly about my going west and had me so beautifully dressed that even my father and mother scarcely knew me. . . .

"I recall my mother's headaches on the trip, and many children dirty and cross, and how we longed for the journey's end."

Like thousands of other women, Melora Espy gave up the security of family ties and old friendships for the promise of a new life in Kansas. "In the year 1853," wrote her biographer, "a young girl of seventeen, even then the Principal of a Young Ladies School in Toledo, Ohio, joined her fortunes with those of her lover, Henry Jefferson Espy, a young lawyer of Sandusky, Ohio; resigned her position as teacher, and went over the Long Trail to become one of the pioneer women of Kansas. To leave permanently one's home and friends, parents, brothers and sisters; to journey a thousand miles, part of the way in an ox wagon, part of the way in a steamboat of the early time, to a strange land inhabited by savages, requires the greatest courage. To forsake culture, plenty, prosperity and peace, for crude living, poverty, adversity and war, requires a poise of soul few possess."

Despite the anguish of parting and the tedium of the long journey west, pioneers continued to emigrate by covered wagon, horseback, stagecoach, steamboat, railroad, and even by foot. For many pioneers the water routes proved to be particularly convenient. After journeying to the nearest departure points along the Ohio or Mississippi River, they boarded steamboats that churned up the Missouri to Kansas. The boats were crowded, the progress was slow and the trip was tedious, but the steamboat remained the most comfortable means of travel, avoiding the jolting passage of the plodding wagons and stages.

As migration increased, the stagecoach became more popular. "The old stagecoach," recalled one passenger, "was built along the lines you so often see now in frontier pictures—two wide seats inside facing each other and a driver's seat high up on the outside front of the vehicle. The baggage was carried on racks at the back and on top. The bottom of the coach was rounded and hung on springs that caused it to rock back and forth in a swaying motion. It was drawn by four horses which were changed every twelve or fifteen miles at stations along the way."

The stagecoach was particularly convenient for the woman emigrant, alone or with children, who followed friends and family westward. However, the trip often proved to be a grueling journey over rough and rutted roads.

In 1867, Carrie Stearns Smith traveled by stagecoach from Kansas City, Missouri, to her new home south of Fort Scott. It was a tiring journey, but also one of adventure and spectacle.

"The stage station," she wrote, "was at a hotel I seem to recall as The Pacific. . . . The stage swung around a corner with a great circling sweep of eight white horses, accoutered in all of harness and ornaments that could catch the sun and the eye. I have often been quizzed as to this statement of eight horses, but I cannot be mistaken; eight seems a superfluity but *there were eight*. It might have been an extra span was being driven to some station below to anticipate a future need of relays. The stage was a Vermont Sanderson, said to be the pioneer stage from coast to coast.

"At last we were all listed and crowded in—wedged would better express the arrangement. The driver cracked his whip and away dashed the beautiful horses. I had been placed by the station agent in the care of a passenger they accosted as Governor Crawford,* a slight invalid-appearing man, wearing a shawl, a fashion not then quite out of vogue. It occurred to me it would have been more appropriate to place the delicate traveler in my care, for he surely appeared the more likely of us two to succumb to the effects of rapid stage travel.

"Our route led south over Westport Road to our first mail station at Westport House, where with a great flourish and clatter of hoofs, we

* That Kansans referred to George A. Crawford (1827–91) as "Governor" was more an expression of frontier courtesy than a statement of fact. In the special election of November 1861, Crawford was elected governor of Kansas, but the state Supreme Court subsequently declared the election illegal. (See A. T. Andreas, *History of the State of Kansas*, pp. 211–12.) In 1864, George Crawford again received the Democratic gubernatorial nomination, but was defeated by the Republican candidate, Samuel J. Crawford. In 1868, Crawford ran for governor a third time, but was once again defeated.

drew up alongside and an exchange of mail bags occurred. Then ho for Shawnee Mission, where at one of the huge original buildings, like formalities were observed. The dashing up and the dashing away from these stations was worthy of a king's retinue, an event that drew small crowds from the immediate vicinity.

"Our route was by no means the shortest distance between more important settlements. We diverged to the southeast and southwest here and there for the delivery of mail or the more practicable fording of streams. Whenever we halted for relays of horses, the traces were loosened, and the released spans marched unled to their long low shed barns, and those to be driven marched each to his accustomed place in front of the stage—not an animal led or driven. Two or three minutes only were consumed in the exchange. . . .

"We reached Paola just at dusk. The hotel was a rude rambling one-story affair, and soon after supper, when fairly abed and about to fall asleep, the sounds of fiddles in the dining-room told that a country dance was beginning. All the sleeping rooms seemed to open out of the dining-room. I occupied one with a lady on her way east to Pleasant Hill. Though very tired, the fiddles, the stamping of stoutly shod feet on the rough floor, and perhaps the excitement attendant on new experiences, kept me awake until 3 A.M., and it seemed I had only caught the merest wink of sleep after dancing ceased, when loud knocking at our door and 'stage leaving!' aroused me.

"I had always been able to dress with real speed, but when I reached the stage at the door, the agent gasped, 'Why, every seat is taken!' And no one of the several men inside offered a solution of the problem. So as I lifted mine eyes to the driver's seat, I managed to beg 'Could I sit with the driver?' The agent put the petition to the one aloft. 'Why, sure,' and I was pulled and hoisted to the seat. I secretly rejoiced. The previous day the presence of a sick child in the stage, poorly cared for by evidently very poor mountain people from Tennessee, had made the journey perforce most disagreeable because of the odor and flies.

"Away we dashed, I fairly holding my breath and the railing at the end of my seat. But the sensation of swift motion and aloftness, the keen air of the October morning's dawn, the unusualness and the unexpectedness of that phase of my journey—it was intoxicating! . . .

"At one point we had forded a stream with a border of brush, and rounding a hill across the ford he [the driver] pointed to a small new grave. Such a sadness possessed me, as I pictured to myself the delay in camp, the suffering of the little one, the absence of medical skill, the death, the burial, and the grief of leaving that freshly heaped mound. But hundreds of such mounds have marked the advance of pioneers. And what stories of grief do they suggest to those travelers who have passed that way."

Later that day, when the Sanderson stagecoach arrived at Fort Scott, Carrie Stearns Smith climbed down from her scenic seat in order to change to another, southbound coach. There was a disappointing delay of a day and a half before an "oilcloth-covered Democrat stage" pulled in for her at four o'clock in the morning.

"I was helped inside and in the darkness we rattled out of the 'Fort,' my only company a roll of freshly tanned leather, the size of a big person's body, placed diagonally across the seats.

"On we clattered, finally crossing several miles of timber on Drywood Creek and at its farthest edge we drew up in the dawn to a log hotel. Here was breakfast. I was chilled by the early ride and asked the Dutch proprietress if I might go into the kitchen to warm. As I drew near the kitchen stove, the swarms of flies on the low ceiling flew down and back with bzz-zz-zz-zz! The housefrau came out with knives and forks from the table where an earlier stage's passengers had eaten, swung around the tea kettle lid and thrust the articles of tableware into the boiling water, hastily drying them on a cloth. 'Heavens!' was my mental ejaculation. 'And I bet on a penny she makes the coffee from that identical kettle.' She did; and I vowed to refrain from coffee, but I was so frozen I verily believe I should have broken that vow if three times that unwashed cutlery had been immersed in that kettle.

"The driver and I breakfasted alone and exchanged brief sentences. Excellent bread, no butter; but lifting the last slice revealed a big grown specimen of cimex lectolarius—familiarly known as bedbug! . . .

"By now the sun was well up. I had made slight acquaintance with the driver, a man of 35 to 40, and I ventured: 'I find the leather unbearable. Cannot I sit in front?' He was quite agreeable. Now I found a different type of prairie, and passing and leaving the few settlers' shacks near Arcadia, we followed the old military road over a barren, treeless stretch of thirty or more miles. There were roving herds of cattle, here and there a bloated carcass. I inquired; 'Flies,' said Mr. Laconic, and further perseverance on my part drew out the details of how an animal, ill-conditioned, often became the victim of concentrated hordes of flies that should have more impartially divided their assiduous attentions among the herd, until the poor beast succumbed, and finally became the most conspicuous object in the landscape. It did not enthuse me at all, even though assured this was bound to become a great stock country.

"Much of the uninteresting stretch passed over that day was later opened up as a great mining region. At this time, however, coal had been found cropping out along creeks or draws in very small quantities, such spots being much favored by campers as furnishing fuel for the campfire where no wood was found.

"The Old Military Road claimed my unaffected interest. For years over this road military supplies had been freighted from Fort Leavenworth, Westport and Missouri points to Fort Worth, Texas, and other places to the southwest. Great herds of cattle and ponies were driven north over this trail. The freightage had been so heavy that for long stretches great cracks had been opened between wheel tracks and often so deep a man's walking stick could be thrust downward and not find bottom. One track had been abandoned, another used until impracticable, then a third, until in places as many as ten or twelve were in existence—all equally worn. This trail is historic, and at one point at least in Crawford County, at Mulberry, where the state line and the public road coincide for a distance with the old trail, the Daughters of the Revolution have placed a tablet commemorating the Old Military Road.

"My driver, after a prolonged interval of silence, mused aloud: 'I suppose I will be hauling you back in about three weeks.' Heavens! 'hauling.' I had never heard the word except as to hauling logs to a mill by chains. Again I queried, delicately. 'Oh, I hauled two young women down to Baxter Springs last summer. They claimed they were going to stay—settlers. But I notice I hauled them back again, over this very road.' My vocabulary was beginning to add new words unto itself."

In the 1860s, a new kind of "hauling" was becoming popular in Kansas: the Kansas Pacific Railroad. Both the Civil War and a growing frontier industry and agriculture had spurred the demand for a transcontinental railroad, and Congress complied, launching, in 1862, the concurrent construction of the Central Pacific eastward from Sacramento and the Union Pacific westward from Omaha. Authorized as a branch of the Union Pacific, the Kansas Pacific line was soon chartered to connect Kansas City and Denver, and by 1863 construction was under way. Advancing rapidly across the state, this system established regular passenger service between Kansas City and Lawrence as early as 1864 and had proceeded westward through Manhattan, Abilene, Salina and Ellsworth by 1867. Slicing straight through Hays and across miles of barren Indian country, the Kansas Pacific finally reached Denver by 1870.

It was in its first year of operation that Mrs. Henry Inman discovered that this spanking new means of transportation was not without its perils.

"In January, 1868, I left my home for Fort Harker, Kansas," she wrote. "In that day the facilities for traveling were not accompanied with the comforts of the present time, but all went fairly well until we reached East St. Louis. There was no bridge then over the Mississippi River, and at midnight I walked over the ice to a boat which took us to St. Louis proper. From there we journeyed on to Salina, Kansas, where our train was waiting to bear us on to Fort Harker, then the terminus of the Union Pacific Railroad.

"It was snowing slightly, but the storm increased, and although Secretary Coburn* denounces the word 'blizzard,' with apologies to him I can substitute no other to express the conditions of the storm we rode into. I had seen picturesque ones in New England, but never where the snow seemed to come from every direction, up as well as down, and seventeen miles west of Salina we became snowbound. The drifts proved too much for our faithful engineer and his engine. So we were left on the open prairie to the mercies of the elements, with complete time for reflection and one entire side of our train buried in snow.

"One passenger car was all we boasted, and I often recall the personnel of that one. Railroad employees, land-seekers—namely 'squatters' as they were then called—furloughed soldiers returning to their respective posts and I, the only woman among them, with a child two years old.

"I often wish I had registered the name of every man, for each one seemed in sympathy with me and made every effort that the situation afforded to do some one little service for our comfort. Yet in a small way I made a slight return and this is how it came about.

"The commanding officer at Fort Harker (for the storm had reached

* Foster Dwight Coburn served as secretary of the Kansas State Board of Agriculture during two terms: 1880–82 and 1894–1914.

there) anticipated the situation [and], knowing that I was on the train, [managed] to get word to me to this effect: I was to use with discretion anything for my comfort and others' with me that I might find in a freight car attached to our train, consigned to the commissary at the Fort. We were here thirty-six hours, and from the first the outlook had been so discouraging that a much less suggestion toward relief would have made me quite happy, so I commenced housekeeping at once.

" 'Uncle Sam' provided bacon and crackers, and the tin washbasin, which had already served the purpose for which it was originally intended, was washed in snow water and was entrusted to no one but myself, the bacon fried in it (and I have never eaten any that tasted better). And our dessert was a little surprise from me. I had brought with me several mince pies (New England ones), carefully packed in my trunk that when my first meal was served in my new home, some one familiar dish would be in evidence. After counting noses I cut the pies so each might have his share, being careful to keep a reserve in case another night of anxiety awaited us—and we soon had occasion to make use of this.

"What we thought an immense drift near the car proved to be a tent. And as the conductor had been regaling us with stories of the border and Indian massacres, one of which had taken place near where we were only a short time previous to this, my anxiety lest I should meet a similar fate of those who had fallen victims was far above normal, when to my relief two railroad laborers, with their horses, broke through the snow, manifesting surprise and delight on finding a refuge so near at hand. One of the horses died but the men seemed in fair condition. As is usual in Kansas, our latch-spring was out, the fire resuscitated, reserve brought forth, and two more made comfortable.

"Late that afternoon our conductor came with the cheerful intelligence that smoke could be seen in the distance, which meant our troubles were nearing an end. A platform car with twenty men provided with shovels literally shoveled us out, took us back to Salina, and Mother Bickerdyke,* who had her home near the station, cared for me until I could go on, which was in two or three days."

* Mary Ann Bickerdyke (1817–1901), familiarly called "Mother" Bickerdyke, was a well-known Army nurse and philanthropist. During the Civil War, she achieved national recognition for her valiant efforts as a Union nurse, both behind the lines and at the front. After the war, she continued her work in behalf of soldiers. Between 1866 and 1868 she raised the funds to

Stagecoaches and railroad trains were convenient for the traveler with few possessions in tow, but for whole families the covered wagon was the most practical and economical means of travel. In a flurry of activity before departure, the wagons were tightly packed with those provisions needed to sustain the family on the long journey; possessions that could not be packed were usually sold. Wedged into the wagon were household utensils—such as skillets and kettles, pewter dishware, lanterns, churns, cookstoves and linens; and farming implements—axes, hoes, saws, hammers and the family plow. Guns and ammunition were also brought along, for hunting and for personal protection. Finally, the travelers painstakingly packed supplies of food and water, including such staples as flour, sugar, salt, bacon, beans, yeast, and vinegar. Occasionally even livestock were tethered to the caravan.

Over the years the prairie schooner—so called because it looked, with its long sturdy frame and high white canopy, like a ship sailing through a sea of grass—became a familiar sight on the frontier. Drawn by a team of horses or hardy oxen, the wagon made its way westward at a slow, walking pace. Usually, the mother and the younger children rode aboard it, while the father and the older children followed alongside. They journeyed on for days and weeks at a time, traveling by day and camping by night and finding sustenance in the fellowship of other travelers.

"There were five covered wagons in our party," recalled Mrs. Edson Baxter. "During our journey we cooked our meals over the fire, Indian fashion, and had a piece of oil cloth spread on the ground for a table; at night some slept in the wagons and others made beds on the ground. . . . We had only one rain storm, and as we were camped near a house the people kindly let the women and children sleep in their house that night. . . .

"Occasionally a horse would get sick, and then it was necessary to lay over for a day, so we would take the big cook stove from father's wagon, which he insisted on bringing to Kansas with him, and set it up, for we always took advantage of such an opportunity to wash and bake. We spent the evenings in talking, telling stories, and singing, and sometimes we would take a walk through towns near where we were camped."

---

settle in Kansas the families of more than three hundred veterans. In later years, she worked to provide relief for the victims of Indian raids, droughts and grasshoppers, and was instrumental in securing pensions for many disabled veterans and Army nurses.

Mrs. Baxter's party was fortunate in having to endure only one rain storm. Often the weather brought heavy winds, sleet or rain. Wheels mired in mud or axles snapped in two meant a sudden halt until repairs could be made. And there were other dangers as well. Beyond each bend was the likelihood of accidents and injuries of all sorts. A broken leg, a snakebite or a cholera outbreak was particularly serious on the trail, where medical help was unavailable. Inevitably, death took its toll among the emigrants, and for the family forced to bury and leave a loved one along the way, these sad moments seemed unbearable.

"Many times I have heard my mother tell of the experiences of the trip," recalled Leslye Hardman Womer. "One that stands out clearly in my memory happened one evening just at sunset, where they had chosen their campsite by a pretty little wooded creek. Just as the fires were well started, another wagon drove up and the folks asked to be allowed to share the beautiful spot for the night. Of course they were always glad to have company and my unmarried aunts were particularly pleased to see a young lady about their own age in the wagon. Visions of a pleasant evening of story telling and singing to the accompaniment of my father's banjo, was in their minds.

"The girls walked around together for a while, talking the usual girl talk, then it began to grow dusk. They remembered the unprepared supper where their help was no doubt needed. The young lady left my aunts and ran lightly toward their own camp fire, swinging her sunbonnet. To reach their fire she had to pass the wagon where the two large horses were tied. As she passed she playfully hit one of the horses with her bonnet and instantly a foot shot out and the girl fell without a sound with a terrible gash in her temple made by the sharp hoof of the horse. She never moved again and was quite dead when her father reached her.

"There was little rest in the little camp that night, and in the early morning a grave was made beside the trail where the body of the young girl was tenderly laid. For a few days the stricken family traveled with my family, but the way soon parted and they never saw or heard of them again."

Finally, the traveler in covered wagon or railroad car or stagecoach would arrive in the county of her destination and face the last lap of her arduous journey. For Lillie Marcks, the seven-year-old whose neighbors had dressed her in finery for the trip, Stranger Station was the gateway to the Kansas prairie. It seemed, at first sight, full of wonders. "[We] were met with lumber wagons to take the entire party to the Bastian home about four miles north on Stranger Creek. Of one thing I am sure, to my mother and me it was a real lark. The road ran along Stranger Creek north, and such a wilderness of willow and other trees, grape vines and hazel brush. Mother would say, 'Oh, how beautiful.'

"As we drove on the prairie, Mother and I could hardly stay in the wagon. The wild flowers covered the prairies in a riot of colours like a beautiful rug. How we longed to gather some. And the gravel beds were new to us.

"And then the hired man said, 'Now we are home already,' and everybody talked, laughed and were happy at a long journey's end. We found waiting for us kind neighbors: long tables of boards were set up out-doors and were soon loaded with food. I did not care about eating, wanted to go back to the flowers and gravel. Took all the children, and such a happy time we had with lovely wild flowers everywhere."

Less happy was the story of Martha Lick Wooden, whose husband and sons had already staked a claim and who arrived at Fort Hays with her two little girls to join them in June of 1878. Her daughter remembered:

"It was night and she was at a loss to know what to do, for she had expected to be met at the train by her husband. He had failed to arrive. She went to a hotel—the best the little town had, but before registering she asked to see the bedroom she was to occupy. She removed the pillow and turned down the sheet and pointed to a bedbug! She refused to stay in that hostelry. Finding another boarding-house, she put up for the night, but declared she was already disgusted with Kansas.

"The next morning early her husband found her back at the railroad station walking up and down and probably wishing she might take the next train for the East, though she never would admit it. He had been delayed and had driven part of the night and yet had failed to meet his little family. There was a joyful time when he found them at the station that morning.

"As soon as the necessary supplies were loaded and the travelers and their baggage stowed in among the boxes and bags, the journey to the claim forty miles away was begun. There was a plain road winding across the prairie for a few miles, then it seemed to lose itself in the thick matted buffalo grass. Mr. Wooden had driven the trail before, and all went well while daylight lasted.

"A stop was made at noon to feed and rest the team, and Mrs. Wooden got her first experience in cooking over a campfire. No more stops were made. Just at dusk the team suddenly began a steep descent and one of those western 'draws' or canyons opened up before her astonished eyes. Nothing like this had she ever seen before, and it was as wonderful as the Grand Canyon of the Colorado seemed to her years after. Darkness deepened rapidly in the canyon and the trail was difficult to follow. Somewhere in its windings the driver made the wrong turn, and after going on for perhaps a half hour, he said, 'Well, I guess I'm lost.'

" 'Lost! Out here on this lonely prairie? And what is that?' said his wife with more of nervous apprehension in her voice than she realized. 'That what? Oh, I guess you hear the coyotes,' he answered. Of all the eerie, dreary experiences, to be lost at night on the prairie on which she had not seen a single habitation all day, then to hear the chorus of coyotes, like hyenas, laughing at one's predicament, this surely was the dreariest.

"Mr. Wooden, who had become more or less prairie wise by this time, turned his team and with lantern in hand, walked ahead of the team as she drove, back to the draw where the wrong turn had been made. After some difficulty the right road—little more than a wagon track—was found and soon the lights of home flashed out."

What force compelled these many travelers to forsake the comforts of their Eastern homes and journey hundreds of miles away into this giant, empty wilderness? What motivated them to endure willingly the seasonal vicissitudes of nature and the daily uncertainties of an uncivilized frontier? Was it the promise of a new life that lured them or some mystical spirit of adventure?

"My memory," wrote Mrs. W. B. Caton, "goes back almost fifty years to a humble home with the library table strewn with literature extolling the wonderful advantages of the new haven for immigrants —Kansas. To me it spelled destruction, desperadoes, and cyclones. I could not agree with my husband that any good could come out of such a country, but the characteristic disposition of the male prevailed, and October 1, 1879, saw us—a wagon, three horses, and our humble household necessities—bound for the 'Promised Land.'

"To say I wept bitterly would but faintly express the ocean of tears I shed on leaving my beloved home and state to take up residence in the 'wild and wooly West.' However, my fears vanished as we traveled toward our Mecca.

"We arrived in Winfield one beautiful Sabbath morning, and to the ringing of the church bells, we wended our way through the attractive hamlet to . . . a beautiful spot on a mound south of the town. As we gazed with rapture over the beautiful valley, encircled by a fine stream of water, we felt that instead of the wild West, we had found God's own country, and were quite content to accept it as our future home."

Beautiful and bountiful, the land was the great lure of Kansas. Some settlers sought freedom, some yearned for prosperity, some craved adventure, but in the end it was the promise of the land that drew them halfway across a continent. Here they could build their own homes, cultivate their own fields and develop their own communities. Undoubtedly, it took a special kind of fortitude to adjust to this harsh terrain. Yet with hard work, imagination and tenacity, the future was theirs to mold. In this new land, God's own country, they reached to the stars through the wilderness.

CHAPTER TWO

Homes of Puncheon, Homes of Sod

The Settlement

"It was such a new world, reaching to the far horizon without break of tree or chimney stack; just sky and grass and grass and sky. . . . The hush was so loud. As I lay in my unplastered upstairs room, the heavens seemed nearer than ever before and awe and beauty and mystery over all."

—Lydia Murphy Toothaker

WITH THE LONG JOURNEY at an end, the emigrants faced the demands of building their homesteads and forging their futures. At first, while the family sought to locate a good homestead site, their home was often no more than their wagon, a tent or a makeshift lean-to. Camped along the roadside, the family set up housekeeping on the open prairie. The meals were cooked over an open fire, and at night the bedrolls were spread out on the hard, dusty ground. For the newcomers, these first days in the wilderness were only a preview of the strenuous life ahead.

In 1873, the Hill family journeyed to Kansas by prairie schooner and pitched a camp on the banks of the Solomon River. In her memoir, Emma Hill described the hardships they faced on their arrival.

"When we crossed the state line into Kansas we were beginning to suffer for water. One night we could find no water for a camp but a farmer who hauled his water six miles gave us a little for supper and breakfast. When we started in the morning he kindly gave us about half a bucketful for each of the horses and told us we would find no water until we got to Belleville. We saw the windmill at Belleville hours before we got there and kept on going until about 2 o'clock. When we drove up to the town well we found a lock on the pump. Water was so scarce that the pump was kept locked to keep farmers from watering their horses. By making inquiries we found that there was a spring a few miles out on the road to Scandia, so we were soon all right.

"When we reached Concordia we found there was no railroad. The wind was blowing a gale so we could not have a campfire. There was no bread in town, so we had to go to the hotel. The baker used an outdoor oven and could not get it hot until the wind went down. Mr. Hill went out and looked around until the bread was baked and he took a supply to camp. That was the last bread we got as there was no bakery in Beloit.

"We wrote to the station agents at Clay Center, Ellsworth and Wilson asking them to notify us at Beloit if any freight arrived. Then we went on to Beloit and made camp on the river bank just below the ford. There Mr. Hill left me with the two boys while he went to spy out the land.

"He came back in about three days with reports. There were three families on the ground, Mr. Callis, Mr. Blakeman and Mr. Elliott. The first two had been there a year or two and were comfortably settled. Mr. Elliott had just come in from Minnesota and was living in a sod shanty. He had spent the summer breaking the prairie and was getting out stone for a house. The house was just started.

"There was a family living near our camp in a one-room log cabin with a dirt floor and they kindly let me come in and make biscuits and bake them in her oven. She had no bread board nor rolling pin and spread a clean newspaper on the rough deal table for me to roll them out on. That cabin surely looked good to me, with a nice clean bed in one corner and a cook stove in another.

"Mr. Hill came back to camp and we loaded up and drove out to Mr. Elliott's and made camp. We left the boys in camp while we mounted the horses and went land hunting. We went out a while that evening and again the next day deciding what we would take.

"The next morning we started to Beloit to buy a cook stove. I was rather helpless around a campfire. It was a cold, raw day with the wind in the north. Poor Tom got tired, so he jumped down off the spring seat and kicked the dashboard with his copper-toed boots and said, 'What for did they make Beloit so far?' I lived on that homestead a good many years and took that long tedious trip to Beloit a good many times, but I think I never took it without remembering what he had said. And I suppose I felt just about like he did when he said it.

"The wind had gone down by the time we got back to camp, and we set up our new cook stove right down in the dry creek bed. I got a good supper, the best we had had for a long time.

"In the morning it was snowing and blowing a gale. Mr. Elliott let us have some poles that he had gotten ready to roof a stable and we fixed up a shelter around the cook stove with horse blankets and old carpet and we did very well. But the oven would not get hot enough to bake. It was too cold to make biscuits so I tried to bake corn bread and when that was a complete failure I threw it away and made some more and carried it over to Elliotts and handed it in and got them to put it in their oven and bake it. I could not get inside as their sod shanty was about ten by twelve with a bed, table, stove, safe and a few chairs. There were five in their family and their friend, Mr. Axtel, with his family from Wilson was there visiting. There were nine people in that small room.

"We got a good breakfast at last, as I could cook on top of the stove all right, and the wind went down towards evening. There is one thing strange about camp cooking, there is never anything left over. No matter how much I would prepare it was all cleaned up. I even learned to feed the dog first to make sure she got anything at all.

"We could do nothing that day but huddle around the stove. But the next day Mr. Hill and Joe and the two Elliott boys went to work and dug a cave in the bank for a stable. They used poles and brush and hay for a roof; broke up some buffalo grass sod, and walled up half of the open side; hung up a horse blanket for the other half; set the stove in one corner, threw hay along one side to make up the beds on. And that all looked good to me.

"The next morning Mr. Hill started for Concordia to take out papers on the land,* expecting to be gone for only three days. When

* The Homestead Act, signed into law on May 20, 1862, became a primary means by which settlers acquired title to their lands. Under its provisions, any person who was the head of a household, including widows and single males, was entitled to 160 acres of federal land. Within six months of his or her initial application, the prospective homesteader was required to have begun improvements for its permanent habitation. In turn, the homestead claim had to be the settler's legal residence for the next five years. After this requisite period, the settler, with the substantiating testimony of two witnesses, was able to officially "prove up" on his land.

he got to Concordia he got notice that the goods were at Waterville, so as he was on his way he went on and got the goods and was gone a week. He had no way to let me know, so I had a rather anxious time. But about 3 o'clock one morning I heard our wagon and knew everything was all right. He came bringing our goods and a few pieces of dimension stuff for doors and window frames, and a few boards, and three bushels of potatoes. Now we were ready to start operations on our homestead."

In locating a prime homestead site, the family sought to find good soil for farming, timber for housing, and water. But the soil and vegetation conditions varied considerably from one part of Kansas to the next. The eastern regions had fertile soil, ample streams and moderate rainfall. With sufficient timber for housing and water for cultivation, this area proved to be relatively hospitable to the pioneering farmer. Traveling westward, however, the emigrants found fewer streams, sparser vegetation and flatter terrain. In some ways, this topography proved easier to cultivate, since there were no forests to clear, no marshes to drain and few stones to extract from the soil. But the serious deficiency of precipitation in the region, coupled with its higher wind velocities and lower humidity levels, placed the western farmers at a serious disadvantage.

In fact, the unending quest for water became an integral part of the pioneer experience. Once the emigrants had settled on their homesteads, a permanent water supply had to be located for both their farming and their personal needs. Running streams and shallow wells provided an ample source of water for the settlers located in the valleys and timbered regions of eastern Kansas. But those who migrated onward to the high western plains were forced to depend on deep underground springs that were troublesome to locate and difficult to tap.

At this time, "water witching" was one popular method of locating underground water supplies. In order to pinpoint a good vein of water, the experienced water witch needed only the forked branch of a peach or willow tree. Stooping low, he took a firm grasp on both ends of the limb and proceeded to pace back and forth over the land. Where there was water, the main stem of the witching rod would bend unmistakably toward the ground to mark the spot.

As a last resort, Ida Gillette sought the help of a local water witch to locate water on her Riley County farm.

"While visiting my brother," she explained, "I found a good sized farm for sale, at what seemed to me a reasonable price. This I bought, paying a small payment down and giving a mortgage for the balance. Of course I did not know until afterwards that the reason that the owners wished to sell was because they had never been able to get any water on the place. That was quite a disadvantage to say the least, but I made up my mind not to get discouraged because I would find water on the farm some place.

"I had never had much faith in water witches and the like but my brother urged me to get an old man who lived nearby who could water witch, and see what he could do. I asked him and he was very glad to do it for me. I was very curious and yet very anxious to know if he really could locate water.

"He took a forked willow stick in each hand and held them straight out in front of him. Where there was water, he said the willow stick would point down immediately. So I watched and waited. Sure enough, after a little wait, as he walked about the grounds, the willow sticks pointed downward and still farther down quicker and at last they went down suddenly. With a sigh of relief, I knew that water was found at last and very conveniently near the house.

"As my brother had just finished drilling a well he sent over the working gang and they were at my place for two weeks drilling the well. The well was 65 feet deep, and there was 11 feet of water. How happy I was when I took my first drink of that cold refreshing water."

Likewise, the regional availability of building materials in Kansas limited the type of house construction from one area to the next. In general, the inhabitants of eastern Kansas found ample supplies of stone and timber to build small but sturdy cabins. Western settlers, on the other hand, did not find traditional building materials and were forced instead to construct their homes out of the prairie sod itself.

The construction of a permanent family home was the first concern of every new homesteader. In the wooded regions of Kansas, the early pioneers sought to find the tallest, straightest trees for their cabins. Chopped and hewn into logs, the timber was hauled to the new home site. After being carefully notched at each end, these logs were then lifted into place, one on top of another. Small sticks and chinks of mud were added to plaster any cracks, thus completing the rough cabin walls.

Often the construction of the new cabin became a festive affair for the entire neighborhood. Always ready to assist one another, the local settlers would join together to help their newest neighbors. While the men set to work building the house, the women gathered to brew hot coffee and bake special breads or cakes for the occasion. For the grateful newcomer, this house-raising party was a warm introduction to the frontier's brand of hospitality.

Hattie Wilson remembered the cooperative construction of her family's first cabin in the valley of Timber Creek.

"My father's and brother's first work was to build a log house," she wrote, "and when they had gotten the logs all out for the walls and 'shakes' (long shingles) split from logs of oak wood and 'puncheon' (long thin boards hewed out with an adz from logs) for the floor, they had a 'house raising' and all the men in the country, for they had gathered in quickly, were invited to help raise it.

"I remember we had eaten most of our provisions up and were waiting to go out to the nearest railroad town to get more, so the only food they had to give the men was cornbread and black coffee with sugar, but they were all in the same situation so they enjoyed and relished it all."

After the log walls were firmly wedged into place, the small one-room cabin was roofed with a frame of rafters and roughly hewn bark shingles. Underneath, the cabin floor initially consisted of nothing more than the bare beaten earth. In time, however, permanent wooden flooring was split from logs and set in place.

"I had a puncheon floor," explained Aura St. John, "and I think but few of you know what that is. They would take a section of saw log about four feet long and split off slabs as thin as they could, from one to four inches thick, and they made a much better floor than dirt. I scrubbed them with a splint broom made from a piece of hickory and they would look so bright and grateful after it. This broom was made by shaving fine splints from the bottom up about eight or ten inches, removing the very center, then shaving from the same distance above down near these at the bottom, turning these down and tying them."

Once the house frame was completed, various openings were cut out for the doors and the windows. At first, an old blanket or a tanned buffalo skin sufficed as the cabin door, but eventually this was replaced by a simple wooden clapboard hung on leather hinges. Likewise, large strips of greased paper served as temporary windowpanes until the family could afford real glass.

Like so many others, Frederica Fischer, the daughter of a prosperous German merchant, left her large and handsome home for a simple log cabin in eastern Kansas. Her daughter recalled: "How different this house was from the three-story house of her girlhood home, with its old pear trees that reached those third-story windows, the girl never dreamed. Imagine her feelings when she first saw the log cabin without windows, door or floor. She thought it was a joke, or perhaps he was showing her a barn, but no, this was to be their home as soon as it could be made livable, and when they spent their first night with neighbors—Mr. and Mrs. Rohm—she learned they too lived in a log cabin. There she was introduced to the method of her future life in a house where living room, bedroom, dining room and kitchen all faced the same direction, for they were all one."

By modern standards, the log cabin was neither beautiful nor comfortable. Usually measuring no more than twelve by sixteen feet, its proportions were certainly confining to the growing family. Nevertheless, pioneer women took special pride and pleasure in making their cabins as cozy as possible. As Lydia Lyons admitted, "The wind whistled through the walls in winter and the dust blew in summer, but we papered the walls with newspapers and made rag carpets for the floor, and thought we were living well, very enthusiastic over the new country we intended to conquer."

In the arid parts of Kansas, dugouts and soddies took the place of the more traditional log cabins. While these western regions lacked adequate timber and stone supplies, the endless miles of prairie turf there became the raw material for house construction. Thick and durable, the tough prairie sod was a valuable commodity to any early homesteader.

For many families, simple dugouts carved in the earth were the easiest structures to build. With their shovels in hand, they literally dug their homes into the sides of hills or ravines. Usually, an entire hillside was hollowed out, leaving only a few small openings for the door and the windows. However, if the mound was not quite high enough, the builders would often dig deep into a bank and then add a front wall and roof of sod bricks to complete the house.

For the most part, the cavelike dugout provided cramped and primitive quarters for the pioneering family. Damp and dark year round, it was practically impossible to keep clean, for dirt from the roof and the walls sifted onto everything. Although its thick earthen walls did afford warm insulation from the cold and strong protection from the wind, in rain the dugout became practically uninhabitable.

"Father made a dugout and covered it with willows and grass," wrote one settler, "and when it rained, the water came through the roof and ran in the door. After the storms, we carried the water out with buckets, then waded around in the mud until it dried up. Then to keep us nerved up, sometimes the bull snakes would get in the roof and now and then one would lose his hold and fall down on the bed, then off on the floor. Mother would grab the hoe and there was something doing and after the fight was over Mr. Bull Snake was dragged outside. Of course there had to be something to keep us from getting discouraged."

Actually, the dugout had drawbacks outside as well as inside. Since its roof was level with the surface of the ground, a dugout carved into the side of a hill was especially difficult to locate. Usually, a single sod chimney or narrow stovepipe jutting out of the ground was the only visible sign of a house underneath. At night, a confused traveler could easily spend several frustrating hours roaming in circles trying to find a particular dugout.

When Martha Lick Wooden pulled up to her prairie dugout after that long, hyena-filled journey from the Hays station (see pages 43–44), she looked over her family's new home with dismay. Years later, her daughter recounted her reaction:

"Home? She had never seen a 'Dugout' or even the picture of one. She was taken into one underground room about fourteen feet square, dug in the side of a bank. The roof was supported by a ridgepole, the ends of which rested in the crotches of two upright poles, and these formed the gables of the roof. The ends of shorter poles rested on the ridgepoles and their opposite ends on the ground; these were rafters. Across them were willows and straw, and on top of all were sods and dirt. It made a good roof overhead, weather proof but not snake proof!

"When daylight came and she had time to 'view' the landscape 'o'er,' she discovered two other dugouts less than a mile away which were the homes of her only neighbors. She knew now why she had not seen any houses all the long road from Fort Hays. 'Bleak and lonely' was her only comment, but she soon fell into line and was using all her energies in making a home and providing for her family."

All too often, however, the flat terrain of western Kansas did not have even the hills and ravines necessary to carve these simple dugouts. With no other materials at hand, the early homebuilders learned instead to create free-standing houses from blocks of the sod they called "prairie marble." Although this type of house was more difficult to construct, it proved to be considerably more practical, comfortable and durable. Over these early years, the sod house became a distinctive style of folk architecture on the Great Plains, a symbol of pioneer ingenuity and perseverance.

In order to build the family "soddy," the settlers first had to stake off a plot of level land. Cleared of grass, the site was smoothed with a spade and packed down hard to form a tough earthen floor. Once the home site was prepared, the builders began the prodigious task of cutting the sod building blocks. Harnessing the strength of several yoke of oxen, they used a special grasshopper plow or sod cutter to slice strips of sod from the earth. A sharp spade was then used to chop the strips into individual bricks. Weighing a full fifty pounds apiece, these blocks generally measured one foot wide, two feet long and four inches thick. Loaded onto the family spring wagon, the chunks of turf were finally hauled to the building site.

In general, the typical sod cabin was constructed by stacking the sod bricks, one layer after another, around the perimeter of the site. Laid with the grass side down, the blocks were normally placed side by side to form walls two feet thick. No mortar or nails were used in the construction of the walls, although loose dirt and mud were often added to fill cracks and crevices. For the cabin door and windows, wooden frames were carefully set in place in order to build the sod walls up around them. Once these walls were completed, the house was covered with a simple frame of cottonwood poles and willow brush, and then topped with additional strips of sod. In all, it took nearly one full acre of prairie turf to provide enough bricks for the average one-room soddy, which usually measured sixteen by twenty feet and weighed nearly ninety tons.

With its massive dirt walls, the sod house provided excellent protection and insulation for the pioneering family. While it remained as cool as a cavern during the hot summer months, it also provided a warm refuge from the numbing temperatures and blizzards of winter. Moreover, the sod cabin was fireproof, capable of withstanding any sweeping prairie fires or flaming Indian arrows.

Yet these houses were by no means luxurious. Like the dugout, the soddy lacked adequate ventilation and seemed perpetually dark, damp and musty. Furthermore, the roof leaked regularly. A heavy rain was liable to soak completely through any sod roof, causing water and mud to drip onto the hapless residents and their belongings.

In Mitchell County, the Brown family had constant trouble with their sod roof. "The roof of the new house was of Kansas dirt," explained Emma Brown, "and when the rains came proved unsatisfactory indeed. We moved into this house about the first of August, 1870, and I felt as happy as a Queen. But a rainy time set in and continued.

"The first of September Mr. Brown took a herd of Texas cattle to Abilene, expecting to return in a few days, but the rains continued and raised the waters in the streams so they could not be forded and, as there were no bridges, he had to wait until the water went down. It was two weeks I was left alone with the children. And the roof leaked!

"Finally when nearly everything in the house was soaked and the fuel gone I went to a neighbor's and found haven in their dugout. But before morning there was six inches of water in it, so we had to make another move. The next shelter was under some boards stood up against a stone wall, [and we remained] there a day and a night.

"How happy we were to have the sun shine out again. I spread all my household goods out to dry and the worst was over when I got them dried and in the house again. But alas, the next morning the rain was pouring down again. However, I had plenty of fuel now and was determined to hold the fort. I raised the leaves of the table and put the children to bed under it and there they slept as sweetly as healthy children sleep."

The dugout and the soddy, though they served the early settlers well, were a far cry from the house most pioneer women had left behind. As Carrie Lassell Detrick remembered: "When our covered wagon drew up beside the door of the one-roomed sod house that father had provided, he helped mother down and I remember how her face looked as she gazed about that barren farm, then threw her arms about his neck and gave way to the only fit of weeping I ever remember seeing her indulge in." Yet in time the women added their own finishing touches to make their simple earthen cabins look like home. Worn carpets, cowhides, or buffalo skins were used to cover the dirt floors, while strips of bright gingham or old newspapers often adorned the rough walls. In the corners, patchwork quilts were draped over beds made of wooden frames and straw-filled mattresses. Dry-goods boxes functioned as tables or bureaus, and old crates or barrels became simple chairs. Traveling trunks were useful as well, serving as makeshift benches, cupboards or cradles.

Emma Hill had warm memories of her first home on the prairie. "In about a week we had a cabin ready to move into," she remembered. "It had a dirt floor and dirt roof, but I tacked muslin overhead and put down lots of hay and spread rag carpet on the floor. I put the tool chest, the trunks, the goods box made into a cupboard and the beds all around the wall to hold down the carpet, as there was nothing to tack it to. The beds had curtains and there was a curtained alcove between the beds that made a good dressing room. So we were real cozy and comfortable."

With the cabin constructed and furnished, the pioneer family was finally ready to start operations on its homestead. Outdoors, they tackled the heavy work of preparing the virgin acreage for cultivation. Indoors, they worked to transform the simple house structure into a warm family home. These new responsibilities did not daunt the newcomers. Enthralled by the open prairie wilderness, they were imbued with a special spirit of adventure and optimism.

"It might seem a cheerless life," mused one woman, "but there were many compensations: the thrill of conquering a new country; the wonderful atmosphere; the attraction of the prairie, which simply gets into your blood and makes you dissatisfied away from it; the low-lying hills and the unobstructed view of the horizon; and the fleecy clouds driven by the never failing winds. The pioneer spirit was continuous in our family."

CHAPTER THREE

Aprons and Plows

Daily Life on the Prairie

"What was the work of a farm woman in those early days? . . . Hers was the work of the Wife and Mother, the Helpmate of her husband, the Home-maker and Home-keeper."

—CLARA HILDEBRAND

IN THE NINETEENTH CENTURY the home was regarded as the proper "place" for women in society, a sphere where women were expected to serve diligently as wives, mothers and housekeepers. For the wealthy woman, this meant a life of leisure; for others, it entailed the endless drudgery of housework and homemaking. Without full legal standing or widespread educational opportunities, most women at this time could not by themselves escape the confines of home and hearth.

To the pioneer woman, home and hearth meant work loads that were heavier than ever. And yet that work was the work of survival. In its isolation, the pioneer family existed as a self-sufficient unit that took pride in its ability to provide for itself and persevere in the face of hardship. Men and women worked together as partners, combining their strengths and talents to provide food and clothing for themselves and their children. As a result, women found themselves on a far more equal footing with their spouses.

"I already had ideas of my own about the husband being the head of the family," proclaimed one pioneer bride. "I had taken the precaution to sound him on 'obey' in the marriage pact and found he did not approve of the term. Approval or no approval, that word 'obey' would have to be left out. I had served my time of tutelage to my parents as all children are supposed to. I was a woman now and capable of being the other half of the head of the family. His word and my word would have equal strength. God had endowed me with reason and understanding and a sense of responsibility. I was going west to try out as a wife and homemaker. How well I have succeeded I leave to those who know me best to tell."

As equally active and capable participants in the family's struggle for survival, women earned the growing respect of their husbands, their children and their communities. In continuing her narrative, Clara Hildebrand went on to discuss the new challenges facing women. "Pioneer life was not all hardship and danger. The outstanding fact is that the environment was such as to bring out and develop the dominant qualities of individual character. Kansas women of that day learned at an early age to depend upon themselves—to do whatever work there was to be done, and to face danger when it must be faced, as calmly as they were able. And there was the compensation of contact with the great new West—a new world—theirs to develop from wild prairie to comfortable homes."

On the Great Plains, the day-to-day lives of the early pioneers were shaped by the topography of the land itself. Unlike other frontier regions, here there were no dense forests for lumbering, no gold reserves for mining, no extensive water routes for shipping. The prairies were endowed with only two essential resources: fertile soil for farming and rich grass for ranching.

The heavy work of transforming the virgin prairies into cultivated farm fields began as soon as the family was settled. Invariably handicapped by poor farming tools and unsophisticated agricultural methods, the homesteaders worked relentlessly to produce enough food and any added income to sustain their families throughout each long year. The land itself, lacking trees and stones, was relatively easy to clear. Staking off the fields, the farmer was soon ready to begin the rigorous process of plowing and planting.

Turning the tough prairie sod was perhaps the most formidable task of all. To cut through the hard ground, a heavy iron breaking plow was indispensable. As Mattie Huffman recalled, "On April 1,

1875, we got to our home near the southern state line. Father had located the place several months before. All the improvements that the place had on it was a meager log house from which the chimney had fallen out. We had barely gotten unloaded when a neighbor man rode up on a donkey and brought us the key to our house. You are no doubt wondering what was locked in the house. Well, it was something very precious—a plow. Father had stored it there after he had located the place. It was to be our means of support. Not a single tree was there; just bare prairie."

Usually, it took the strength of several yoke of oxen and several hardy farmhands to push the plow through the rigid soil. Turning a strip of sod twenty to thirty inches wide, the farmers were ready to sow their seeds. "We prepared the soil for planting with a breaking plow," explained Mrs. J. H. O'Loughlin, "and then used an ax or hatchet to make a hole in the sod, then dropped the seed and closed the hole with our heels. The ground squirrels got part of our seed, but we had very good crops the first year. The next year we ran the sod cutter over this ground, harrowed it, and then seeded it with wheat."

In testing the fertility of their lands, the settlers experimented with such crops as tobacco, hemp, cotton, oats, barley, rye and sorghum. Despite these attempts at diversity, however, they relied heavily upon wheat and corn for their most substantial harvests. In general, corn became the principal crop of the eastern and northern portions of the state, while spring and winter wheat proved particularly well suited to the more arid plains of central and western Kansas.

All too often, a family's first efforts at farming were filled with frustrations. As one woman wrote, "It is difficult today for us to realize what it meant to the first people of Kansas to settle on the broken prairie that had so recently been the homes of Indians, buffalo and other wild things. None of the settlers knew the rich possibilities of the untried fields with their wealth of grain and fruit, when the prairie was untilled and unlimited. Nor did they imagine the hard work, hardships and pests."

For the Shepard family, the first years of farming in western Trego County were difficult ones. Writing in the 1920s, daughter Jessie looked back on those uncertain times. "My parents were Augustus Shepard and Millie M. Shepard," she wrote. "They came to Kansas from a farm in New York state in March 1879. The rest of the family, consisting of my two sisters and myself, came the following fall. Soon my father bought a ranch in Trego County and a large number of sheep. The regulation Sod House was put up and real ranch life began.

"Methods of farming, farm tools even, the western way of handling stock, all were so different from eastern ways that my father, who had always been successful with sheep, soon found his first venture in Kansas a disastrous failure. After that it was wheat, corn, cattle, dairying, hogs, poultry. How much hard work that meant for the women folks only those who have tried it can understand.

"Soon death broke up our home circle and mother must henceforth assume all of the heavy cares and responsibilities of a big ranch, some of it mortgaged, some free and clear, and play the uncertain game of farming and depend on hired help to get the work done.

"Pioneering those days meant for us the expense of wheat put in by hired labor or sometimes on shares, watching the fields develop in all their spring beauty (provided the grain wasn't all blown out of the ground during the winter), grow and ripen into acres of golden loneliness, and then standing helplessly by during a thunder storm followed by hours of burning hot sunshine that fairly cooked the kernels in the heads. An even quicker and more thorough method of destruction was hail.

"One year in particular I recall. It was along in the nineties. We had a large field of corn as fine as corn could grow. One Sunday we drove around the field admiring and rejoicing. It was like a garden, not a weed to be seen and all in the tassel. To us it looked like payment, then came a hot wind and by sundown that corn wasn't worth cutting. Grasp a handful of leaves and you could powder it all up in your hand almost like charred paper. Such things happened far oftener than a crop was grown successfully and harvested without some loss or other.

"One year cinch bugs took the corn. That was the year we had a bunch of about sixty hogs, doing well too, and after the corn was ruined we could hardly give them away.

"Such years as that it was that dairying and poultry saved the day. Butter and eggs, what would people have done without them? But no matter what happened we always planned on next year being a good year and never quite gave up, for along with all the hard work and worry we had lots of fun and good times. Everybody else was facing the same hard times."

At this time, women assumed an active role in the daily farm work.

Faced with a chronic shortage of labor on the frontier, the working family needed all the help it could muster. When the strength of the frontiersman and his sons proved inadequate, the mother and the daughters assisted with the traditionally male tasks of planting and harvesting, tending livestock, hauling water, gathering fuel, and even hunting.

According to Clara Hildebrand, "The pioneer Kansas woman shared her husband's work and interest in the garden, the orchard, the crops and animals of the farm; she worked in the garden and gathered its products. She knew just how each vineyard or tree in the young orchard was coming in. She shared in the hopes for a bountiful crop as the field things sprouted and grew green and tall. Did a horse, dog or other farm animal get badly gored, cut or wounded, hers was the task to cleanse the wound and take the stitches that drew the torn edges together."

For the pioneer woman, procuring the family's daily water supply was a regular part of the household chores. To many women this meant ladling rainwater from an outdoor cistern or drawing bucket after bucket from the nearby well. On more arid lands, a housewife had to trudge a mile or more to the nearest running stream. Filling huge wooden buckets or barrels, she then made the long haul home again. "A prime need was water in the hot weather," recalled J. C. Ruppenthal, "The spring, about half a mile or more distant, was the nearest source of good water. Happily this was clear, cold and of good quality, without tang. Mother began her part in hard labor that endured thereafter almost unremittingly for fifteen years, and that without doubt brought her worn-out to the grave at the age of 58 years. A yoke was made to place across the shoulders, so as to carry at each end a bucket of water, and then water was brought a half mile from spring to house. Both father and mother carried water thus from day to day. When the ponds near the house contained water after showers, this was dipped up for washing and other purposes, but water to drink and to cook with was held to a strict requirement of cleanliness and purity, and used from the spring only, until the well was in shape to yield ample supply."

Gathering the family's fuel supply was another heavy chore. Without any ready source of coal or firewood, the early settlers were forced to devise practical but unconventional fuel substitutes for their heating and cooking needs. Scouring the prairie for anything burnable, they relied on assortments of dried twigs, tufts of grass, hay twists, old corncobs and woody sunflower stalks. By far the most popular sources of fuel, however, were the abundant chunks of dried dung left by grazing herds of cattle and buffalo. In dry weather, the pioneer housewife and her children roamed the grasslands in search of these cow and buffalo chips. Stored in old gunnysacks, the chips were stacked in a dry corner of the family cabin to be burned throughout the long winter months.

In 1879, Emma Smith and her husband, E. T. Smith, staked a claim along the South Sappa Creek. Anxious to build the first campfire on the new homestead, the newcomers could find only shovelfuls of cow chips for fuel. "E. T. and his father set the cook stove on the ground near the creek," explained Emma, "but what could we burn for fuel? There was not a tree nor even a bush in sight to furnish us with fuel. But 'Grandpa' was elected to supply our needs, so taking a basket and pitchfork he started out and soon returned with a well-filled receptacle of what they called 'Chips.' Well, I thought I could do almost anything other people could do, so I put on my mittens, and attempted to make a fire. Then I knew why grandfather needed a pitchfork—his fuel was too wet to burn. But I soon learned by experience how and what to gather to make a fire. 'Chips' were plentiful, as the plains had for years been an open range, first for buffalo then for cattle in great herds which roamed at will over the prairies. The sod house and cow chips were two great factors in making possible the settlement of this country at so early a date."

In general, however, it was the daily housework which consumed most of a woman's time and energy. The prairie housewife put in long hours cooking, cleaning, sewing, laundering and gardening. With the most limited of supplies and without mechanical conveniences, she required diligence and ingenuity for even the simplest chores.

"That the rearing of a family now is a task worthy of the effort of any woman, no one can deny," maintained Harriet Adams. "But the difficulties of the present day are largely due to artificial conditions and luxuries. In the time mother was guiding her household, it was the necessities which made up the bulk of her labors. In thinking over the things mother had to work with, there come forcibly to mind the things she never had to use. Plumbing of any description never lessened her steps. Electricity was unknown, and no house she ever occupied was heated with a furnace."

In particular, the preparation of the family's meals and food supplies took up a large portion of her working day. Few ready-made supplies were available to families isolated on separate homesteads. Although general trading stores eventually opened with a limited quantity and variety of stock, the settlers' chronic shortage of funds reduced their buying power. As a result, the working mother resorted to her own skills and ingenuity to produce the basic food staples.

"The provisioning of a large household," continued Harriet Adams, "required constant attention and foresight. Fruit, when it could be obtained, was preserved, dried and canned. Vegetables were stored and meat preserved and smoked, and all the bread and pastries were made in the kitchen. The aroma of mother's favorite blend of coffee, Mocha and Java, as it roasted in the oven on Saturday mornings still lingers delightfully in my memory of spicy odors."

For the most part, simplicity and monotony characterized the regular diet. Limited in large measure by their own harvests, the settlers relied heavily on corn, wheat and potatoes as their basic staples. During lean times, corn emerged as the primary ingredient of their diet. After all, corn grew abundantly in Kansas, and its versatility made it particularly practical. Eaten plain or cooked as bread, grits, mush, pudding or pancakes, corn was a regular feature of every pioneer table.

Since the wheat harvest was more uncertain from year to year, white flour for baking was considerably harder to come by than the flour ground from corn. Nevertheless, the wheat, when boiled plain or baked into biscuits and flapjacks, did help to stretch the daily food supply. "Our living at first was very scanty," recalled Ida Saxton Moser, "mostly corn coarsely ground or made into hominy. After we had raised a crop of wheat and had some ground, we would invite the neighbors, proudly telling them we would have 'flour doings.' Next it was 'chicken fixings.' And when we could have 'flour doings and chicken fixings' at the same meal we felt we were on the road to prosperity."

On festive occasions, the meager corn and wheat supplies were often baked into special breads, cakes and biscuits. Bessie Wilson recalled one such occasion. "When it was known that Mr. J. B. Jackson was to be married at Ellsworth on September 6, 1875, some of the neighbors planned a surprise for him and his bride on their return. Mother was asked to bake a cake for the affair. In consequence, we ate our bread without butter for several days in order that father might have enough to take to the store and exchange for the amount of sugar necessary to make a cake. This he did, covering the sixteen miles horseback. Mother's was the only cake at this important gathering, and despite the fact that she had no recipe to go by, and that she used sour milk and soda in the making, it was pronounced by those who partook as being all a bride's cake should be."

In addition to their own harvests of grains and vegetables, the pioneers occasionally supplemented their diet with the few fruits that were native to the plains. On hot summer says, the housewife and her younger children often scoured the countryside for any wild berries, grapes, apples or nuts. "Oh, what flavor and fragrance!" reminisced Mrs. F. M. Pearl. "Blackberries were plentiful over in Doniphan County along Missions Bluff, also some wonderful plums. Supposition was that roving Indians brought them from the east and dropped the seed at one of their camps, for they were by no means wild. One variety in size, shape and color was that of a small lemon, another very large red and all told were several distinct varieties.

"There were also wild gooseberries, wild grapes, chokeberries, pawpaws, wild crab apples, hazel nuts, and hickory nuts, if you went far enough to get them, but the one lone fruit on the prairie was the globe apple, which was made into preserves and was very much appreciated on account of the scarcity of fruit.

"Some of the other necessary things gathered was the Mullen plant to be made into candy to ward off winter colds, also horsemint and catnip for teas."

Meat too was a regular part of the daily fare. Many frontier families raised an assortment of barnyard animals in addition to their field crops. The family milking cow provided a daily supply of milk for butter and baking, and poultry was raised for fresh eggs and meat. The barnyard hogs were butchered and smoked, providing a good supply of bacon, ham and salt pork. In addition, small herds of sheep and cattle often grazed on the rich prairie grasses.

At the same time, the prairies also provided the settlers with a bountiful array of wild game for hunting and trapping. "Many years ago," explained Sarah Hammond White, "the resources of this new country were Buffalo, Deer, Wild Turkey and Antelope, Prairie Chicken, Quail and many fur-bearing animals. The settlers subsisted on wild game for meat, particularly Buffalo and Prairie Chicken. The Buffalo roamed at will in western Kansas and woe to the travelers who encountered a herd of them when they decided to go south in the fall of the year as was their custom. In the fall the men usually went west and killed our winter supply. Some of it was dried and hung up to be used as we needed it, and the best parts of the animals were allowed to freeze and put away for winter use. We needed no expensive butcher shops at this time as each family was provided with this buffalo meat, and the prairie chicken was an agreeable change. I can still hear that peculiar noise the prairie chicken made when they went forth in the early morning for their morning meal. But the prairie chicken, like the buffalo, were ruthlessly slain and it is no wonder that after sixty-five years have elapsed they are almost extinct."

Once the animals were killed, skinned and butchered, the housewife took on the work of preserving the meat. "The family supply of meat was killed and cured at home," recalled Clara Hildebrand. "There was the butchering, the cutting and rendering of lard, grinding of sausage, salting and later smoking the meat."

Some of the meat, of course, was kept fresh to be fried plain or simmered in hearty stews, though few pioneer women in the early years had the convenience of wood- or hay-burning stoves. "Our foods were of a coarse variety," explained Sarah Hammond White, "and we had to resort to a very crude way of cooking it. Cook-stoves were unknown in the territory. We used kettles suspended from a wire over the fire-place and boiled most of our food; baking was done in an iron kettle about four inches deep and two and one half from the ground, supported by three iron legs. This baker, as it was called, was covered with an iron lid upon which coals of fire were placed, and the baker was placed on coals of fire too, and I want to say no malleable stoves ever baked better biscuits."

Along with the regular farming and cooking chores, the housewife and her daughters devoted much of their time to sewing. Since ready-made clothes were generally unavailable, virtually all the family's clothing was sewn by hand. Hours were spent stitching new skirts and trousers, darning socks, knitting sweaters and embroidering the household linens.

In the dusty fields and open trails, there was little need or use for elegant fabrics or fashionable frills. Instead, clothing was kept simple, designed for practicality and economy. Women got through the year with only a few drab dresses of faded gingham or calico, a sunbonnet and a plain muslin apron or two. Likewise, men wore simple uniforms of denim overalls, dark cotton work shirts and old dusty caps. Sturdy leather shoes or boots were difficult to come by. Heavy socks and long woolen mufflers were knitted for the cold winter weather, and old coats and shawls brought from the East were used year after year. "For some years," wrote one woman, "a new calico dress was good enough for the best, also cotton hose and calf skin shoes. Most of the children and many grown people went barefoot in the summer time. The leaders of fashion favoring long dresses, low necks and short sleeves were never seen then. Those who could afford a hat treasured it for the Fourth of July. No one thought of going anywhere bareheaded."

Sunday's best was usually no different from this plain workday garb of calico and denim. Simplicity governed, and it was quite a novelty to see a woman dressed in elegant clothing. "Our neighbors were none of them cultured," wrote Carrie Detrick, "and had little if any education, and mother's books were the wonder of the neighborhood. Her clothes, too, were silk and she wore real shoes every day, and nothing like her handsome kid wedding shoes had ever been seen here. I remember one pretty Irish girl who came to mother with tears in her eyes, and begged the loan of those shoes to wear to a dance. She felt sure that she could land a certain dashing cowboy if she could only have proper clothes and shoes."

Faced with a frequent scarcity of cloth, the frontier family often produced its own yarns and wools. In her reminiscences, Mattie Huffman described the long process of producing the winter woolens:

"Since people there did their own weaving of cloth, most everyone kept a small bunch of sheep. One year I remember that a woman sheared ours. She would catch a sheep, tie it, then throw it on the shearing table with ease. That is, it looked easy to me. The wool had to be washed before it could be treated. We always did this at Fall Creek, which was near our house. It was beautifully clear and clean where the water ran over the falls. This process of washing was fun for we children. I now had two brothers, and it kept us all busy to prevent the wool from floating on down the stream after it was sufficiently washed.

"When the wool was dry, we picked it; that is, took out all the trash and burrs. Next we arranged it in rolls about the size of a crayon chalk pencil a yard long, then it was ready to send to the carding machine. Mother would spin the rolls into thread, first on a broach at the wheel, and then made them into skeins. (She had a very large spinning wheel, also a loom for weaving.)

"The next process was the coloring of the yarn. That was an interesting time for me. Mother had a sister who lived on the adjoining farm. She would bring her yarn so that they might work together. It was difficult to get the blue dye just right, as it had to be kept warm and watched over for several days. The red dyeing was easy; also the dark brown made from walnut bark. They would peel the green bark off the trees in the timber and dry it for dye. Sometimes they bought dye stuffs such as logwood for black, madder powder for red.

"I presume that most of my readers would have no idea what my aunt was about to do when I tell you that she would gather quite a number of corn shucks, cut them in two cross-wise and sit down with her lap full of them and a quantity of yarn. Then she would begin winding the knitting yarn on these shucks; about twelve inches on each one, and leaving about as much yarn between each two. When the entire skein was so prepared on the shucks it was then put into the dye. When it was taken out, if the dye was red, for instance, next to the shuck would be the natural white color of the yarn, next to that a pink shade, and next or on the outside it would be red. This was the manner of making what they called clouded yarn."

Emeline Crumb also prepared her own dyes for coloring homespun wools and unbleached muslin. Like the Huffmans, she followed old family recipes for extracting dyes from wild plants and tree barks, producing muted shades of yellow, gray and brown. In describing the home dyeing of cloth, she wrote:

"This was a more intricate process than either making soap or Hulled Corn. The native plants and barks were used. Many women had receits handed down, but the ingredients could not always be obtained. Good browns were produced with walnut bark, when properly set. The Confederate Soldiers' Uniforms were colored with the hulls of butternuts—hence, 'Butternut Brown.'

"A good dark slate or grey was secured by walnut bark, set with sumac 'bobs.' The seed head of sumac has a frosting of very tart acid. Golden Rod was used for yellows—the tint called 'Nankeen.' Rusted iron—or iron fillings—set some colors. Mother used the grit in the grindstone trough for that.

"A bolt of strong unbleached muslin, after passing thru the dyes, made quite nifty dresses, much like the Indian head goods of the present day. And oh, how it did wear—till a girl became so tired of washing and ironing that same one-piece dress, it was a relief when the pony ran against the gate post and tore a huge hole in the skirt. The Indians used many kinds of roots, barks and berries, making lasting colors, equal to the Persian. But they were not inclined to impart their secrets to the Pale Face."

Since ready-made fabrics and clothes were hard to come by, most settlers resorted to refashioning old clothing and household items into garments for the whole family. Hand-me-downs stretched their meager wardrobes as each worn garment was passed from one child to the next. The family trunks were stripped of old dresses, suits and shawls for usable scraps of fabric. Blankets, sheets and linens often provided material for new shirts, skirts and trousers. Even heavy grain sacks proved useful. As one woman declared, "Someone had said that the real pioneer in Kansas didn't wear any underwear, but this was not true of the Ellis County pioneer, and the clothes lines with undergarments advertising I. M. Yost's High Patent Flour were the best evidence."

For the cold winter months, animal skins were carefully preserved by the settlers to be fashioned into heavy leather coats, hats and shoes. The tough hide of the buffalo was particularly useful, as Anna Heaney explained. "The buffalo was indeed their savior. Buffalo robes shut out the terrific cold of the western winters. The bedding that had seemed so ample in the wooded, hilly Ohio country seemed pitifully scant in the little log cabin on the wind-swept prairie. Coats and caps and mittens and leggings were made of this leather, and here the shoemaker's skill in handling leather stood them in good stead."

Like other women, Alzada Baxter had to contend with the shortage of new garments and fabrics. Emigrating to Kansas in the late 1850s, she learned to use her own skills and ingenuity in replenishing the family's wardrobe. As Ada Musgrave, a family friend, recalled, the clothes were fashioned from a variety of different household materials:

"To dress in style was not thought of in those days. Mrs. Baxter told that to get clothing sufficient to protect the body from the cold of winter and from the heat of summer was the only thing thought of. Mrs. Baxter said she very often made shoes, or rather moccasins, for her family from buffalo hides. Several times she traded little trinkets to the Indians for the moccasins. She knitted stockings for the whole family. When Mr. Baxter's shirts, which he had brought with him from the east, wore out, there was no material with which to make new ones. Mrs. Baxter was not long daunted by a simple thing like that but made up a supply of shirts from the canvas which had been used as wagon covers on the trip from the east.

"The problem of trousers for the men was another thing to be taken care of. When the Baxters came to Kansas they expected to have large grain crops and consequently brought a large number of grain sacks with them. The name 'Baxter' was stamped in red across the sacks. As there was no grain to put in the sacks, Mrs. Baxter cut them up and made trousers for her husband from the material. There was no danger of him being lost with his name brightly stamped across the seat of his trousers. Straw hats were made by braiding seven strands of straw and then sewing the braids together by hand. Hats were also often made of buffalo, wolf, and other animal hides. The ingenuity of Mrs. Baxter was taxed to the utmost to find ways of keeping her family properly clothed, but she always won out."

In addition to sewing the family clothing, the housewife devoted a good deal of her spare time to making the household blankets, linens and coverlets. Often sitting at the fireside on quiet evenings, she spent hours stitching window curtains, embroidering table linens, stuffing down pillows or knitting blankets and lap robes. Best of all were the beautiful handmade quilts pieced together with odd bits of calico, muslin and other fabrics.

India Simmons remembered her mother's many creations. "Such quilts!" she wrote, "Appliqued patterns of flowers and ferns, put on with stitches so dainty as to be almost invisible, pieced quilts in basket or sugarbowl or intricate star pattern, each one quilted with six or more spools of thread, the patterns of the quilting brought out in bare relief by padding with cotton each leaf or petal or geometric design; soft, fleecy, home-woven blankets; linens woven from their own flax and embroidered deep in scalloped and cut-out-designs; coverlets, in the blue and white rose pattern, or in the red, white and blue colors with the 'Liberty Tree' woven in, as well as the date of her birth; but crowning joy! a WOOL CARPET, for which she herself had spun and dyed the wool and designed the pattern for the village weaver."

In keeping the family supplied with clean clothing, even the simple chore of laundering proved laborious and time-consuming. On the frontier, most housewives lacked the convenience of boilers and wringers. Instead, they were forced to rely on iron kettles filled with hot water and soft soap. Water, always in short supply, had to be hauled in heavy buckets from the nearby well and hung over the fire to boil. Using a washboard and a stiff brush, it then took vigorous scrubbing and pounding, along with plenty of soft soap, to rid the clothes of ground-in dirt and stains. Once clean, the garments were hung on the line or spread along fences and shrubs to dry in the hot Kansas sun.

At this time, the soap itself was a scarce and valuable commodity. Only by collecting scraps of fat and preparing special ashes was the family able to produce a limited quantity for its personal and laundering needs. As a pioneer, Emeline Crumb followed an old New England recipe for the making of her soft soap. "Soap making was a complicated matter. First, if one was to have good results, it was necessary to burn the right kind of wood. This was hickory as first best, with white oak second. Walnut and other woods, giving a dark ash, were useless.

"A leach, or Hopper, was constructed, of rived clap-boards, set upright on a board platform, with their lower ends converging, and spaces between the boards battened with narrower strips. This platform was grooved around the outer edge, just as is one for cider making. The upper parts of these clap-boards were held in place by a frame with posts at each corner. Then a liberal bunch of straw or hay was placed in the bottom of the hopper. The ashes were put in when taken from fire places or stoves each day, always being careful they contained no fire, for there was always danger of fires getting started on the prairies. If much rain fell, boards were used to cover the leach, it being desirable the ashes should be all collected before they were wet down.

"When the hopper was full, a depression was made in the middle, and clear water poured in each day, until at last the lye began to drip from the groove in the platform. A wooden bucket or stone jar was set under to catch the drippings. When the family did not possess these convenient articles, father went to the woods, cut a proper log, and hewed out a trough, which answered the purpose, just as it did to also water stock, or rock the baby for a cradle.

"If the ashes were leached slowly enough, the lye would be very strong. To be perfect, it should bear up an egg. A fresh egg—not an addled one, which will float anywhere.

"When a bright day came—in the right time of the moon—father set the big soap kettle in the back yard, and brought plenty of dry wood near. All the grease and scraps of fat trimmings that had been collected during the year were brought to the place. In the case of grease which had been tried out, such as that from the entrails of hogs, or saved from the cooking, it could be made up at once. There were likely to be some pounds of meaty scraps and rinds, and these were first cooked in a weak lye, by the most particular housewives. When thoroughly cooked, water was put in a wooden tub and the mess turned in and set aside to cool. The debris settled in the bottom, and a mushy grease on top was partly made soap, later to be used as was the more pure grease. When the grease was thus all prepared, the real presiding genius was called to put the finishing touch.

"A noted painter was once asked, by a fellow artist, what he mixed his paints with to produce such wonderful results. The reply was 'BRAINS.' And this was one ingredient of pioneer soap making.

"The grease being in an indefinite state, it was a matter of experienced judgment how much to put into the kettle of boiling lye. Not infrequently some eastern dame was invited to superintend the process, who invariably brought her knitting along, and sat in the hickory bottomed rocker, out in the sunshine near the soap kettle, telling of bygone days when men hunted bears and women fought Indians in their absence. When the soap was declared done by the best authority present, it was carefully ladeled into a wooden tub containing a few quarts of water, covered and left to cool. If a little salt or rozin had been added it would be hard and could be cut into bars for drying as hard as soap. Turned into a firkin or barrel, and in which it remained until used, it was the popular soft soap. The kind housewives used to scrub their tables and floor. Not the sort used later by politicians."

In addition, women also took on the responsibility of keeping the family healthy. For the pioneers, disease was an insidious adversary. Weakened by poor nutrition and substandard living conditions, they were highly susceptible to illnesses of all sorts. At best, cleanliness was difficult in the confines of a one-room soddy or dugout. Qualified doctors were scarce, hospitals were virtually nonexistent and medical supplies were difficult to obtain. As a result, settlers by the score fell victim to cholera, malaria, smallpox, typhoid, pleurisy and pneumonia.

Among the young, malaria was particularly devastating. Spread by mosquitoes, it attacked its victims with severe chills and fevers. Like others, Minnie Mickel remembered her childhood bouts with the ague. She wrote: "As is usual in new countries where much land is newly broken, there was a great deal of sickness of a malarial nature. Few families escaped the ague and fever. We had our full share of 'the shakes' and were all taught to take our quinine before the days of capsules. Many were the plans to try and disguise the awful bitter, but with indifferent success. Sometimes the whole family would resemble a temporary hospital with all the nurses sick.

"In the better understanding of maturity I often think what burdens father and mother bore of poverty and work and care, which I though willing could not share. I remember their sad, anxious faces when the dark angel seemed to hover over some of us."

Sometimes, however, even a sudden case of the ague seemed to have its practical side. Remembering her father's illness, Anna Biggs wrote: "Malaria or ague, as they called it then, was the bane of the early settlers' lives. When Mr. Biggs was so with it that Mrs. Biggs had to cut the wood, she put the baby behind him on the corded bedstead where his shiverings joggled the baby off to sleep. The early settler in Kansas couldn't waste even an ague chill."

In the home, it was the women who assumed the major burden of nursing and caring for the sick. With calm deliberation, they used what little medical knowledge they had to treat their stricken families. Old-fashioned remedies and potent herbal brews were concocted to ease their patients' pains and cure their ills. Often, these medicinal recipes had passed through family generations. Wild herbs and plant roots of all sorts were brewed into teas or beaten into poultices to quell chills and calm fevers. Along with quinine for the ague, the pioneer mother administered sassafras tea for fevers and buttercup tea for asthma. Strong doses of whiskey, kerosene or turpentine served as antiseptic solutions, while raw beef slabs or live chicken flesh were used to draw the deadly poison from a snake bite. Occasionally, the ailing settlers were even lured by the promised cures of patent medicines.

Along with her special home remedies, Sarah Jayne Oliver made her family follow a strict diet and a hygienic regimen to prevent undue illnesses. Her daughter, Katherine Elspeth Oliver, recalled her mother's determination to keep the family fit:

"My mother loved Kansas from the first. We, her children, have often marvelled that she who had been 'brought up' to the conventional refinements of life and its ordered ways, prepared neither by training nor anticipation for the life of a plainswoman, should have adapted herself so readily to its demands and have conceived a keen zest and pleasure in her new experiences and life, that in all its vicissitudes she should have distinguished herself so gallantly.

"I challenge anyone to produce a situation of more surprise and dismay than the discovery of four youngsters, following their first search for that native delicacy wild gooseberries, frantic with a rash of unknown character. Provisional aid in the form of every remedy known to past experience was administered. It was no ordinary case of 'jiggers.' The children were covered from head to toe and near to spasms from their sufferings, before a neighbor of longer residence came to the rescue with diagnosis and remedy.

"As to ague, malaria and the other maladies common to the new country, mother met them valiantly. Mother should by rights have been a doctor. Treating the sick was a real gift. While seeking health for her husband she had become acquainted with the homeopathic form of medicine—new in those days. Her little box of homeopathic remedies and her skill in diagnosing spared the little family the ravages suffered by many from native maladies, while her advice and aid was of service to the entire neighborhood.

"Father and mother had also, at one of the early-day sanatoriums or 'water cures' of the East, been inducted into the new and simple forms of diet and the science of water hygiene and cure and they became in turn ardent adherents of the same. Our parents felt, and rightly so, that the family regimen, directed on these lines, was largely responsible for bringing us all to adulthood in wholeness and vigor. It required something like Spartan qualities on the part of my mother, I am sure, to persist in a simple diet of cereals, graham gems, vegetables and fruit as staples in a neighborhood where tables groaned with those tempting delicacies hot biscuits, salt pork, fried potatoes and pancakes.

"Although we were exceedingly loyal to the family principles and felt in our hearts that they were of superior character and as such to be staunchly supported, our comparisons when returned from a meal at the neighbors' when we had been permitted to feast generously upon the fare of the Philistines must have been somewhat hard for our parents to bear. That Spartan touch in my dear mother's character! It was very real and needed for her day and her experiences—a firmness holding no flavor of coldness—it was a fine reinforcement indispensable in the rearing of a family."

Oftentimes, women were called on to take care of ailing neighbors as well. Traveling to nearby homesteads, they delivered the newborn, soothed the ill, treated the wounded and even dressed the dead for burial. "Mother's nursing ability," recounted May Crane, "was not confined alone to the home. She would ride on horseback to the home of a sick neighbor, often taking with her the baby, if her services were required for a length of time. She assisted at births and deaths in many homes and in her calm way was a tower of strength to many in trouble. It was always so easy to tell mother one's troubles and even easy to confess one's sins. She always saw all sides and nothing seemed to horrify her, for she always made allowances for human frailty."

When Amy Loucks and her husband, William, moved to Lakin in 1879, the nearest doctor was seventy-five miles away. Knowledgeable in a few basic medical practices, she often served as the local surgeon, midwife or nurse to the surrounding frontier community. In a tribute to her valiant efforts, Amy Loucks's son wrote these words:

"Probably no woman in the history of the pioneers of Western Kansas could have contributed more to the welfare and happiness of humanity during that period than my mother, Amy M. Loucks. She was born August 18, 1843, in Western Pennsylvania, where she was reared. She received a high school and academic education and taught in the public schools. Through association with a brother who was a practicing physician, she became interested in the science of medicine and surgery, and also gave considerable study to those subjects.

"In 1866 she was married to William P. Loucks, and in 1879 they moved to Lakin. At that time, Kearny County was unorganized territory. It was entirely a 'cow country,' there being no substantial settlement. There were no schools, churches or other organized society. The nearest doctor and the nearest approaches to civilization were at Dodge City, seventy-five miles away. The Santa Fe Railroad had extended its line through Lakin in 1872.

"Mother's ability and helpfulness made her a friend to all who were in distress. She treated their injuries, nursed them to health, or said a prayer at their deaths. To show her resourcefulness and ability, we may relate a few instances:

"A man had been scalped by the Indians and left on the prairie for dead. He was found and brought to Lakin. The scalp had not been entirely removed, but it was pulled down over his eyes. She replaced the scalp, stitched it with a fiddle string and common needle, and nursed him back to physical health, communicated with his relatives in the East and sent him to them. Although the poor fellow lived for many years, he never regained his sanity.

"One time a posse summoned her to treat a badly wounded prisoner. With a small vial of carbolic acid as an antiseptic, a knitting needle as a probe and a pair of common pincers, she removed the bullet and saved the man's life. At another time, with a razor as a lance and her embroidery scissors, she once removed three fingers from the crushed hand of a railroad brakeman.

"In those days the railroad ran an immigrant train. One day the conductor telegraphed Mother to meet the train on arrival at Lakin. She found a woman who was about to become a mother, and before she could be removed to a private place it was necessary for my mother to perform the office of midwifery on the freight truck on the depot platform.

"A railroad wreck occurred near Lakin in which several employees were killed and many passengers were injured. Mother administered first aid to a score or more before the arrival of a special train from Dodge City carrying the railroad surgeon. In appreciation of this act, H. R. Nickerson, the division superintendent, and later president of the company, gave her a pass, which courtesy was extended to her as long as he was connected with the railroad.

"As was her wont, she was ministering to the sick when she contracted the disease that took her life, and she passed out March 12, 1905, one son and her husband having preceded her. The words of comfort to her remaining son and host of friends were taken from Matt. 25:34: 'Come ye blessed of my Father, inherit the kingdom prepared for you from the foundation of the world. . . . For I was sick and ye visited me. . . . Inasmuch as ye did it unto one of the least of these, my brethren, ye did it unto me.' "

For these women, life was far from easy. The endless hours of back-breaking toil left little time for rest and leisure. Day in and day out, they worked in the house and in the fields to produce the basic necessities of life and to build a future for their children. At first, the heavy work load seemed almost unbearable; it was physically exhausting and emotionally draining. Over the years, however, most women learned to abide the drudgery and monotony which filled their lives. They developed a certain fortitude and resilience which enabled them to withstand the privations and overcome the hardships.

One woman, turning her thoughts back to those days of toil and tribulation, had only praise for the tireless efforts and unyielding strength of the pioneer mother. "Much has been said and written of the life of the Kansas pioneer, but woman in her unfading laurels has stood the acid test. Theirs were the lonely days spent in the little cabins working and striving to advance their cause for humanity's sake. Lonesome and homesick, the little Kansas mother stood at her post of duty, wife, mother, neighbor and friend to all in those early days."

PART TWO

CHAPTER FOUR

Days of Valor
Fighting the Wild

"Imagine, if you can, these pioneer women so suddenly transplanted from homes of comforts in eastern states to these bare, treeless, wind-swept, sun-scorched prairies with no comforts, not even a familiar face."

—LIZZIE ANTHONY OPDYKE

FOR SETTLERS LIKE THE OPDYKES, Kansas was a harsh and formidable environment. Settling miles apart from one another, the emigrants faced the starkness of the wilderness alone. Deprivation, isolation and desolation were facets of everyday life for men and women alike.

To the pioneer woman, the day-to-day uncertainties of wilderness life proved especially harrowing. During the working hours of the day, her husband was frequently too far out of range to respond to any call for assistance. Furthermore, circumstances often required him to leave his family for days or weeks at a time. Setting off on trading or hunting expeditions, the frontiersman left his family unguarded with only the hope of his safe return.

Such long absences were wearing for the waiting mother. Burdened with both the maintenance and the protection of the family homestead, she could rely on no one but herself. In these lonely circumstances, she fought the wilderness with her own imagination, skill, common sense and determination.

Allena A. Clark had her own ways of coping with a lonely day or a sudden emergency. Her daughter Esther remembered:

". . . the unbroken prairies stretched for miles outside, and the wistful-faced sheep were always near at hand. Often mother used to go out and lie down among them, for company, when she was alone for the day.

"When the spring freshets came, the sheep were on the wrong side of the river, and it was my mother who manned one of the three wagons that went back and forth across the rising waters until the last sheep was safely on the home side. She has told me of the terror that possessed her during those hours, with the water coming up steadily to the wagon bed. To this day, there is a superstitious dread of water in the heart of every one of our family.

"Mother has always been the gamest one of us. I can remember her hanging on to the reins of a runaway mule team, her black hair tumbling out of its pins and over her shoulders, her face set and white, while one small girl clung with chattering teeth to the sides of the rocking wagon and a baby sister bounced about on the floor in paralyzed wonder. I remember, too, the things the men said about 'Leny's nerve.' But I think, as much courage as it took to hang on to the reins that day, it took more to live twenty-four hours at a time, month in and out, on the lonely and lovely prairie, without giving up to the loneliness."

That loneliness, usually borne with dignity and silence, could at times express itself in unexpected ways. Mary Furguson Darrah recalled a time when "Mr. Hilton, a pioneer, told his wife that he was going to Little River for wood. She asked to go with him . . . She hadn't seen a tree for two years, and when they arrived at Little River she put her arms around a tree and hugged it until she was hysterical."

Nightfall, blanketing the prairie in a dense, boundless blackness, brought an even keener sense of solitude to the pioneer home. The profound silence was broken only by the occasional chirr of a cricket or the gentle swish of the tall prairie grass—or by the call of the wild. For it was during the black nights that the howl of the coyote and the wolf spread terror throughout every frontier homestead. Often roaming the plains in packs, these rapacious animals would attack without provocation or mercy.

"In the summer of 1872 and '73," recalled S. N. Hoisington, "the gray wolves and coyotes were very numerous. It was not safe to go out across the prairies without a weapon of some kind. My mother was a nurse and doctor combined. In early girlhood she used to help her brother mix his medicines, and after she came to Kansas people came for miles for her to doctor their families.

"A man by the name of Johnson had filed on a claim just west of us, and had built a sod house. He and his wife lived there two years, when he went to Salina to secure work. He was gone two or three months, and wrote home once or twice, but his wife grew very homesick for her folks in the east, and would come over to our house to visit mother.

"Mother tried to cheer her up, but she continued to worry until she got bed fast with the fever. At night she was frightened because the wolves would scratch on the door, on the sod and on the windows, so my mother and I started to sit up nights with her. I would bring my revolver and ammunition and axe, and some good-sized clubs.

"The odor from the sick woman seemed to attract the wolves, and they grew bolder and bolder. I would step out, fire off the revolver and they would settle back for a while when they would start a new attack. I shot one through the window and I found him lying dead in the morning.

"Finally the woman died and mother laid her out. Father took some wide boards that we had in our loft and made a coffin for her. Mother made a pillow and trimmed it with black cloth, and we also painted the coffin black.

"After that the wolves were more determined than ever to get in. One got his head in between the door casing and as he was trying to wriggle through, mother struck him in the head with an axe and killed him. I shot one coming through the window. After that they quieted down for about half an hour, when they came back again. I stepped out and fired at two of them but I only wounded one. Their howling was awful. We fought these wolves five nights in succession, during which time we killed and wounded four gray wolves and two coyotes.

"When Mr. Johnson arrived home and found his wife dead and his house badly torn down by wolves he fainted away. . . . After the funeral he sold out and moved away."

To apprehensive settlers, the coyote was not the only terror of the night. Prairie fires, sweeping furiously across the plains, were a constant worry to families isolated on separate homesteads. From late summer through the autumn months, the endless miles of tall prairie grass became a vast tinderbox, dry and brown from the scorching summer weather. It took only a quick spark from an untended campfire or a passing train engine, or a stroke of lightning, to set the countryside ablaze. Within minutes, great clouds of heavy black smoke would fill the autumn air, and the skies would redden from the brilliant inferno below.

"In those days of endless sweep of prairies," wrote Agnes Barry, "when the tall grass became dry from premature drying from drought or early frost, it was a signal for close vigilance in watching the horizon all around for prairie fires. A light against the sky told of a prairie fire in that direction and great anxiety was felt if the wind happened to be in your direction. At times the fires would be such that the flames could be seen creeping up the hillsides, and would spread over great stretches of ground. The Saline River which almost surrounded our place was considered a security, but sometimes the gales of wind blowing masses of loose grass or weeds would cause the fire to 'jump' the river. Excitement was keen whenever the fires were seen, and the men always took wet sacks and hastened to fight the flames, sometimes working for hours before it was under control."

For protection against the fires, most homesteaders plowed wide strips of ground around their property. Although these furrows were designed to halt the spread of any fire, they were not always foolproof. Sweeping flames carried by a stiff wind could easily jump a fire guard and threaten homes and fields alike. In this regard, the frontier family was always on guard and stood ready to battle any sudden fire. At the first sign of smoke or flames, they raced forward with buckets of water, pails of dirt, and wet blankets or grain sacks to help douse the flames.

Lillian Smith well remembered the many nights spent fighting fires which threatened her family's farm. "Many a time my mother stayed up all night watching the red glare of the prairie fires in more than one direction, in fear and trembling that they might come swooping down upon us asleep in our little log cabin. However, she was always prepared. As soon as she would see the fire getting close, away we would go with our buckets of water and rags tied to hoes, rakes and sticks, wet them and set a back fire to meet the monster coming, so when it reached our line we would stand still and wait until we knew it had passed us by for that time.

"There were no barns then, so frames for sheds and stables were constructed of small trees cut from the timber, and haystacks were built beside them for walls, the tops covered with hay, in that way making good shelters for cows and horses. With such things that close to the house, one can realize in what a position we would be in case one of those prairie fires had reached them."

Harriet Walter also had vivid memories of the fires which threatened her family's farm in Lincoln. "One spring a heavy smoke was seen in the southeast over towards Minersville, and Mr. McIntyre, as was the custom of every man when the fire was not near his home, grabbed a sack and went to meet it. His neighbor, George, living a mile south, had a very cross cow and everyone in the community was afraid of her, as she did not hesitate at all to use her horns on anyone except her owner. So, when Mr. McIntyre came bounding down the hill from the north, he was frightened nearly to death to find that he had almost leaped on this cow. It was hard to tell which was the more frightened, the cow or himself, but he certainly felt a great relief to see the cow turn tail and flee.

"As he advanced to meet the fire he found a great many of the neighbors already fighting, with blackened faces and smarting eyes. Before it was put out an old Irish woman, by the name of Porter, was burned trying to save her possessions, and our home was saved with the fire a little more than a mile away. Another time one came from the northeast crossing our farm diagonally, burning quite a bit of hay and the hedge trees which had been set with a great deal of care and labor around each forty of land.

"One day in May I was gathering wild flowers on a hill opposite our house when I discovered fire creeping along the roadside and almost to a meadow which was in front of our house. The grass there was very tall and rank, and I knew, child that I was, that if the fire ever got in there our home was doomed. What would you have done? Well, I took off my petticoat and beat till I was exhausted but every spark was out.

"The worst scare that I ever had by fire, though, was when a little girl of eight. We had been out with father burning off the pasture as was the custom of every spring, because the grass grew so rank and the new growth would come on quicker if the old was burned off. So on Saturday evening, as there was no wind, we all assisted in the 'burning off.' Sunday afternoon the wind veered to the north and a cowchip which had smouldered unnoticed was blown into some trash along the hedge row and the mischief was done.

"My father's feed lots were perhaps an eighth of a mile south of this hedge row. I've forgotten what the fence was made of, but I think of six-inch plank. One thing I remember vividly and that was the wind break which was one hundred feet long, and the sheds were of prairie hay. I realized only too well what that meant. My childish mind was filled with horror as I ran to my father to tell him the awful news. He sent me to a neighbor a quarter of a mile away for help and I ran, gasping for breath when I arrived. The men succeeded in saving all the stock except one small calf which ran back into the flames. My, what a brawling and turmoil there was though, because all animals seem to be crazed by fire."

In 1877, Anna and Jacob Ruppenthal brought their five children to a homestead ten miles north of Wilson, Kansas. Like other families, the Ruppenthals experienced the trials and tribulations of farming on the wide-open prairie. As J. C. Ruppenthal later explained, prairie fires were a constant source of worry:

"In the days of endless sweep of prairie, of grass without limit for many, many miles, the ripening of the grass in early fall or its premature drying from drought was signal for renewal of nightly vigilance in watching the horizon all around. Every light against the sky told of a prairie fire in that direction. The direction of the wind, either from or opposite the direction of such fire, or sidewise, the unsteadiness of wind with possibility of veering so as to bring fire toward the home—all these were noted. The last act at night, after seeing that the children were all asleep, and all quiet among the livestock in sheds, pens and corrals, was to sweep the entire horizon for signs of flame.

"Many times, on awakening in the dead of night, the room was light with reflection from the sky, shining thru uncurtained windows from some fire ten or twenty or fifty miles away. Often in the small hours mother watched from window to window to see if the light died away, indicating that the fire had gone out, or had grown brighter threatening a wider scope of blackened prairie behind it.

"At times the flames themselves were visible at night up to twenty or twenty-five miles away, as they crept up hills in the buffalo grass, or flared longer in redtop bunch grass, and when the fire rolled down into a hollow in big blue stem grass, though the flames might not be seen, the general red glare in the sky told somewhat of the heat and light from the tall grass below. Despite the fear inspired by a prairie fire, there was a fascination to watch a fire by night, advancing, brightening, showing masses of solid flame or myriads of tiny jets that flickered and went out, to flash again farther along. At times the silhouettes of men fighting could be seen against the background of distant flames.

"Some freighters, in revenge for the shutting off of the road by the Twin Groves by Philip Gabel, set fire to the dry grass between Dry Hollow and our log house. We new settlers were without the slightest notion what to do. Father hastily turned the livestock loose. The wagon was drawn onto a patch of plowed ground near the house. Household goods were hastily carried out to the same place of refuge.

"Then father took a shovel and started toward the fire raging in flames in tall blue stem grass in the creek bottom 80 rods away. A man dashed up on horseback and called to him to drop his shovel and get some wet grain sacks. At once the five children huddled on the plowed patch were admonished to stay there. Mother and father each seized the 'American extra heavy A seamless' white grain sacks, dipped them into water to wet them well, and then hastened toward the fire.

"A number of neighbors came too, and perhaps a dozen or so in all fought the flames for hours and finally subdued them, though considerable good timber was burned over and fine young trees killed. In this fight with fire, fear lent power to mother and she fought without stopping, heeding nothing of the admonitions of the men fighters who assured her she need not work so hard. She wet sacks and carried sacks and smote the flames of burning grass, even as any of the men, and ventured to the thickest and hottest of the line where the fire ate steadily into the dry grass.

"Several years later a similar prairie fire swept down on the east side of the homestead. Again mother pressed to the front and labored there until all danger was past. For the several women who gathered but took no part she had a feeling very akin to contempt, tho not disclosed to them. For her, there was danger and she saw nothing but to exert every ounce of strength to beat out the fire."

Women gradually learned to cope with prairie loneliness and to cherish whatever neighboring was possible. "There was just a cotton-wood cabin on the farm," recalled Anne Bingham, "with one room and a loft reached by a ladder. There was not a tree nearer than the little creek, and our nearest neighbor lived in a 'ravine' out of sight about a half a mile away. We were as much isolated as if we were miles from a neighbor, and not a dwelling in sight. I never saw a light from a home at night all the time we lived on the farm.

"Our home in the ravine was miles from the highway, but I had the satisfaction of knowing that when anyone came to see us, they did not come from convenience on the way, but really did want to see us. Then we were not troubled with tramps. But I did wish many times that we lived on the road to relieve the loneliness and besides in case of accident or sudden illness or snake bite."

The isolation of frontier living seemed particularly alarming during times of unforeseen crisis. Sudden accidents, illness, or death often became terrifying ordeals when the nearest neighbor or town lay many miles away. Pregnancy and childbirth involved particular apprehension for the pioneer woman and her family. During pregnancy, adequate medical supervision was totally lacking. Likewise, the expectant mother often had very little female company to console and guide her through any difficult times. Worse yet, an unbalanced diet, a heavy work load and poor housing conditions placed serious physical handicaps on the pregnant woman and her unborn child as well.

Childbirth itself was often the most difficult time of all. For the most part, women struggled through labor and delivery with little assistance. While a practicing physician was occasionally available to them, blizzards, floods or other mishaps often delayed him until it was too late. In many communities, the tireless hands of an experienced midwife brought some relief to the new mother. Yet all too often the woman isolated on her homestead found no medical help forthcoming. Instead, she relied only on the assistance of an anxious husband, a concerned neighbor or an older son or daughter.

One woman, Mrs. A. S. Lecleve, did not have even this much help. As her daughter, Annette Lecleve Botkin, shyly explained, "My parents settled in Rice County, Kansas, in 1873. Their house was three miles from the nearest neighbor. Ellsworth or Sterling was their nearest trading point, both over sixteen miles away.

"It was the last of July, and my father was thinking of the long winter ahead, and perhaps the blizzards to come. And at that time there was not a tree in sight. The little four-room frame house (at that time the only frame house in the county) had to be kept warm, for there were a couple of little children already in the home and the stork was expected to make his appearance again in a short time. So my father arose early and started on his all-day trip to Mule Creek to get a load of wood. Mule Creek was about seventeen miles away.

"He had no sooner gotten out of sight, than my mother knew that the stork, being an undependable sort of bird, had decided that it was time to leave his precious bundle. Now that was a terrifying situation. Alone with two babies, one four and the other eighteen months, not a neighbor that could be called, no doctor to be gotten.

"So my brave mother got the baby clothes together on a chair by the bed, water and scissors and what else was needed to take care of the baby; drew a bucket of fresh water from a sixty-foot well; made some bread-and-butter sandwiches; set out some milk for the babies. And when Rover had orders to take care of the babies he never let them out of his sight, for at that time any bunch of weeds might harbor a rattlesnake.

"So, at about noon the stork left a fine baby boy. My father arrived home about dusk with a big load of wood and congratulating himself that he would at least have some wood to burn on very cold days. My mother, having fainted a number of times in her attempt to dress the baby, had succeeded at last; and when my father came in he found a very uncomfortable but brave and thankful mother, thankful that he had returned home with the precious wood, and that she and the baby were alright."

In these difficult times, the pioneer mother experienced many such long and lonely hours awaiting the return of her husband from his daily expeditions. During her first years of pioneering, Anne Bingham composed, in the romantic diction of the time, an account of the quiet expectancy and dread she felt as a young wife. Fifty years later she sent the account to Lilla Day Monroe, noting that she spent "days and days of it when my husband was obliged to go to town":

"The day is gone. The sunbeams slant across the room and shadows lengthening out of doors are further thrown upon the grassy hillsides, almost enfolding them in fond embrace.

"A woman sits alone. Her work is done and she looks anxiously at the time to see if the hour has not arrived when her loved one will be at home, for she has been alone all day with just a little child to bear her company.

"The hours fly fast when work employs, but tired hands and anxious heart must give up now, and watch the distance down the road as far as eye can reach. The dear one is so prompt to come, that she can measure out the time almost that he will be away.

"He is not yet in sight. She rests her straining eyes, shading them with her hands from the rays of the setting sun.

"The minutes go so slow and he should be here now. Oh, what if something may have happened and she would never look into those dear eyes again. She cannot bear the thought and her own eyes grow dim with gathering tears.

"The little child draws near and seeing the anxious look tries to comfort, saying, 'Don't worry, Mama, Papa'll come soon.' The dog shares in the longing for his master, and trots along the path, stopping to listen for the tread of the horses' feet. He crouches low, and finally springing up, pricks up his ears and barking joyously, bounds away to meet the moving object just coming into view, across the span between the clumps of trees.

"As the fond absent one draws nearer, the woman's anxious look is lessening and tears are almost falling in blessed thankfulness.

"The sun has gone below the western horizon and dewy fragrance falls upon the valley. She whose lonely hours were filled with loving thoughts and anxious heart wears now a happy look and says when he is near enough to hear, 'I am so glad that you are safe at home.' The loving child raises her tiny face to get the welcome kiss and greets her papa with 'I knew that you would come, dear papa, I knew that you could come.'

"The scene is changed and now the woman looks no longer, for her dear family is all away, to come no more. She now looks forward to the time when she will go to them. All her hours are lonely now and memory only brings her sad and mournful thoughts of bygone days."

CHAPTER FIVE

Days of Darkness
Fighting the Elements

"There were many tearful occasions for the tearful type. There were days and months without human fellowship, there were frightful blizzards, drouth destroying seasons . . . and many pitiful deprivations, but there were also compensations for the brave, joyous, determined pioneer."

—LULU FUHR

FOR ALL THE TERRORS of isolation or attacking wolves, the frontier family soon learned that its worst enemy was nature itself. In Kansas, each season carried its own perils. Spring might favor the farmer with sunny skies and balmy temperatures; yet often melting snows and spring rainstorms caused torrential floods that menaced home and field alike. Tornadoes, with their deafening roar and deadly funnels, often ripped across the land, obliterating everything in their path. Summer, in turn, was apt to unleash droughts and hot winds that withered the crops and crippled the fall harvest. Plagues of grasshoppers devoured entire cultivated fields and miles of prairie foliage. Finally, the bitter winter season brought numbing temperatures and crushing blizzards.

Dwarfed by the endless sweep of grass and sky, the frontier family found little protection or relief from these seasonal adversities. Out on the empty plains there were few trees to shade them from the sun, no boulders to shield them from blinding snow or ice, no caves to shelter them from rains and biting winds. Resourcefulness and ingenuity were the only weapons against the indifferent elements.

The settlers fortified their homes with special storm cellars. They devised primitive irrigation methods to combat droughts, dug fire guards to halt the spread of fires, and even invented their own contraptions to trap and suffocate locusts. Sudden crop losses were harder to cope with; often, whole families would have to comb the prairies for anything edible.

During such times, the sharing of common hardships and hopes created a strong sense of cooperation and community. The settlers offered each other solace, companionship, a helping hand. Yet ultimately their determination in the face of hardship emanated from their own persevering faith in God and in the future. "We were able to laugh together over the deprivations we suffered," wrote Mary Darrah, "with always a vision for the future. The pioneers as a rule were that kind of people."

For Emma Mitchell New and her growing family, life on the plains of central Kansas was far from easy. Over the years, they suffered one heartache after another in a seemingly endless struggle against fire, drought, Indians, blizzards, and even death. Yet through it all, Emma would not give in to the perils and privations surrounding her. Without remorse or self-pity, she never ceased to fight the odds. A devastating flood was one of her worst trials:

"A terrible storm and cloudburst came upon us and we lost almost everything, except the cows and an old team in the pasture. It came on the twenty-third of July. We had a nice cow barn put up and that day they put up a stack of millet the whole length of the barn. It commenced to rain in the afternoon, but in due time we started the children to town with the milk. It was a general downpour and the creeks were commencing to rise. So my husband started out to meet the children and get them home in safety. My husband said to the children, 'We will be good to the ponies tonight and put them in the cow barn and give them some nice millet.' They hadn't been in the house very long before we discovered our cellar was full of water from the outside door, and the well curb and toilet were gone.

"The creek was up to the house and still pouring down. My husband investigated and found that the underpinning of the house was going and that we had to get out. We took a lantern and matches and some blankets, and started for the side hills. When we opened the door to get out, the water came up to our necks. We had a struggle to get out and I can't tell to this day how we ever made it but the Lord must have been with us. My husband carried the baby girl in his arms as high as his head. We soon got out of the deepest water, as there was a turn in the creek. We went by way of the horse stable and found we would be safe in it. Still the water was up and it was pitch dark. The matches were wet, so we couldn't light the lantern.

"We stayed there until the storm abated and the water went down. Then we started out to see if we had a home left and to our delight, even in such a mess, we found it still standing. It was still dark and we couldn't see what havoc the storm had made for us. We found some dry matches and lit the lamp. Such a deplorable sight words can't express. We couldn't shut the door when we left the house, so the kitchen was full of rubbish and everything had been swimming in the high water. Many things were up side down. When the water went down there was an inch of mud all over the carpets and floors.

"When daylight came it was a sad sight to behold. Our cow barn and ponies were swept away, also our stack of millet. Practically everything we had was gone or ruined: machinery, wagons and nice garden. Back of the house was a nice patch of potatoes, but it washed them out clean and the soil as far as was ever plowed. Our ponies washed down stream about sixteen miles to the Saline River before lodging. When they were found, they were still tied to the same ridge pole. We did not have much to eat for breakfast, as all our food and groceries were in a cupboard in the kitchen and everything was ruined in the cellar. Even the water was not fit to drink."

The winter was perhaps the most debilitating of all the seasons. At times it seemed interminable. For days and weeks on end the temperature hovered at zero, and often it plummeted to twenty degrees below. Compounding these freezing temperatures was an almost ceaseless wind that whipped across the plains, often reaching over fifty miles per hour. To the settler unaccustomed to such climatic extremes, this numbing weather became almost unbearable.

A winter blizzard was an awesome spectacle. Without warning, dark billowing clouds roared across the skies and unleashed blinding bursts of snow. "They came with a mighty blast," recalled one witness, "sweeping with almost the strength of a cyclone, raking the life of stock and sometimes human beings."

Isolated in its cabin, the frontier family braced itself against the onslaught of ice and snow. Wrapped in heavy overcoats and thick woolen blankets, they huddled around the fireplace for warmth. Yet the searing gusts of wind outdoors seemed to penetrate every crack and crevice of the prairie house. Sleet pounded against the windowpanes, and drifts of snow piled up higher and higher against the door. Outside, the woodpiles became deeply buried in snow, the food bins stood caked in ice, and whole herds of starving cattle were lost from view. In all directions, the prairie lay enveloped in a boundless and impenetrable whiteness.

"As I sit today," wrote Josephine Middlekauf, "and look at the snow-drifts and think of the snow-drifts of earlier days, these are mere 'make-believes.' After a blizzard would rage for forty-eight hours or more, with nothing on the prairies in the way of houses, barns or fences to hold the snow, it had a clean sweep in to town and piled up against woodpiles, barns and fences six and eight feet deep. Communication with the outside world would be completely cut off for ten days and two weeks at a time. All traffic would be tied up until two or three hundred men could dig an opening through the snow that would be drifted full without the protection of snow fences."

For Ary Johnson's family, the nightmare of one sudden blizzard was not easily forgotten. According to one daughter, "New Year's morning in the year 1886 gave the promise of being one of the lovely days of western Kansas, but about one o'clock the clouds began to darken the skies and by night were very heavy; snowflakes beginning to fall very lightly at about six o'clock and by ten o'clock everyone realized that the country was in the grip of a terrible blizzard, the wind blowing a gale and the snow coming in a blinding rush. By morning, nothing could be seen, and in order to care for the stock in the barns, it was necessary to draw a rope from house to barn. The cold was so intense that fires had to be kept going in the house day and night, and many people suffered from a lack of provisions and fuel.

"This continued for four days. Cattle on the range could not be cared for and it was not possible to search for them until after the fourth day of the storm. Losses were extremely heavy, and searchers would find them frozen to death, some with their mouths frozen shut, some with their feet frozen. It was only with the greatest difficulty that progress could be made through the large drifts, and men on horses were frequently compelled to get off, make their way as best they could through the drifts and then pull the horses to them by a rope previously tied to their heads. The snow made everything look alike and it was only by the aid of familiar posts or fences that one was able to keep from getting lost. A week after the storm, searchers saw steam coming from a drift and found 100 head of cattle that were in good shape, all that was left of a bunch of 500."

The November 16th blizzard of 1871 roared abruptly out of unusually warm autumn skies. Caught unawares, the settlers awakened to a magnificent onslaught of snow that continued to bury the countryside for three long days.

Helpless travelers caught in the gale were blinded by driving snow and quickly lost their way. Among them was a young English bride on a honeymoon hunting expedition. Annie Gilkeson, writing in 1908, described the desperate plight of the plucky bride:

"We called her Stormy Petrel to designate the manner of her coming to us, although the warmth and sweetness of her disposition forbade the thought that anything rougher than a sunbeam had ever crossed her path. Slight, petite, yet of perfectly moulded form, dark eyes and light hair, she was indeed most charming in appearance. Everyone who came in contact with her fell promptly in love; a victim to her grace, beauty and vivacity of manner.

"Until the time we made her acquaintance, her history had been as follows: Born in Merrie England, the daughter of a prosperous manufacturer, she had received all the advantages which wealth can bestow and was in consequence a thoroughbred gentlewoman. Her father unfortunately fell a victim to drink, and the family—a large one—soon found themselves in straitened circumstances. Our heroine was a brave little woman, so she resolved to strike out for herself into the world in company with the two brothers who had planned to seek their fortunes in America.

"The early spring of 1871 found them in sunny Kansas, this State offering them alluring prospects, especially in the line of climate. Farming seemed to them an ideal mode of occupation, involving little labor, and no knowledge of the subject whatever, the modus operandi being simply to scratch the ground, drop in the seed, and allow the climate to do the rest. About a hundred miles inside the State, they located three claims, built a rude little house on the bare prairie, and proceeded to farm.

"Our little lady was as well versed in the duties of housekeeping as were her brothers in the wiles of agriculture, and all together they made sad work of it. She, however, had a faculty of accomplishing whatever she set out to do, and was resolved to profit by practice. Well, our young Englishmen tilled the soil, according to their light. They scratched the ground and planted the seed, then sat down on the shady side of the house to smoke their pipes, and watch the crops grow. The winds blew, the sun shone, but the rain came not—neither did the crops.

"About this time there appeared on the scene another young Briton. He also had heard of the fame of Kansas, over in old England. His coming was hailed with delight by our homesick young friends, and they gladly made him welcome. It was a pleasure even to talk about the cool shady lanes of dear old England, while here the soil was parched and baked by the wind and sun. Before many weeks had passed the little God Cupid had added his presence to this small abode on the sunbaked plains, and very soon Petrel became a bride.

"When autumn came, the hope of a fortune reaped from bountiful harvests was dead in each heart. From further west, however, came the report of buffalo which swarmed the plains. A cruel slaughter of the noble beast was then being carried on both for pleasure and profit. It afforded royal sport for such men as the Duke Alexis of Russia, who was here that winter. Our young friends became inflamed with new zeal. They would yet win their fortunes, and in a way congenial to their tastes, for hunting is a sport dear to Englishmen.

"They disposed of everything not necessary to a camping outfit, and early in November started out. The weather was warm and balmy, such weather as only Kansas can show at this season. Petrel still accompanied the party, making this her bridal trip, one sweet lady attended by three chivalrous knights. It was like a merry picnic party, all remembrance of failure blotted out by the high hopes which ran riot in each youthful breast. Fox hunting in old England was a mere bagatelle in comparison to the grand sport they were going to have in hunting such big game—and then for profit too.

"Petrel, being a true sportswoman, entered heartily into all their enthusiasm, and although she knew she could not partake in the actual hunt, she could at least keep the camp and share their triumphs. They enlivened their way by snatches of song and merry jest, and many of the beauties of the old homeland, which had hitherto been so poignant, faded into oblivion. They could even be thankful that its rain and fog were not present to mar the comfort of the smooth, hard ground over which they travelled.

"Suddenly, in the midst of all their mirth, they noticed a small, fleecy cloud passed over the sun. This was speedily joined by other innocent-appearing little clouds, and a chill came into the summer air. Petrel donned her natty little jacket, and the men turned up their coat collars. The singing ceased, however, and they moved quickly on, anxiously watching the sky, and the ever-thickening gloom.

"After a time some little flecks of snow drifted lazily down, melting as soon as they touched ground. Our party laughed at this, for the season was not yet far enough advanced to bring forth any serious storm; and, too, the land agents had assured them that Kansas never had any severe winter. The snow continued to fall, but in the same gentle, desultory manner.

"Presently they came in sight of a long, straggling line of tree-tops, which marked the trend of a little stream. Night was coming on, so they concluded to pitch their camp on the banks of this creek. In the morning this flurry of snow would be over, and they could pursue their way rejoicing. After preparing some supper as best they could in the steadily falling snow, they made camp as comfortable as possible and retired to rest, fully expecting to see a clear sky on awakening.

"During the night, the air became freezing cold, the snow fell yet more thickly, and the wind blew in fierce gusts. When morning broke, and our friends looked out from their beds of uneasy slumber, the wind was blowing a gale, and they found themselves nearly buried in snow. To prepare any breakfast was a physical impossibility; so, having observed the evening before a little town about a mile from where they camped, they decided to strike for it and obtain supplies. By some strange process of reasoning they concluded that it was safer to have Petrel remain where she was than to risk the journey. Tucking her into the wagon as snugly as possible, they bade her be brave, until their speedy return.

"It was with great difficulty that they made their way through the drifted snow, into the town, and several hours passed in the accomplishment of this feat. They supplied their wants as speedily as possible, and then started on the return journey, fearful that by this time Petrel might be suffering with cold; but 'man proposes and God disposes.' They had reckoned without their bearings.

"The wind, having increased in fury each moment, seemed to come from every quarter of the globe at once. It swirled about them with rush and power, driving the cutting, blinding snow into their faces so that they could see only a few feet ahead of them. They fought the baffling snow with desperate courage for the entire day, and when night came on they had not yet found their camp. Heart-sick and weary, they realized that it would be futile to continue in the darkness and the still raging storm, and, guided by the lights, returned to the little village. Traveling in a circle as lost people usually do, they were not far from it.

"Very early the next morning they mounted their tired horses and resumed the search. The storm had by this time abated, but they were almost crazed by the fear that Petrel when found would be frozen to death.

"And how had it fared with her during all the long, weary hours of the day and night? As the wind grew colder, she drew around her all the covering she could find, and as the day wore on and her rescuers did not return, she satisfied her hunger with a few biscuits she could reach. For drink, she had only to put out her hand and gather a little snow. What her feelings were during all this terrible day and night can better be imagined than described. She was a courageous little woman, but she knew the country around her to be infested with Indians. What if they should find her before her own loved ones could, and carry her off?

"She was becoming numb from cold in her cramped position, and when at last the morning dawned again, she found herself completely buried in the snow. She had no fancy for a premature burial, so proceeded to dig herself out. By climbing on some boxes in the wagon, she was able to get her head and shoulders above the snow, then, like Noah's dove, she looked forth for a place to land. All around her was a smooth, unbroken surface of snow, and nowhere could she see a place to put her foot.

"She knew that as the wagon was buried out of sight it devolved upon her to do something to make her whereabouts known, so she put a red scarf on the end of an umbrella and hoisted her flag of distress. Some hours later this was what the searchers spied. At the sound of their shout a curly head soon appeared beside the flag, and the shout became a joyful cry. Very soon they had broken a way through the heavy drift, and had the numbed and half-frozen little woman in their arms, with a fervent 'thank God' for finding her alive.

"The young husband took her on the horse with himself, and as she was so weak and exhausted they stopped at the first house to which they came. It proved to be the home of a widow who lived with her son on the outskirts of the town. Here she was tenderly nursed and petted by the dear old lady, and it was she who christened her—the Stormy Petrel."

For the farmers struggling to wrest a livelihood from this harsh land, the summer was a particularly critical period. Dependent upon fertile soils, warm sunshine and ample rainfall, they worked the fields in anxious anticipation of what each year's weather would bring.

In the main, the sunny skies of Kansas blessed the farmer with consistently warm temperatures throughout the summer months. In fact, summer temperatures often soared to one hundred degrees or better. Adequate rainfall, however, was considerably more unpredictable from year to year. For most crops, an annual precipitation rate of about twenty inches was necessary to ensure any substantial harvest. While the annual rainfall in the area often reached this level, summer droughts were a serious and persistent problem for the settler who lacked any viable methods of irrigation.

The first marked drought in Kansas occurred in 1860, when for sixteen long months prairie farmers subsisted without a single measurable rainfall. From June, 1859, until November, 1860, a merciless sun and hot gusty winds beat upon the parched landscape, withering crops and vegetation everywhere. Even the hardy prairie grasses succumbed to the blistering drought. Everywhere springs, streams and wells dried up and stranded the settlers without the basic water supplies necessary for their personal and farming needs.

In its wide sweep, the drought reached into the cupboards of every home. Most settlers had not yet accumulated adequate cash reserves, but relied primarily on their crops for a livelihood. In the course of the long drought, they had depleted their granaries of any wheat and corn reserves and were consequently unprepared for the widespread crop failure. Distressed at the condition of their hungry children, pioneer mothers scoured the countryside for wild berries, acorns, nuts and grasses, while their husbands set off on distant hunting expeditions.

Having recently settled in northeastern Kansas, the young family of John and Mary Belts was particularly hard hit by the drought of 1860. Laura Elizabeth Belts later recollected the desperate efforts of her parents to save the family from starvation during the bitter winter months:

"Tonight my memory turns back to the early days in our beloved Kansas. . . . All went well for a time, but the rains ceased to come and the weather grew hot and all the vegetation dried up. Night after night we could see the lightning flash all around the horizon, but it was only heat and not the forerunner of rain. By and by, hope failed the stoutest heart and how we were to live the long cold winter through was a problem not easy to solve. Fifteen months without a drop of rain and the country new, no surplus corn and wheat in the bins as now, made the bravest heart despair.

"My father made up his mind he would drive up into Iowa where there was plenty to spare and get a load of corn and flour. So he set to work to make mother and we children as comfortable as possible. He killed some hogs that had gotten into fair shape on nuts and acorns, of which was a good supply, cut and hauled a big pile of wood and then, bidding us be brave, he left us, telling us he would be back in three weeks, but it was nearly three times that long before he got back.

"Not long after he left, it began to snow, and how it did snow and blow and drift. It drifted until there was a snow bank nearly as high as the little cottonwood house and entirely around it, and packed so hard we children could run on it like it was ice. The fences were all hidden under the snow.

"How the days dragged on and how fast the scant provisions disappeared in spite of my mother's care. Our cows had strayed away and mother would not let my brother go hunt them lest he perish in the deep snow. Some kind neighbors came and cut a fresh supply of wood. My brother and I had gathered a big supply of walnuts and stored them away, and then came a day when there was nothing to eat but the nuts and pork. My baby brother, about two years old, would not eat such food and he cried for bread, and there was none to give him. That was more than my mother could bear and she broke down and cried. It was the only time we children saw her other than brave and hopeful all through those long, trying weeks. The cold was intense, and the wind fierce, and the wolves would come and fight with our dogs right on the door stone, and how it would frighten us.

"One night, about ten o'clock, my father got home, and I remember I had gone to bed hungry that night, so my mother made some biscuit dough and baked it on the griddles in front of the fireplace, and she then wakened me so I could eat some and see my father, but when I saw him I said, 'That is not my papa, my papa is white.' He had had to dig his way through the snow, and the intense cold had frozen his face until it was dreadfully discolored.

"Now we had plenty and the neighbors came for miles to borrow flour and none were sent away empty, for they had all been so kind to mother and her helpless little ones. Soon after that the states began to send in aid, and it was not long until the men and boys were wearing clothes made of the sacks in which the aid was sent, and it was not uncommon for them to have a stripe down the leg saying, 'S. C. Pomeroy Kansas Aid.' But what did they care, the worst was over and the next year the crops were immense and we were happy. People who came to this glorious state in the fifties suffered many privations, but we were all poor alike and there was a 'brotherliness" that was sweet and is a pleasant memory."

As their aspirations withered with the last drops of moisture, thousands of pioneers across the plains faced hopeless poverty. In that one year alone, more than thirty thousand people fled the state. This mass emigration in itself was a bitter blow to the development of the region, reducing its population by nearly thirty percent. In the long run, both discouraging publicity about the drought and the resulting exodus deterred migration to Kansas for many years to come.

Nevertheless, some two thirds of the Kansas settlers steadfastly refused to give up hope. Determined to remain on their lands, they managed to carefully ration meager food and clothing supplies among their families and friends. And these diehards were not entirely bereft. Alarmed at their widespread suffering, state legislatures, church organizations and concerned individuals across the nation rallied to their plight. Within a short time, various relief associations were organized to help the victims reseed their fields and rebuild their farms.

Thadyus Hyatt, a New York philanthropist, was the primary impetus behind the initial drive for assistance. After personally visiting the stricken areas, he organized a statewide relief system to distribute provisions within each county. Returning to the East, he solicited more than eight million pounds of provisions, including carloads of clothing, boots, wheat seed, and food. In addition, a total of $83,869 was collected to defray the costs of packing and shipping the goods.

Reverend John Armstrong Steele brought his young family to Topeka at this time. Distressed at the poverty and misery of the surrounding communities, he ministered to the area with both material assistance and religious guidance. His daughter Matilda recalled the sorrows of that time and paid tribute to his persevering efforts:

"My father, Rev. John Armstrong Steele, and my mother, Catherine Hampton Steele, came to Topeka with their family of eight children in 1860 from Illinois. . . . There was not a tree nor shrub nor fence. Our house seemed to be in the open prairie and around it was that yellow clay soil so noticeable to strangers and so well remembered by old settlers. No spear of grass grew there. No shade, no fruit, no flowers, and worst of all, no rain, for this was the year of the great drouth in Kansas. It needs no descriptive adjectives, and no dates to make any old Kansan know what it meant. Since then dry spells have destroyed this crop and that, sometimes at one end of the season and sometimes at the other, but the drouth of 1860 swept the calendar.

"Most of the water used by the people was hauled from the river, which was quite as muddy then as it is now. It cost forty cents a barrel and when allowance was made for dirt which settled in the bottom, that was quite expensive. Most of the wells went dry and there was such a scarcity of anything green that had not apples and vegetables been brought by wagon from Missouri, we would have, like the wells, dried up. In June there was a hard shower, and the hopes of the disconsolate people revived, but alas, showers came no more. That was the only rain for sixteen months.

"When the hot winds blew like a simoom for days together, and no clouds scudding across the blue sky made grateful showers, one could almost believe that what had been in late geographies called 'The Great American Desert' was within walking distance. The leaves on the trees shriveled and dried up, and every living thing was seeking shelter from the hot rays of the sun. The earth opened in great cracks several inches across and two feet deep. We used to play these were earthquake crevices and scores of imaginary people met an untimely end.

"As there is an end to all things, so the long hot summer drew to its close. Through this trying time during which sorrow and sickness had come to our family, my faithful father kept on with his work, preaching and visiting, and encouraging the now thoroughly homesick people, many of whom were preparing to go back from whence they came, rather than face the dread possibilities of the approaching winter.

"In November, my father went back at his own expense to Illinois and Indiana to solicit aid for starving Kansas. He was very successful. Quantities of food and clothing were sent which were distributed by a committee of business men, and the timely aid saved much suffering.

"It was a long, very cold winter, and we were thankful that we had fuel to keep us warm and plenty of food at our house. To be sure, our principal diet, the Irish potatoes, froze, but they were kept frozen until they could be used. Potatoes were not to go to loss while many people were living on parched corn. Counted among our luxuries were a few pounds of butter sent to us by our relatives in Illinois, but jams and jellies, there were none."

Often, excessive rainfall could be just as devastating as any sweeping drought. Set against the stark terrain, the summer storm was a dazzling spectacle with its violent claps of thunder and brilliant flashes of lightning. Yet this beauty was deceptive. All too often, the western squall drenched the parched plains with more water than the ground could absorb. Worse yet, atmospheric blasts of ice-cold air sometimes turned the rain into hailstones as big as marbles. Pulverizing fragile crops and eroding precious topsoil, these downpours could quickly shatter any prospect of a full harvest.

"I remember driving over to the [Groves] ranch one beautiful day in early spring," wrote Susan Proffitt. "The great acres gave promise of an unusual harvest of feed for the thousands of white-faced cattle grazing contentedly in the pastures. A more beautiful scene I never saw.

"Spring gave into summer, and in August at the close of a hot day when the grasses seemed to wither and the cattle bunched up near the creek and well and no air seemed to stir the leaves on the trees, all nature seemed still with an ominous stillness. A mass of black clouds loomed up in the west, distant thunder rumbled, the clouds gathered fast, taking on a greenish hue, thunder boomed and lightning streaked the sky and cut through the landscape and then with a rush and roar came the hail, devastating everything.

"After the storm has passed, the Groves ranch was damaged thousands of dollars, the acres of feed was beaten into the ground, there was no pasture for the thousands of white faces, and next day I drove out to the ranch. Mrs. Groves was with her husband on the ranch and met us with a smile and greeting so bright that we almost forgot her great loss. When we did speak of it, she smiled and replied, 'It is bad, but our neighbor has suffered a heavier loss than we.' This reply was characteristic of her; in her busy life she always had time to listen and sympathize with others, but of her own troubles she seldom spoke."

Droughts, winds and hailstorms were not the only summer terrors for the pioneer. The grasshopper, voracious and marauding, inflicted still more misfortune. As one woman lamented, "All, or many, of the elements of nature seemed to work together to discipline the early Kansas settlers, they were not allowed to grow soft with ease and luxury, and as though hot winds, droughts and Indians were not enough, the grasshoppers came along and did their part."

During the first twenty years of its settlement, the Kansas frontier was relatively free from any sizable grasshopper infestation. Although grasshoppers had aggravated the farmer in relatively small numbers from time to time, they had not been a particularly serious problem. As a result, the pioneers were largely unprepared for the massive onslaught of the insects which would literally eat their way across the state in 1874. In fact, the infestation was so overwhelming and devastating that the year was later identified as the "Grasshopper Year."

In the beginning, 1874 seemed to have the makings of a very good year. "In the spring of 1874," wrote Mrs. Everett Rorabaugh, "the farmers began their farming with high hopes, some breaking the sod for sod corn, others plowing what had been broken the year before, sowing spring wheat, corn and cane, and with plenty of rain everyone was encouraged at the present. The neighbors would meet at some little one-room house and put in the day visiting and eating buffalo meat boiled, and cornbread and dried 'apple sass' that some relative back east had sent, and the men talking about the bumper crop they were going to have that year."

Although the summer had been typically hot and dry, the crops were growing well. By August, the wheat and the oats were mostly in the shock, and the lush green pasture grasses gave promise of fat and healthy herds of cattle. For the farmers evaluating their prospects, a plentiful harvest seemed assured. But their anticipation turned to despair as millions upon millions of grasshoppers blanketed the sky. "They looked like a great, white glistening cloud," recalled one bewildered pioneer, "for their wings caught the sunshine on them and made them look like a cloud of white vapor." Swooping down on the fertile fields, the insects began a feast of destruction.

"August 1, 1874," explained Mary Lyon, "is a day that will always be remembered by the then inhabitants of Kansas. . . . For several days there had been quite a few hoppers around, but this day there was a haze in the air and the sun was veiled almost like Indian summer. They began, toward night, dropping to earth, and it seemed as if we were in a big snowstorm where the air was filled with enormous-size flakes."

Alighting to a depth of four inches or more, the grasshoppers covered every inch of ground, every plant and shrub. Tree limbs snapped under their weight, corn stalks bent to the ground, potato vines were mashed flat. Quickly and cleanly, these voracious pests devoured everything in their paths. No living plant could escape. Whole fields of wheat, corn and vegetables disappeared; trees and shrubs were completely denuded. Even turnips, tobacco and tansy vanished.

"When they came down," remembered Mary Roberts, "they struck the ground so hard it sounded almost like hail. Father had tried to get a start in fruit trees as soon as he could, and we had a greengage plum tree in our yard that was full of plums that were almost ripe, but it was thought too green to pick yet. We had to postpone dinner while 'all hands' gathered garden stuff and plums to save them. We picked every plum, as they would soon have all been devoured by the hoppers had we not done so.

"There was a watermelon patch in our garden and the melons were quite large and long. They were not ripe, so we could not save them, but by the evening of the second day they were all gone. I think we found one or two pieces of rind about the size of the palm of our hand in the whole patch. Such enormous appetites they had! In a few days they had eaten every green thing. They soon had every twig on every tree or bush eaten off and the trees were as bare as in midwinter."

Stunned by the continued onslaught and desperate to save what little remained, the pioneers grabbed whatever coverings they could find to shield their crops and shrubbery. Out came the bedsheets, blankets, quilts and shawls. Even old winter coats and greasy burlap sacks were ripped apart to spread over precious vegetables. Yet these coverings proved useless; the grasshoppers ate straight through the cloth or wormed their way underneath. As the settlers soon learned, these creatures would stop at nothing.

"They devoured every green thing but the prairie grass," continued Mary Lyon. "They ate the leaves and young twigs off our young fruit trees, and seemed to relish the green peaches on the trees, but left the pit hanging. They went from the corn fields as though they were in a great hurry, and there was nothing left but the toughest parts of the bare stalks. Our potatoes had to be dug and marketed to save them.

"I thought to save some of my garden by covering it with gunny sacks, but the hoppers regarded that as a huge joke, and enjoyed the awning thus provided, or if they could not get under, they ate their way through. The cabbage and lettuce disappeared the first afternoon;

by the next day they had eaten the onions. They had a neat way of eating onions. They devoured the tops, and then ate all of the onion from the inside, leaving the outer shell.

"The garden was soon devoured, and when all of these delicacies were gone, they ate the leaves from the fruit trees. They invaded our homes, and if our baking was not well guarded by being enclosed in wood or metal, we would find ourselves minus the substantial part of our meals; and on retiring to bed, we had to shake them out of the bedding, and were fortunate if we did not have to make a second raid before morning."

Within hours, no part of the countryside was left unscathed. Having eliminated all the crops and foliage, grasshoppers by the thousands moved on into barns and houses. Besides devouring the food left in cupboard, barrel and bin, they attacked anything made of wood, destroying kitchen utensils, furniture, fence boards and even the rough siding on cabins. Window curtains were left hanging in shreds, and the family's clothing was heartily consumed. Craving anything sweaty, the insects took a special liking to the handles of pitchforks and the harnesses of horses. Lumbering cattle stood by helplessly as the pests crawled all over their bodies, tickling their ears, eyes and nostrils. Young children screamed in terror as the creatures writhed through their hair and down their shirts. Men tied strings around their trouser cuffs to keep them from wriggling up their legs.

Lillie Marcks was a child of twelve when the grasshoppers scourged these prairies. In her memoirs, she relived the anguish of witnessing the unexpected devastation of her family's homestead. "Several days before the plague of grasshoppers, my father and his hired man, Jake, came home from the near-by village with tales of trains that could not start or stop because the tracks were slick with crushed grasshoppers. So thick were the grasshoppers that the sun could scarcely be seen.

"One morning, I had a chill and shook for hours. Mother made a pallet for me on the floor near the front door and covered me. I fell asleep. After a long rest, I awoke burning with fever. Mother had placed a wet cool towel over my face to reduce the fever. The sun was shining over my pallet and I felt so ill. Oh dear! Then Jake's voice rang loud and clear. 'Mrs.! Oh, Mrs.! They're come! They're come! The grasshoppers is here! You can jes' see the trees bein' ett up!' I raised the towel from my face and eyes, looked toward the sun. Grasshoppers by the millions in a solid mass filled the sky. A moving gray-green screen between the sun and earth.

"Riding his pony like the wind, father came home telling us more tales of destruction left in the path of the pests. They hit the house, the trees and picket fence. Father said, 'Go get your shawls, heavy dresses and quilts. We will cover the cabbage and celery beds. Perhaps we can save that much.' Celery was almost an unseen vegetable in that time and place—they wished to save it. They soon were busy spreading garments and coverings of all sorts over the vegetables.

"The hired man began to have ideas. Everyone was excited trying to stop the devastation. Bonfires began to burn thru the garden. 'Now I'll get some of them,' Jake said. Picking up a shovel, he ran thru the gate. Along the fence they were piled a foot deep or more, a moving struggling mass. Jake began to dig a trench outside the fence about two feet deep and the width of the shovel. Father gathered sticks and dead leaves. In a few minutes, the ditches were filled with grasshoppers, but they soon saw the fire covered and smothered by grasshoppers. Think of it, grasshoppers putting out a fire.

"Ella, my five-year-old sister, was shooing and beating them off the covered garden by means of a long branch someone had given her. I was ill and so excited over all of this battle and could only be up a few seconds at a time. Then all at once, Ella's voice rang out in fear. 'I'm on fire!' Forgotten was my fever. I ran to the door and saw a flame going up the back of her dress. In less time that I can tell this, I ran to her and tore off her dress from the shoulders down. Then I turned and looked at the writhing mass of grasshoppers on the garments covering the vegetables and called, 'Ma! Ma! Come here! They are eating up your clothes!"

At least the clothes the grasshoppers ate in the Marcks household were on the ground and not being worn. Adelheit Viets was not as lucky: "The storm of grasshoppers came one Sunday. I remember that I was wearing a dress of white with a green stripe. The grasshoppers settled on me and ate up every bit of green stripe in that dress before anything could be done about it."

For the beleaguered settlers, the devastation continued long after the grasshoppers had moved on. To their dismay, everything reeked with the taste and odor of the insects. The water in the ponds, streams and open wells turned brown with their excrement and became totally unfit for drinking by either the pioneers or their livestock. Bloated from consuming the locusts, the barnyard chickens, turkeys and hogs themselves tasted so strongly of grasshoppers that they were completely inedible.

"Hearts were heavy," lamented one victim, "every bit of our crops gone for that year, and how were we to live? The question was solved in various ways. Some were still hopeful and stayed there to try again. Some gave up and went 'back home.' We sent back home and borrowed money to buy wheat to feed horses and pigs, going many miles east to find the grain."

To make matters worse, the insects had deposited their own eggs in the soil before departing. By the following spring, hordes of grasshoppers hatched and continued the onslaught. "One day the whole earth began to crawl and move," wrote one woman, "grasshoppers by the millions were hatching, pale sickly-looking white bugs at first, and once more they mowed down all of God and man's work." This time, however, the farmers had time to replant their crops, thus preventing any repetition of the wholescale destruction.

With the pestilence finally behind them, the stricken homesteaders tried to overcome their troubles and resolutely confront the future. "How shall I describe that time?" wrote one woman. "Life made miserable in so many ways, for in that memorable year of 1874 life was wretchedly uncomfortable, we were poverty stricken, without the means to sustain life through the coming winter. In those days, there were no aristocrats on Spring Creek, we made the most of our circumstances and of one another. Life was yet before us, and it was the same danger that threatened us all: *hard times.* The men went to work with heavy hearts and put in cane and millet for the winter, and kind friends in the East sent us 'aid' such as bedding and clothes, food and shoes. We lived principally on cornbread, cornmeal, coffee, gravy, sorghum for sweetening, and the men smoked grape leaves for tobacco." In true pioneer spirit, she added one more recollection: "Life was worthwhile, even then."

CHAPTER SIX

The Clashing of Cultures
Indians

"Hearken well to what I say. A long time ago this land belonged to our fathers, but when I go up to the river I see a camp of soldiers, and they are cutting my wood down or killing my buffalo. I don't like that and when I see it my heart feels like bursting with sorrow."

—SANTANA

SPEAKING THESE WORDS in 1867, the Kiowa chief echoed the frustrations and bitterness of the Indian people.* Disrupted by the continual extension of the country's western borders, the indigenous tribes struggled unsuccessfully against a white nation that was determined to conquer them. For two centuries they had seen their homelands gradually usurped by white settlers, their game reserves eliminated by white hunters, and their nomadic life style disrupted by a white government that failed to understand their needs or appreciate their culture. Weakened in strength and in spirit, the Indian people were pushed off their native lands and eventually herded onto isolated Western reservations. While some tribes acquiesced peace-

* For the full text of Santana's speech at the Medicine Lodge Peace Council of 1867, see the account of Henry M. Stanley, *Kansas Historical Quarterly*, Vol. 33, No. 3 (Autumn, 1967), p. 282.

fully, many more vowed to fight the white man until the bitter end. It is their story of resistance and proud determination that became one of the most compelling chapters in the development of Kansas and the American West.

Until the middle of the nineteenth century, the federal government regarded the various Indian tribes as separate and independent nations. Under this policy, all land concessions made by these Indian nations were to be effectuated by formal treaties with all the stature of international covenants. Such negotiations were to be conducted only by official government representatives and the tribal leaders. Once formulated and signed by both sides, a treaty was to be submitted to the United States Senate for formal ratification.

Although these land treaties were well suited to the needs and the policies of the American government, they offered the Indians few benefits in return. On the whole, the Indian people were slow to comprehend the full meaning of the relinquishment of title to their native lands. By tradition, the American Indian had little conception of either individual or tribal ownership of land—it belonged to nature, just like the waters of the river and the clear skies above. The tribes were free to occupy and control their territories, but the land itself was not theirs to buy and sell like a simple commodity. As a result, although the Indians did yield to government threats and promises, they were slow to understand that their concessions would exclude them permanently from their homelands.

In addition to these conceptual difficulties, the tribal leaders had trouble enforcing treaty provisions and guaranteeing their promises. Traditionally, the Indian tribe had functioned as a loose democratic organization, without a rigid hierarchy of authority or a legal system. Within the village council every male warrior had the right to speak his own mind and make his own decisions. Since tribal members were not compelled to adhere to the commands or the promises of their leaders, the formal treaties were easily ignored.

Neither did the American government meet *its* promises. Though the government had the authority to prevent territorial transgressions by its people, it was often unable or unwilling to restrain land-hungry citizens from wide-scale violations of the Indian treaties. Over the years, infringements on both sides of the treaties fueled the fires of mutual hostility.

Initially, the hostilities between whites and Indians were confined to the eastern portion of the country. But the United States gradually acquired Indian lands and pushed the native tribes farther and farther west. By 1825, it was evident that the nation would need all the land area east of the Mississippi River for its steadily increasing population and developing economy. Conveniently, the Great Plains to the west were considered at this time to be unsuitable for white habitation. Since few people believed that Americans would ever covet these arid grasslands, it seemed logical to give the area to the Eastern Indians in exchange for their lands.

In this regard, Secretary of War John C. Calhoun proposed the first definitive Indian policy to President James Monroe. Under its provisions, those tribes living east of the Mississippi River would be forcibly moved to the country west of it. By forbidding any white citizens to enter this territory the government would guarantee to the Indians perpetual ownership of their new Western lands. Enacted by Congress in 1830, the plan for Indian removal was carried out under the vigorous prodding of President Andrew Jackson. Throughout the 1830s and early 1840s, the American government thus created a special Indian frontier that was intended to permanently separate the white and Indian peoples.

It is not surprising that the Indians themselves became increasingly resentful of this arrangement. For Eastern Indians, the move meant transporting entire tribes and all their belongings hundreds of miles. Wrenched from their ancestral grounds, they were forced to abandon the hills and valleys, forests and rivers which were fundamental to their culture. Heartbroken, the Indian people set out on the long journey westward to a strange and arid land.

To the native tribes of the West, the removal policy seemed equally objectionable. Up until this time, the vast Kansas prairies had been the undisputed territory of several nomadic tribes. For centuries the Kansa and Osage tribes had controlled the eastern portion of the area, while the Pawnee had roamed the central plains. To the far west, the high plains had been the traditional hunting country of the Cheyenne, the Arapaho, the Kiowa and the Comanche. Disturbed by the sudden influx of Eastern tribes, these native Indians resented an encroachment upon their rightful lands and game reserves.

At the same time, white violations of the boundaries established by the government caused further indignation among the Indians. White pioneers, eager to migrate westward, had resented the government policy which excluded them from the Great Plains area. Despite legislative proscription, increasing numbers of explorers, miners and adventurers trekked across the territory throughout the 1840s and early 1850s. By 1854, new land treaties were signed with the Indians to provide for the legal white settlement of the Kansas and Nebraska Territories. Once again, the Indians were uprooted in the name of U.S. growth and development.

In order to provide for a gradual settlement of this area, the initial treaties had provided that no Kansas lands would be occupied until they had been officially surveyed and opened by the government. However, the white settlers, without regard for their Indian neighbors, typically ignored these legal restrictions and staked their claims across the territory. At the same time, the Homestead Act of 1862 and the construction of the railroad further encouraged the rapid settlement and development of white communities on former Indian lands. For the beleaguered Indians, the harassment of the white man, coupled with the near-elimination of vital buffalo reserves, doomed any prospect for peaceful survival in their native lands. In the end, they found themselves uprooted once again, this time to be pushed southward into the unsettled territory which is now Oklahoma.

However, for a number of years before this final move southward, the Indian tribes remained in Kansas, living side by side with the white settlers. Although their underlying antagonisms were still strong, they existed in relative harmony. Outbreaks of violence occurred from time to time, but increased military policing of the area minimized contact between the pioneers and their Indian neighbors.

On the whole, relations between the white and Indian peoples were characterized as much by cultural misunderstanding as by racial hostility. In the white man's view, the Indian had always been a savage, uncivilized element of the wilderness. The settlers, having been unsuccessful in their attempts to convert the "red man" to their own civilized ways, usually isolated themselves from direct contact with the tribes. Accepting the popular stereotypes of the "savages," most pioneers did not attempt to understand Indian customs or appreciate Indian culture. When Gertrude Burlingame witnessed a tribal war dance, performed on a special day of pomp and pageantry, she reacted with both fascination and profound fear:

"The most interesting event of that time to me was a government payment to the Pottawatomie Indians [a payment for the purchase of title to their lands]. It was to be held at Silver Lake, and after the payment the Indians would give us a war dance and everybody was invited.

"Well, the payment came off in the morning and then the dinner and then the braves went to their tents to dress for the dance, or rather to undress, for when they came out of their tents they only had on a breech cloth and a coat of red paint, and some feathers stuck in their hair. A large circle was marked off for the dance.

"When the time came, the tom-toms struck up their weird, hideous music and all at once the Indians came rushing out of their tents, brandishing their tomahawks and yelling their war whoops. For an instant my heart stood still at the sight, and then I remembered the Government troops that were nearby which had been sent down from Fort Riley to guard those payments. On they came. The Indians were often called 'red devils,' and they certainly looked it. They got in the circle, one behind the other, and the dance was a sort of hop with their bodies all bent over and their piercing eyes looking in every direction, like they were looking for the enemy, holding up their tomahawks and every few minutes joining in their war whoops that nearly shook the ground. It was a sight never to be forgotten."

In many ways, fear played a large role in the settlers' dealings with the Indians. Although few families personally experienced intimidation or violence by the Indians, the stories of distant Indian attacks were frightening. Rumors of Indians on the rampage became a part of every pioneer's experience. At night, the frontiersman slept fitfully with a rifle by his side. The housewife left alone was easily disquieted by any sudden noise or mysterious shadow. No Indian, whether friendly or not, ever seemed completely trustworthy.

"In our frontier experience," recalled Mary Gettys Lockard, "the thing that continually harrowed the feelings of myself and my mother was the fearful dread of Indians. This was particularly true of my mother, who of necessity was left at home alone so much with the smaller children while my father was freighting or on hunting trips.

"We had been told that there were no hostile Indians in Kansas, but just the same we could remember the horrible tales of Indian depredations further west that continued to sift in to trouble us. We had a book that gave some of Jim Bridger's* philosophy, and in one place he was quoted as saying, 'Wha're you don't see no Injuns, tha're

* James Bridger (1804–81) was a famous mountain man, fur trader and guide to the Far West. In 1825 he journeyed to the Great Salt Lake, becoming perhaps the first white man to reach its shores. In 1843, he and a partner, Louis Vasquez, built Fort Bridger in the territory which is now Wyoming. This fort, located on Black's Fork, became an important way station and supply point for emigrants bound for Utah, Oregon and California.

they are the thickest.' That gave me the fixed idea that Indians rose up from the ground at times and killed everybody in sight. We children talked about Indians so much it got on my mother's nerves not a little, and she had hard work trying to stop our chatter about them."

Although the more warlike tribes of the high western plains were actively hostile toward the white interlopers, most prairie tribes approached the settlers with purely peaceful intentions. The Indians were by nature a friendly and sociable people, and, much to the consternation of the wary homesteaders, they became persistent visitors at the cabin doorstep. Unaccustomed to the formal etiquette of white society, they felt free to wander into any dwelling, whether it was a fellow tribesman's tepee or a white man's dugout. Without bothering to knock, they marched in and made themselves at home.

"Yes, the Indians were in evidence everywhere," continued Gertrude Burlingame. "I was told they were harmless, but I did not like the way they had of stalking into the house unbidden or of looking in at the windows. In Leavenworth, we had the Delawares, a short stocky-built Indian who dressed in buckskin suits with leggings and mocassins to match and they always rode ponies. But in Topeka, we had the Kaws, a tall raw-boned Indian, who always wore a red blanket.

"I still recall how scared I was in my first experience. It was warm and my windows were open and I was combing my hair. My hair was then very long, thick and even, and as I drew the comb through it and looked up to the mirror before me, which was opposite the window, I saw reflected two big Indians, one had just gotten inside and the other was climbing over the window sill. Well, I thought of course they were after my scalp and I screamed and ran out the door into the hall, nearly knocking Col. Holliday [a guest] over, who had heard my screams and was coming to my rescue. He caught me and asked me 'what was the matter.' I could barely gasp, 'Indians.'

"The Colonel went into the room and found the Indians laughing heartily and they said, 'Squaw heap fraid.' 'Heap fraid.' The other one said, 'Squaw heap scalp,' and he measured off the length of my hair by his two arms and said, 'See, see, heap scalp.' The Colonel came out and said, 'They want to see your hair,' but I shook my head and not on your life would I have gone into that room."

The Indians were openly intrigued by the white man's sedentary ways. For them, the pioneer cabin was filled with an array of strange furnishings, unusual sounds and wonderful aromas. Paying no attention to their disconcerted hosts, the visitors often proceeded to examine methodically every nook and cranny. They rummaged through the trunks and drawers, poked at the chairs and peered into the mirrors. They marveled at the turn of the spinning wheel and listened intently to the rhythmic chime of the clock. Moving on to the kitchen, they examined the cooking utensils, pried open the storage bins and helped themselves to the food.

Looking back on those trying moments, Aura Viola St. John recalled their insatiable curiosity. "One day three squaws rode up, jumped off their horses and came right into the house. They did not speak to me or act as if they saw me, but proceeded to investigate the room. They went all around looking at everything and when they came to my dish cupboard, made of dry goods boxes with a curtain in front, they pulled back the curtain and looked long at the dishes, pointing laughingly and jabbering. Much the most interesting thing they found altogether, they looked long at the bed with its pieced quilt and pillows with white cases, something so different from their blankets spread on the ground."

Even the white papoose was a source of fascination. "One day we went strawberrying on 110 creek," continued Aura St. John, "this was on the Indian reservation. My baby Hattie was eight months old. In the afternoon, several squaws came riding up, and when they saw the baby they jumped off their ponies and gathered around me, laughing and saying, 'Oh, petite papoose.' They think a white baby is something wonderful and I am not sure they had ever seen one before. Finally one of them held up her hands and what did that baby do but go right to her. They laughed and passed her from one to the other until I began to be very uneasy, for I considered my baby girl a very desirable piece of property, and motherlike I feared they would think the same and jump on their ponies and ride away fast and furious."

The Indians would often go begging from house to house for food. They were apt to stalk uninvited into the family kitchen and demand tastes of the freshly baked breads or the roasting meats. The frantic housewife, frightened by their unrelenting demands, would hastily offer them plates of food just in order to get rid of them. Many a dinner was sacrificed to appease these hungry visitors.

"The Osage Indians used to come to our camp frequently," wrote Hattie Wilson. "[One time] an Indian chief (I think his name was 'Chetopa') asked for some of my mother's fresh bread. She gave him a roll. He stuck his finger through it and handed it back, much to our disgust, [for we were] hungry and wanted it too, but had not been allowed to have it. My sister Mary and her family were there at the time, and he pointed to her and said to my mother, 'She you papoose,' then to my sister's baby and said, 'She you papoose.' I've always remembered that."

During the late 1860s, Kansa tribesmen were frequent visitors at the Chase County home of Caroline Pinney Hays. Although their social calls were always friendly ones, Mrs. Hays could not overcome her sudden trepidation at the sight of Indians on her doorstep. Noting that her mother was a timid woman by nature, Grace Hays Blackburn later described her apprehensions:

"Mother never could quite conquer her fear of the Indians but she became more or less accustomed to their appearance, and never turned them away quite empty handed when they came begging for her cornmeal or 'boggie meat' and they soon learned to speak of her as the 'heap good squaw,' which name she earned from heaping up the little pan she used for dipping up cornmeal for them. She was always startled when an Indian face would suddenly and noiselessly appear at the window or door, and although she soon learned that they meant no harm but were only curious to see into the room, she never could conquer the sudden fear that gripped her heart.

"At one time, five hundred Kaw Indians, on their way from the reservation near Topeka to the Indian territory, camped within half a mile of our house. Of course, these Indians were friendly, almost too much so, as they would beg for anything from a chicken to a bit of ribbon or bright colored bead.

"One day an old squaw came begging for chickens, and mother good-naturedly sent the children out to catch one, but the only one they could lay their hands on was an old setting hen. Mother handed the hen to the squaw, who, after feeling about the anatomy of the fowl and noting the prominence of its bones, threw it on the ground and walked indignantly away. This was the nearest Mother ever came to offending the Indians.

"A neighbor woman, Mrs. Manly, who had not a particle of fear of the Indians, was taking some ashes from her cook stove when happening to glance up was startled for an instant by the face of an Indian pressed flat against the window pane. Like a flash, she hurled the shovel, which she had in her hand, straight at the face of the Indian, shattering the glass and thoroughly frightening a much astonished Indian, who never stopped running while in sight of the house.

"The Kaw Indian boys were always eager to engage in jumping and running races with my brothers, Charley and Dick, and other neighbor boys, and while they never boasted when victorious, the sparkle in their black eyes was proof of their satisfaction.

"Mother experienced one Indian scare which she did not soon forget. Among the animals owned by the family was an old sorrel horse named Snort. The children were very fond of him and would often all ride him at once. This faithful old animal was subject to colic and when seized with one of these attacks would roll on the ground in agony. Father and Mother knew what to do for him when he had one of these 'spells,' and always kept medicine in the house for his relief. It was no small job to apply the remedy, but the old horse, who was gentle as a kitten, always submitted to the treatment with the best grace possible.

"One day Father had gone to Cottonwood Falls in the wagon with wheat and corn to be ground into flour and meal. This was an all-day trip, and Mother was at home with the two younger children, Madge, five years old, and Dwight, just a baby. Happening to look toward the timber which was about half a mile from the house, Mother saw old Snort rolling on the ground. Leaving little Madge and the baby, she took the medicine and started for the old horse.

"Uneasy at having to leave the children when she had gone about two thirds of the way, she looked back, and to her terror, she saw some Indians, armed with guns and bows and arrows, between herself and the house. Sick with fear of what might have happened to the children, she dropped the medicine and turned and ran back toward the house. She was accosted by a big Indian, who pointed with his large knife toward the timber and asked, 'See Deer? See Deer?' Shaking her head, she hurried back to the house, forgetting in her fright that when about half way to the house she had had a glimpse of a fleeing deer.

"Running into the house, she sank down exhausted when she saw the children were safe and unharmed. Little Madge could not understand Mother's fright when she gasped out, 'Indians! Indians!' "

Not all pioneer women regarded the Indians with a terror like Mrs. Hays's. In 1858, Christina Phillips, a young woman whose family had emigrated from Scotland when she was a child, married a Mr. A. M. Campbell and settled in the new town of Salina with her husband and brother. Delia E. Brown told of the time when the young bride was the only white woman in town:

"While her husband and brother were busy with the many things that go to the settling of a new country, Mrs. Campbell took charge of the store, trading with the Indians, for pelts and furs. She had great patience with the Indians, but was very firm and straightforward in her dealings with them, thus commanding their respect for the 'White Sister,' as they called her. No whiskey was ever sold or given to the Indians in Salina. And early in her trading with them Mrs. Campbell resolved that there should be no Sunday trading. Her husband and brother tried to discourage her in this, saying, 'The Indians will not understand.' But she persisted, until finally when they would come from their reservations and, not knowing anything of the days of the week, would send a rider with this query, 'Big Father's Day, no swap?' and if it was Sunday it was all right, there was 'no swap' until the following day.

"Mrs. Campbell has said, if it had not been for the friendship of the squaws she does not know how she would have survived those first years of loneliness in the little new town on the Smoky. When questioned as to the Indian sense of humor, and as to whether they ever laughed, Mrs. Campbell tells this amusing incident. This was the day of the enormous hoop-skirt, and one day she noticed three squaws, after they had done their trading, curiously regarding her feet, and wondered what was wrong. Finally one squaw a little more courageous than the rest came to her, and lifted her dress a little way, then her white petticoat, then asked her to lift her skirts higher, when she did, and says Mrs. Campbell, 'After seeing those squaws laugh until the tears rolled down their cheeks, at my hoop-skirts, no one could possibly doubt the Indian's sense of humor. . . .'

"One day as Mrs. Campbell was sitting quietly at her work, her three small children in the room with her, she saw two Kaw Indians running toward the house, pursued by drunken soldiers. The Indians—who were of the friendly tribe—rushed into the house, and she had just time to lock the door and seize her gun, when the soldiers commenced pounding on the door, demanding the Indians and threatening to shoot. She called to them not to shoot or they would kill her children. This, however, made no impression on the soldiers, so she pointed her gun at them and told them she would shoot the first one who tried to enter the house. Seeing she meant all she said, they began to weaken, and just as Mr. Campbell, who had noticed some disturbance, came from his work, the soldiers left. The Indians were then free to leave, expressed their gratitude, and said, 'No forget,

White Sister,' and went to tell of the incident to other members of their tribe. . . .

"During those early strenuous years, Mrs. Campbell was almost doctor, lawyer, merchant, chief, as the old rhyme goes; helping the Indians in their troubles, trading with them, administering simple home remedies when they were ill. One day an Indian brave came to her telling her his squaw was 'heap sick.' Not knowing how ill she was, nor the nature of her illness, but thinking whatever was the trouble a mild dose of castor oil would not hurt her, she sent this remedy. Next day, seeing the brave return, she was somewhat frightened, fearing her remedy had not proved successful, but was reassured when the proud brave told her, 'Heap good medicine, two papoose.'

"Late one afternoon Mrs. Campbell saw three Indian women coming toward the store, and as they invariably did their trading in the mornings, she was somewhat surprised, and asked Mr. Campbell if he would not see what they wanted. Mr. Campbell returned in a few moments, saying, 'No me, White Sister.' She then went to them, as she did so they said, 'Come to meet, good bye,' and laying their heads on their hands, to show that it would be one night before they would be home, said, 'One sleep, go home.' Then one of the women took from the bosom of her dress a little package, and opening it brought out a little gold ring, and placing it on Mrs. Campbell's finger, turned and left. And says Mrs. Campbell in telling of this, 'No words can express what that little gold ring meant to me, the love and kindly feeling that was in the hearts of those three Indian women has been a very precious memory to me.' "

Over the years, dealings between the pioneers and various Indian tribes were not uniformly tranquil. Although the tribes that roamed across the eastern and central prairies were generally friendly, the nomadic western tribes were implacable. The most troublesome of all were the Comanche, the Arapaho, the Kiowa and the Cheyenne. Bold and warlike, they refused to accede to the usurpation of their ancestral lands or to the slaughter of their buffalo.

The Plains Indians were hunters by tradition, depending primarily on the buffalo for their livelihood. The buffalo supplied not only food but leather for their clothing and tepees and fur for heavy wraps, rugs and blankets. For centuries, the lush grasslands of the Great Plains had provided the Indians with teeming herds of buffalo. In fact, an estimated thirty million head of buffalo roamed the Plains in the early 1800s, and in 1850 at least twenty million remained. But by 1870 the great American buffalo was virtually extinct.

The eradication of the buffalo was one of the most unfortunate chapters in the history of Western settlement. During the early years of the Kansas frontier, white hunters engaged in the wholesale slaughter of the thundering herds. While homesteaders butchered buffalo for their winter food supplies, professional hunters, including the famous Buffalo Bill Cody, were hired to provide meat for railroad construction crews and hides for commercial tanneries.

In addition, plains buffalo hunting became a popular sport over the years. Railroads promoted special hunting excursions, and, from time to time, visiting dignitaries were encouraged to try their hand at hunting. Even the Grand Duke Alexis of Russia, son of Czar Alexander II, journeyed to Kansas in 1872 to hunt these prized animals.

As the buffalo slaughter continued, the Western tribes became increasingly desperate to retain their lands. By the 1860s, the enmity between whites and Indians erupted into open hostilities. Angry tribesmen raided railroad crews and border settlements, while anxious homesteaders armed themselves in defense.

In 1864, the massacre of hundreds of Cheyenne by government troops at Sand Creek, Colorado, was the spark which ignited full-scale warfare. In the months and years that followed this tragic episode, Indian marauders carried out a relentless campaign against the settlers of western Kansas. Travelers on the Santa Fe and Smoky Hill Trails were attacked and murdered, and many settlements in the valleys of the Solomon and Saline Rivers were plundered and destroyed. There were many hard casualties on both sides of the conflict.

Alarmed by the continuing depredations, pioneer families lived in constant dread. At the first rumor of trouble in the vicinity, they prepared to defend themselves and their properties. While many families fled to nearby towns or military forts, others congregated in neighboring homes for protection and comfort.

Lavina Gates Chapman, accompanied by her husband and three small children, arrived in Ottawa County in 1863. In those early uneasy years, their home often became a refuge for frightened neighbors.

"One time the Indians were on the war path and were coming down the river and everyone was much frightened. Mr. Kirkby and

Mr. Falliber, who lived across the river from us, said, 'The Indians are coming, we will go to Chapman's dugout.' So they took the young baby, only three days old, of Mrs. Kirkby's, and Mrs. Falliber taking two other children, one on her back and one in her arms, and struck out for the river. Mrs. Falliber said for them to wait till she took the two children over, then she would come back for the baby. She plunged in and had almost reached the opposite side when she heard a splash and looking around she saw Mr. Kirkby's head coming up out of the water. Mr. Falliber being so frightened by thinking he heard a war-whoop told Mrs. Kirkby to get on his back while he carried the baby in his arms. He bravely started over and probably would have crossed all right but his feet became entangled some way and he stumbled and fell, the baby underneath. But they up and scrambled for shore, all being thoroughly wet, but no one was seriously injured as I gave them dry clothes as soon as they reached the dugout. I put Mrs. Kirkby to bed and gave her a ginger and she was all right. I spread quilts on the floors that night for beds, and all that could get on a quilt were bedded while the men were watching for the coming of the savages. I cooked a breakfast the next morning for fifty-two."

Although the Chapmans and their neighbors were not disturbed at this time, a later encampment of hundreds of warriors in the vicinity renewed fears in the settlement.

"In February, 1865," Lavina Chapman continued, "husband was going with some neighbors to kill buffalo for their hides. . . . When they went out in the morning to hunt they found Indian signs in the country. They shunned them all day and [at night made camp] on Spring Creek. They built just fire enough to fry some meat and boil coffee. All seemed well and all had gone to bed except one who was hovering over the coals, the fire being mostly extinguished, when listen! There was the crackle of brush and an Indian walked in upon them. He gathered up some sticks and placed them upon the embers and blew them into a blaze and rubbed his hands over the fire.

"By that time the camp was all astir. The Indian, still rubbing his hands, raised up and gave a war-whoop. Mr. White said that his hair just stood up like bristles and they told the Indian he should not do so again. The Indian bent over the coals and picked up some more brush and had a good blaze. Still rubbing his hands and shaking with the cold, he raised up and gave another whoop. The Indians began to come in on them thick and fast, and the white men started on the run without their shoes, leaving teams and all. The Indians did not follow them far, as it was so dark, but stayed with the teams."

As the Indian attacks intensified, the government moved to expand its military policing of the frontier. Accordingly, Army troops waged a relentless campaign against the warring tribesmen, and additional military fortifications were established at Wallace, Hays, Harker and Dodge to provide greater protection for the beleaguered settlers and the vulnerable railroad construction crews.

In 1865, Fort Wallace was established on the western borders of the state. Located along the Smoky Hill River, this isolated outpost accommodated up to five hundred soldiers at a time. In the summer of 1867, a band of three hundred Cheyenne, led by the fierce chief Roman Nose, attacked the post. Company G of the Seventh Cavalry mustered its forces and charged the Indians, but the government forces were greatly outnumbered and suffered heavy losses in the ensuing battle.

At the time, Lieutenant David B. Long, aided by his stalwart wife, Harriet Sage Long, served as the chief steward in the fort hospital. Their daughter, Cora Belle, later recounted their efforts during that tragic day as many badly wounded soldiers were brought in for treatment:

"The summer of 1867 was a very critical one, many depredations were committed. The Indians made it difficult for the building of the Kansas Pacific Railroad that was being extended to Denver. In August, the Indians attacked the overland stage station at Pond Creek 2½ miles west of Fort Wallace, the horses and mules were stampeded and made a dash for the fort, with the Indians in close pursuit.

"One company of the 7th Cavalry and a few men of the 3rd Infantry went out to meet the Indians, a hard fight followed, for the Indians were well mounted and well armed and out numbered the soldiers three to one, they drove the command back to the Fort, with quite a loss of killed and wounded.

"Sargt. Williams of Co. 'G' got separated from the company and was shot in the head, stripped of his clothing, heart cut out, nose cut off, hacked and split and scalped with 16 arrows shot into his body. It was a horrible sight. Three men had arrows shot into their bodies which could not be removed without first shoving them through and cutting the fastening which held the barb and drawing the shaft back. Two of these men recovered, but it was impossible to save the third one.

"One poor fellow staggered into the Fort with his scalp hanging—the Indian had been killed before finishing his job—the scalp was sewed into place, dressed and I am glad to say healed nicely, leaving only a slight scar. Mother had been appointed Hospital Matron and was of great assistance in caring for these poor suffering men."

In addition to its military maneuvers, the government continued to negotiate with the tribes. In 1865, peace talks were held along the Little Arkansas River just north of the site of Wichita. After heated debate with hundreds of Indian representatives, new treaties were drawn up to limit Indian hunting grounds and establish reservations. The talks, however, did little to curb the warfare, and within the next two years alone two hundred settlers were killed.

In October, 1867, the peace negotiations were reconvened at the site of an old Kiowa medicine lodge. While government representatives conferred with the chiefs of the Comanche, the Kiowa, the Arapaho, the Cheyenne and the Apache, thousands of tribesmen camped nearby. The Indians, still bitter about the Sand Creek massacre, decried white encroachments on their lands and game reserves. The government agents cited Indian violations of the land treaties and denounced the tribes for their continued hostilities. Although new treaties were signed, these agreements again proved ineffective. The Indian wars continued to disrupt the frontier through 1868, and by the end of the year two hundred more settlers were added to the death toll.

At this time, Mitchell County was in constant agitation. Officially established in February, 1867, the county was first settled by pioneers in the fall of that year. By the following spring, the white settlement of the area had enlarged and the first clusters of cabins were erected along the banks of the Solomon River.

The hostilities in Mitchell County reached a climax during the summer of 1868 as restless bands of Cheyenne and Sioux looted homes and terrorized the settlers. In August, the tribesmen gathered near the mouth of Plum and Asher Creeks to plot their offensive. After a long parley, they swept down through the Solomon River Valley, forcing the local residents to hastily congregate for protection.

On August 12, the warriors made their first attack. It was a typically hot summer day, and one could see for miles in the clear morning sunshine. At this time, the Bell and Bogardus families—among the first to settle in the county—had gathered together in alarm at the Bells' small cabin. Bracken Bell, his wife, Elizabeth, and their one-year-old daughter, Ella, were there, along with David Bell, his wife and two young sons. In addition, David Bell's two nieces, Esther and Margaret, were visiting from Willow Springs. Years later, Matthew Bogardus related the events of that day to a friend, Carrie Gates McClintic.

In the early-morning hours, she reported, as the families set about their chores, a huge cloud of dust, kicked up by horses, suddenly appeared on the western horizon. Esther and Margaret Bell, playing in the yard, watched uneasily as the figures drew closer. Indians dressed for war with bright paint, headdresses, bows and spears approached at a fast gallop. In terror, the girls rushed into the cabin to warn their uncle.

"Things began to happen almost as soon as the Indians arrived," wrote Carrie McClintic. "Bracken Bell and David Bogardus were killed. Bracken Bell was holding his daughter Ella in his arms when he was shot, and the little daughter was cut on the head with a knife or some other sharp weapon. Mr. Bogardus was whipped to death by the Indians after he was shot.

"The house was rifled of everything the Indians wanted and Esther and Margaret Bell were strapped on horses with the other plunder. An attempt was made to place Mrs. Bogardus on a horse but an old dog took up her fight. The Indians attempted to kill the dog but failed. Finally, Mrs. Bogardus cried 'Soldiers' and this seemed to scare the Indians away. Mrs. Bell was placed on a horse, but when a short distance from the house, she jumped from the horse and started to run back but was shot by an Indian.

"The Indians, with Esther and Margaret Bell in their charge, crossed the river to a mound where they held a pow-wow. They traveled the rest of the day towards the Saline River on which they camped that night. The Indians fixed a tepee for Esther and Margaret and placed robes on which the girls slept.

"The journey was continued the 13th but during the afternoon the Indians thought they saw soldiers. The two girls were taken off their horses and left with a squaw while the Indians scouted. The Indians returned towards evening, took the squaw with them, and left the two girls on the prairie.

"They wandered down to the river and found an old vacant dugout. They stayed there that night and the next day they stayed by the river until about four o'clock when they were found by [neighbors].

"The burial ground is on west Asher Creek. Eight people were buried at this place as follows: David Bogardus, Bracken Bell and his wife Elizabeth—these people were killed by Indians; other people buried there are Benjamin Bell, Elizabeth Farrow and two children, one a Farrow child and the other a Nicholas child. This burial ground is the first laid out in Mitchell County and is now marked with a marble monument and a woven wire fence six feet tall around the burial ground."

The Cheyenne and Sioux tribes continued their aggressions throughout the fall of 1868. A series of assaults in neighboring Cloud and Ottawa Counties created widespread panic among the frontier communities. Among other atrocities, the capture of two young women, Sarah White and Anna Brewster Morgan, caused particular alarm.

The first of the two kidnappings occurred along Granny Creek west of Concordia. It was a quiet September afternoon and the White family was busy with the daily chores. Benjamin White was at work in the fields, while his wife and seven children were tending the house and garden. All of a sudden, four burly Indians appeared as if from nowhere. Entering the small cabin, they demanded food from the startled housewife. Believing the tribesmen to be friendly, Mrs. White readily acquiesced to their pleas, and a hearty meal was quickly prepared.

The Indians' intentions, however, were far from friendly. After devouring the food laid before them, they suddenly turned on their hosts. Two warriors grabbed seventeen-year-old Sarah, while the others attacked her shrieking mother and sisters. The house was quickly ransacked and its furnishings were destroyed. Within minutes, Benjamin White lay dead and young Sarah was whisked away as a prisoner.

Sioux warriors captured Anna Brewster Morgan one month later. In 1872 she related the events of her capture to a neighbor, Lavina Gates Chapman. "I was a bride," Anna explained, "my maiden name was Brewster. My brother and I were orphans. Mr. Morgan and I were married September 24, 1868, and I always went with him to the field. On the morning of October 23, it being very foggy, Mr. Morgan thought there was no danger, so he told me that I could stay at the house and do what work I most needed. While I was busy at work, I heard the clatter of horses' feet and rushed to the door to see what was the matter. There were our horses near the door, snorting and looking back. I could not see anything, and thought that Mr. Morgan might have been hurt and managed to free the horses. So I slipped the harness off at the corner of the house and strapped on my revolver. I mounted one horse and led the other and started in search of him.

"I came to the river and the coast seemed clear. I rushed down into the river and started up the opposite bank. The Indians saw me coming and lay flat on the ground until I was right among them, when they jumped and grabbed my horse by the bridle. They had all risen to their feet and there seemed a regiment of them. Everything turned dark to me and when I came to consciousness, I was in a strange country among the hills, bound tight to my horse. They travelled until night, and then camped on a creek. Another band of Indians came in soon after, having a Miss White as their captive, having captured her somewhere near Concordia.

"Then they took us to their village and put a guard over us. They made us do menial service such as carrying wood from the creek for the more favored squaws. We obeyed all orders and gained the confidence of the Indians. During this time, we were laying by a supply of dried buffalo meat so we could escape for civilization the first opportunity presented.

"The warriors came in one day from the warpath and had a big pow-wow. When all was quiet we crawled out past the guards unnoticed. Then we struck the Indian trail and travelled for dear life. We travelled until morning and then hid in some secluded spot where we could see the Indians passing to and fro on the trail seeking for their lost captives. When night closed in we again took the trail and repeated the same until one morning we saw a light on the hill and knew it must be Fort Dodge. We thought it best to keep hidden until the soldiers came out, but we were so hungry to see a white face that we agreed to pass on.

"[We] had not travelled over a half hour when the Indians recaptured us. I fought hard and said I would not go back. But they took me by main force and whipped me and bound me onto the pony. They took us back to the Indian village and they were more strict with us, giving us no privileges whatever. We felt that we would never gain our liberty as we settled down to hard work.

"An Indian chief proposed to me and I married him, thereby choosing the least of two evils and never expecting to see a white person again. My Indian husband would come in from the warpath bringing many things he thought would please me. The squaws were now waiting on me, bringing me wood and laying it down at my door. All my Indian husband expected of me was to tend his horse when he came in off the warpath. He would throw the lariat to me, and I would picket out his horse. I began to think much of him for his kindness to me, and when they brought the news that there were two white men in the camp, I did not care to see them. I was surprised to see my own brother walk into the tent. I had on Indian garb.

"The government had captured five Indian chiefs and was going to hang them. Only on one condition would the government free them, and that was to free myself and Miss White. The Indians took young Brewster and White down to their village, where they found their sisters. There were many things that I have not spoken of. We were piloted back to the Fort, where the officers' wives took us in charge and furnished us with clothing from their own wardrobes. We were then sent to our former homes. After I came back, the road seemed rough, and I often wished they had never found me."

Anna Morgan seemed unable to forget her months in captivity. To make matters worse, she gave birth to a son only a few months after her rescue. Fathered by her Indian husband, the child died at the age of two. For Mrs. Morgan, unhappiness seemed to fill the coming years.

An acquaintance, Emily Harrison, later wrote: "Mrs. Morgan's story is a pitiful one. . . . Miss White, on her return, took it as an awful incident well over, made a little income from rehearsing her story to interested writers, sold her photograph, married a good man and let time haze her memory. When they returned to their homes they were besought by newspaper men and book writers to give an account of their experiences, and furnish their portraits for publication. This Mrs. Morgan refused to do. . . . She considered it a disgrace, and that a relation of it only added to the infamy. Her brother, Mr. Brewster, felt as she did. Mrs. Morgan was a beautiful woman, yellow hair, blue eyes and a lovely complexion. She lived for some years, but her mind gradually failed and I was told she died in an asylum."*

General George A. Custer, in *My Life on the Plains,* wrote about the capture of Anna Morgan and Sarah White in political terms: "It was the story of oft repeated outrages like these, but particularly of these

* Emily Haines Harrison, "Reminiscences of Early Days in Ottawa County," *Kansas Historical Collections,* Vol. 10 (1907–8), pp. 627–28.

two, that finally forced the people of Kansas to take up arms in their own defense. . . . so earnest and enthusiastic had the people of the frontier become in their determination to reclaim the two captives, as well as administer justly-merited punishment, that people of all classes and callings were eager to abandon their professions and take up arms against the traditional enemy of the frontier." The stolen women may have fired a spirit of war among the settlers, but Anna Morgan's account and Emily Harrison's observations make us realize how complex the personal truth of the capture really was. Though Emily Harrison attributed Anna's melancholy after her rescue to "disgrace," somehow Anna's own words keep ringing in our ears: "I often wished they had never found me."

By 1870, the Kansas prairies had become relatively quiet. The military campaigns of 1868 and 1869 had gradually quelled the hostile Indians of the western plains. One by one, they were forced to accede to the government's demands. Relocated on reservations in the Indian Territory, the tribes unhappily resigned themselves to an alien way of life. As the last tribes were pushed southward, an end to the depredations seemed certain.

In the fall of 1878, however, the prospect for a permanent peace in western Kansas was suddenly shattered. On the night of September 9, one final war whoop was sounded as a band of more than two hundred Northern Cheyenne escaped from their reservation at Fort Reno. Dissatisfied with the poor living conditions and meager rations furnished by the government, they were determined to return to their homeland in the Dakotas. Led by Chief Dull Knife, the restless warriors, accompanied by their squaws and children, journeyed into Kansas. Throughout September they swept northward across the state, murdering homesteaders, plundering property, and spreading terror.

Alarmed, the western settlers dispatched frantic requests for arms and military protection. However, the United States troops, under the command of General John Pope, were slow to recognize the extent of the danger and thus failed to capture any of the marauders during their month-long flight across the state. In the end, nearly forty pioneers were killed, scores of white women were brutally assaulted, and an estimated $100,000 worth of property damage was committed before the Indians were finally overpowered near the Dakota border.

PART THREE

CHAPTER SEVEN

A Social People

"Don't think that all our time and thoughts were taken up with the problems of living. We were a social people. We never waited for an introduction or invitation to be neighborly, any day or any night might see a wagon load of neighbors drive to the door and introduce themselves. And they never stayed a less time than the day, and possibly all night. Our houses were small but they had a wonderfully expansive quality, and I never heard of anyone being turned away for want of room."

—MARY LYON

TO THE HARD-WORKING FAMILY of the frontier, social visits brought a treasured time of relaxation and companionship. While the adults chatted together, comparing notes on crops or livestock or sharing confidences, the children would scamper off to play in the barnyard or explore the nearby creek bed. In the late afternoon, everyone would sit down to supper, and afterward there might be group reading, singing or storytelling by the fireside.

Passing travelers were as welcome to the pioneer home as visiting neighbors. A family of new settlers arriving at nightfall would be greeted with fresh coffee and a newly stoked fire. "The pre-eminent law of the land was hospitality," wrote Anna Biggs Heaney. "No stranger was ever turned away from the shelter afforded by the little log cabin. A buffalo tallow candle burned all night in the unshaded window to light some luckless wayfarer to warmth and shelter. Many a time it served its merciful purpose.

"One night twelve people spent the night here. Two wagon loads with eight people were caught in a blizzard and only the deeply rutted freighter roads served to keep the leader somewhere near the trail. The man, whose name was Johnson, said he was about to give up when he saw the light of our log shanty. They made it in and a vigorous hello brought an answering hail from the house. More buffalo chips were piled in the old cook stove, and soon eight tired, cold, hungry, exhausted women and men and children were eating buffalo steak and drinking 'coffee' made from parched corn and sorghum sweetening.

"Mother took her own little son and the woman with the smallest baby in with her. The other two men and two of the children bunked crosswise in the trundle bed. The two men visitors took their blankets to the rude loft of the cottonwood boards laid across the rafters for a place of storage. Father rolled in his army overcoat and a buffalo hide beside the stove while small Stella slept snugly on the table with her head on the flour barrel. And none of the guests of the hotel had to ring for ice water, because every once in a while a ruder-than-usual blast sent icy particles through unchinked crevices to sprinkle the weary sleepers."

Although most travelers stopping in the night were just ordinary families on their way westward, unsavory characters were encountered from time to time. Kate Aplington wrote: "I was alone all day, and half frightened lest vicious-minded stragglers might annoy me. I had no gun, but kept a cup of cayenne pepper and a corn-knife within reach. I knew I could make things hot and interesting for a tramp!" More trusting was Theoline Plummer, an early resident of Muscotah, who recalled one suspicious stranger who wanted lodging for the night:

"One evening at dusk, a tall, ungainly-looking woman, queerly dressed, carrying a heavy satchel, came to our door and asked permission to stay all night. She said that she was alone and did not like to stay at the hotel. She looked tired and travel strained. I told her to come in. Soon afterward, she asked permission to go to bed. When the Doctor [Theoline's husband] returned from the country, he thought she must be a queer duck, but probably she was all right. She guardedly kept her satchel near her head so that she could readily place her hand on it. When we got up in the morning, she was gone.

A short time afterward we learned that our strange visitor was the noted bandit, Jesse James, in disguise."

Old friends and relatives emigrating from back East were always greeted with outstretched arms and warm rejoicing. Bringing special letters or packages from home, these travelers reported the latest home-town politics and told of recent births, marriages and deaths. In turn, the family entertained their guests with stories of their new life and their new friends in Kansas. For the homesick woman severed from her roots, these special visits brought the past just a little closer and often made her uncertain life on the prairie seem more bearable.

In the Oliver household, relatives visiting from their hometown in New York were frequent guests. Always welcome in the family cabin, they were entertained in the evening with family suppers, storytelling and musical accompaniment. Katherine Elspeth Oliver remembered: "What pleasure their coming brought! What eager anticipations—excitement—what plans! The guests were introduced to every pastime and interest of the new country and were invariably enamored with it. The nights were the best of all. Our elders sat about and talked of people and things 'back East' and happenings present and past in that tribal center, Fergusonville, every relative on both sides of the family having apparently taken a fling at education there. We children grew up with the conviction that our parents' former home was a sort of lesser heaven distinguished by personages and felicities far beyond those our prairie home afforded.

"My father was, I am sure, the original 'good mixer' and as a host was irresistible. My mother while more reserved was the soul of hospitality and her table in spite of 'new fangled ideas' regarding diet was renowned. She was especially happy in her gift—music. She had received a generous education in the piano and together with a natural appreciation and facility her playing was a thing of rare pleasure.

"Her little melodeon set up in the crude new home became a shrine of delight to the family and to the neighborhood as well. I have never seen more graceful or instant response than she was wont to give to a request for music, whether from a family guest, a child, or some crude stranger under our roof for the night and hungry for the solacing and almost forgotten pleasure of music. 'Certainly,' she would reply and rising immediately would seat her self before the instrument (later it was the wonderful new rose-wood piano come all the way from New York City and smelling wonderfully).

"Mother always played from memory. She played the lovely old airs—not so old, then—'Annie Laurie,' 'Silver Threads Among the Gold,' and others, popular negro melodies, in lovely arrangement—quaint 'whimsies' to make the children laugh, and the operas: Lucia Di Lammamoor, Il Trovatore and the others. Mother played with beautiful technique and lovely interpretation.

"Our Sunday nights were best of all. Mother used to play as we sat in the twilight and far into the dark, the lamps unlighted. Musingly, her fingers drifted over the keys, weaving from memory a rich medley. Then when the lights were brought someone found the 'gospel hymns,' and crowding the piano we sang."

Picnics were always a favorite time for neighborhood socializing. Local families would often gather for lunch on Saturday afternoon or after church on Sunday. Weather permitting, they would congregate outdoors in the churchyard or along a nearby river bank. The picnic was a community affair, with each family packing baskets of chicken, ham, breads, relishes, cakes and pies. Often, the men hunted buffalo or butchered hogs to be barbecued fresh over an open fire. After a leisurely lunch, there were ball games, foot races or community sings. The old folks often sat visiting in the shade, young couples strolled through the grassy fields, and the children played games of jump rope, tag or hide-and-seek.

For everyone, the afternoons spent together were a special time for making friends, sharing news, and relaxing from the week's work. As Mary Lyon, continuing her remembrances, wrote, "And then the lunch! A gathering of Kansans was, then, as now, a failure without a lunch. When the baskets were unpacked, there was always a plentiful supply, perhaps the cake was sweetened with sorghum, and as this was before the pure food agitation,* the coffee might have been adulterated with rye or beans, but there was nice bread and butter, cream for the coffee, fried chicken, either prairie chicken or the domestic variety, delicious boiled ham, pickles of various kinds for relishes, an abundance for all, and I do not remember of any failure of appetite or complaint of indigestion.

"Ours was a favorite place for social gatherings. We had a nice grove on a creek, that was an ideal place to picnic, and then we had

* At the turn of the twentieth century, national controversy over impure and adulterated food led to the passage of the Pure Food and Drug Act. Enacted in 1906, this legislation prohibited the adulteration and mislabeling of foods or drugs shipped in interstate and foreign commerce.

such a commodious house with a great big room 14 by 16 feet—with a floor, which was a fine place for dancing. Our door was never locked, and it happened sometimes that there was a party at the house and a picnic in the woods when the host and hostess were away."

Holidays were always a popular time for community celebrations, and the Fourth of July was typically the most joyous of all. As one woman observed, "The fourth of July celebrations of those days were the meeting place of the whole county, where once a year old friends met and new friends were made and new settlers were welcomed to the county." Across Kansas, every prairie community observed Independence Day with its own blend of patriotic ceremonies and carefree activities.

The day's affairs usually began with services at church or speeches delivered in the village square. A parade followed, with a winding line of children and adults marching to the beat of a drum or singing to the tune of a flute. Often a makeshift band was assembled to add a more harmonious accompaniment for the festivities. Invariably a community supper was planned for the afternoon, and afterward children of all ages joined in games and races. In Harriet Walter's recollection, it was all in a day's fun:

"We always got up early in the morning because we wished to hear the salute which was fired in every town at sun up. Gunpowder was exploded on an anvil if the town did not boast of a cannon of the Civil War. This salute could be heard many miles away and we listened closely as the sound reached us, now from this town and then another.

"In the meantime, the chores were quickly done, and early breakfast served and an overflowing lunch basket filled. Father harnessed and hitched the driving team up, and they had real driving teams forty and fifty years ago. Little flags were fastened to the bridles and on the buggies and the harness wrapped with bunting and all piled into the wagon. What a day it was. Everyone went. You passed a neighbor or a neighbor passed you.

"How our hearts thrilled as we heard the military band which played the Patriotic airs. We didn't hear much music then. At eleven o'clock there was a parade led by the flag bearer and band. Then there was a float filled with as many little girls as we had states, little girls dressed in white with sashes and caps of red, white and blue, representing each state of the Union. In front holding the flag was the loveliest being on earth—the Goddess of Liberty—dressed in white, a silver starry crown on her head and her long hair waving in the breeze. They sang America and the Star Spangled Banner. Do you wonder then that our hearts were thrilled and that we were proud of our country and our hearts were filled with patriotism?

"At noon a basket dinner was served. Neighbors gathered together in congenial groups and at two o'clock all drifted to the bandstand for 'the program.' There was more band music and singing. A little girl spoke and then the military band escorted Judge Brown to the stand and he delivered the address. About five o'clock we went home tired but happy."

The Fourth of July celebration often continued on into the evening. Many communities purchased fireworks to start off the night's festivities. This display was usually followed by a community dance held in an open barn, schoolroom or courtyard. With all the young people joining in, the dancing continued long into the night.

Anna Evans Carlton recalled how the evening festivities of her first Independence Day in Kansas turned out to be more exciting than anyone had bargained for: "The first 4th of July celebration that was ever advertised in our part of Kansas was held at Douglass, in south Butler County, and I remember it well. The bills announcing this big event were written by hand on large sheets of paper, not printed as they are now, and read as follows:

> A great 4th of July at Douglass, 1871, everybody is invited to come and bring filled baskets and buckets. There will be a prominent speaker present, who will tell of the big future in store for southern Kansas. Grand fire works at night! Eighteen dollars worth of sky rockets and other brilliant blazes will illuminate the night! There will also be a bunch of Osage Indians and cowboys to help make the program interesting. After the fire works there will be a big platform dance, with music by the Hatfield Brothers.

"And truly the fire works proved to be the most exciting that we ever witnessed. As there was not a single building in the little town that had a roof fit to shoot them from, a wagon was drawn up in the middle of the street, and the explosives placed in one end of the wagon box, and a long board placed in the rear and slanting upward, so that when shot off they would shoot up into the air. Lanterns were hung all around this wagon, and the crowd of over 100 people were gathered around the wagon so that nothing would escape them, when suddenly the pile of explosives caught fire. Sky rockets were darting in all directions among the crowd, and there was a regular stampede of Indians and cowboys and people trying to get away as fast as possible."

On the frontier, weddings were a special time for neighborhood rejoicing. If possible, the wedding ceremony was conducted in the local church with a minister officiating; in the absence of a preacher, the wedding took place in the bride's home. A local justice of the peace or county judge united the young couple, while friends and relatives, crowded into the cramped quarters, looked on. Afterward, the newlyweds and their guests were entertained in typical pioneer fashion with a blend of music, food and dancing.

Although resources were slim and elaborate weddings seldom possible, the frontier bride and her family "made do." Jessie Hill Rowland described one such home-style wedding at which her father, a local justice of the peace, officiated:

Hear the mellow wedding bells—golden bells!
What a world of happiness their harmony foretells!

"Great must have been the contrast of a Kansas pioneer wedding and the one thought by Edgar Allen Poe. No doubt the happiness was all there but there could be no ringing of bells to announce the fact. My father, being one of the early pioneers and a justice of the peace, was called upon many times to report 'Wilt thou, Mary?' and 'Wilt thou, John?' Then came the test of trying to live happily ever-after.

"On one of those occasions my father was asked to preside at a wedding ten miles away from our home and my mother received an invitation to accompany him. Upon arriving at their destination they were ushered down six steps into a dugout, where the mother of the bride was preparing a wedding feast. There was but one room and the furniture consisted of two chairs, one with only two rounds to the back and bottomless. A bed made of scantlings, a board table, a short bench, a stove and a motto hung over the door, 'God Bless Our Home.'

"There was no floor, and a sheet had been stretched across one corner of the room. The bride and groom were stationed behind this, evidently under the impression it would not be proper to appear until time for the ceremony, but they were in such close quarters and the sheet was so short it put one in mind of an ostrich when it tries to hide by sticking its head in the sand.

"Mrs. Brown, we will call her, was grinding something in a coffee mill but arose to receive her guests with all the dignity of the first lady of the land. She placed one chair for my mother and one for my father; seating herself upon the bench, she continued turning the coffee grinder. Soon after some of the neighbors came in and at the appointed time the bride and groom emerged arm in arm from behind the temporary curtain and stepping forward to where my father was sitting, all became quiet and he pronounced the words that made them one.

"Soon after all sat down to the wedding supper. The sheet that hung across the corner of the room was taken down and spread over the table for a cloth. Mrs. Brown's efforts at the coffee mill had turned out some delicious coffee, made of dried carrots. There were seven different kinds of sauce, all made out of wild plums put up in seven different ways. The rest of the menu was quite simple and consisted of plain bread and butter, and fried pork. The table was shoved close to the bed and three sat on that side while three sat on the bench. The chairs were occupied and two or three kegs finished out the number of seats.

"After supper the bridegroom took my father to one side and asked him to accept some potatoes in payment for performing the ceremony. He readily consented and returned home."

A bride arriving suddenly from the East could expect an even more makeshift arrangement, as Emma Adair Remington recalled: "Travel being so uncertain then, Dan's bride-to-be* arrived unexpectedly from New York. As no arrangements had been made for the wedding, Dan hired the stagecoach driver to take them to the Rev. S. L. Adair's cabin, where the ceremony was performed with the Adair household witnessing from their beds, as the hour was late and all had retired for the night. They then went to their own cabin, where the bride was greeted by the newly butchered hogs hanging from the rafters, there being no safe place outside to put them. Imagine a bride of today joyously accepting such a reception to her new home."

Happily, not all brides were subject to such crude and hasty cere-

* Daniel R. Anthony (1824–1904), brother of the noted feminist Susan B. Anthony, was married to Annie E. Osborn on January 12, 1864. At this time he was mayor of Leavenworth, Kansas, a post he served from 1863 to 1866.

monies. Mrs. J. H. O'Loughlin remembered a more prosperous frontier wedding:

"Not everyone in western Kansas was poor in those early days and some of the prosperous new comers in 1876 were German-Russians. In 1881, when Carley Howard was sheriff, a girl by the name of Barbara Corbey came from Munjor to do house work for his family. Her family were German-Russians and were well known in Hays. When Barbara was married, she had a big wedding celebration at her home in Munjor and most of the Hays people were invited. The bride wore a changeable green silk dress which Mrs. Howard had brought back from Germany and which she had folded into a bustle when she came through the customs. The parish priest was called away, so the wedding festivities continued for five days until the ceremony was performed. Several beeves had been butchered for the occasion and a special table with fancy cakes and decorations was set for the Hays people. The bride and her family had a separate table with a large bowl of soup and meat in the center from which all were served. The guests took turns eating, drinking and dancing the hoch-zeit with an occasional nap at the home of the near neighbors. Whiskey was passed around after each dance and the men smoked their long-stem pipes even while they were dancing. Every man danced with the bride, and greenbacks were pinned all over her dress by the guests."

To all but the most puritanical pioneers, dancing was a favorite pastime. Every neighborhood get-together, wedding celebration, housewarming party or holiday festivity seemed to include hours of waltzing and square dancing. Moreover, special community dances were held regularly, to the delight of every young couple.

"During the five years we lived on the farm," wrote Annie Gilkeson, "I do not remember one religious service being held in the town, but I do remember the dances that were frequently given and to which I was sometimes allowed to go. There I learned to 'Swing around the circle, Balance all' and dance the Virginia Reel, which I thought the most fun of all."

The neighborhood dances were held in any convenient place. Sometimes the local schoolroom, courthouse or livery stable was cleared for the evening; otherwise a bare plot of ground or an abandoned cabin sufficed. The settlers, dressed in their Sunday best, began arriving early in the evening. It was an affair for the entire neighborhood, young and old alike. Women came with their children in tow, elderly grandfathers and spinster aunts joined the party, and young couples arrived arm in arm. Since the men invariably outnumbered the women, single ladies were particularly welcome.

In fact, there was such a large surplus of bachelors in early Hays that the annual town ball was held in their honor. "The big social event of the year," explained Josephine Middlekauf, "was the Bachelor's Ball that held sway for many years until the bachelors became husbands. One of the Balls was a masquerade and Archer, the Costumer, came from Kansas City and dressed us up. Hill Wilson, Simon Motz, Henry and Frank Krueger, A. D. Gilkeson, Dr. G. B. Snyder, L. F. Eggers, Frank Montgomery, Billy Murphy, Charlie Kaufholtz and Charlie Oderfield were some of the bachelors and I must not fail to mention 'Jimmie' Conwer who always promised himself to be a millionaire, having a black and gold dining room and spend his winters in Honolulu. He went to Colorado and made good every promise."

At most dances, a collection plate was passed among the guests to pay the local fiddler hired for the evening. Drawing his bow, the fiddler signaled for the men to choose their partners, and the dancing began. A grand march often opened the party, to be followed by endless rounds of the polka, the Virginia reel, waltzes, and square dances. As the caller led the dancers through the whirling steps, the onlookers tapped their feet and clapped along to the music. Large bowls of punch and plates of cakes or cookies refreshed the guests and kept them dancing long into the night.

In Hays, a grand ball given by the commander of the nearby fort was the highlight of one year's social season. Catherine Cavender, stationed there with her family at the time, vividly recalled the excitement of that special night:

"We of the Fort had been so well and so often entertained, our post commander, Major D. M. Vance, decided to give a grand ball and invite the whole country. He asked Colonel Pennypacker for the regimental band. The bake house was run night and day, the big ovens turning out bread and roasts and pies and cakes. The ladies of the Fort made salads and fancy dishes and Tommie Drumm sent over loads of liquid refreshments that were not home brew.

"The big problem was girls. With a full Company, nearly all dancing men, at the Fort and the many men from the towns and the ranches, there would be about ten men to each girl, so the two daughters of the Forage Master, who were the only girls of the Fort, and I were appointed as a committee to rustle girls for the ball. If they had no escorts they were to be chaperoned by the wives of the 1st and 2nd Lieutenants of the Company. And the ambulances were to be sent for them and take them home again.

"The night of the ball, it was found that one young lady of our list had not been sent for and no one seemed to know just where she lived. We started out about 8 P.M. to find the young lady, a daughter of Judge Humphrey. We were told the Humphreys lived northwest of town and we drove all over the earth or so it seemed without finding them.

"After a time we found a man who volunteered to *show* us the house, and he did, but we couldn't see it. 'There 'tis,' he said, pointing to a stove pipe sticking out of the ground. The Humphreys, evidently hearing our approach, opened the door. A dark figure appeared in the yellow glow of a magic cave. 'Hey, Judge,' called the man, 'here's some gals come to take your gal over to the doings at the Fort!' The house was a Kansas dugout down a few steps and built against a bank of earth with windows and a door in front. We found it very comfortable inside with a carpet on the floor and lace curtains at the windows.

"When we reached the ball with Miss Josie, the grand march was over, but as we danced 'till the 'wee small hours' in those days, there was plenty of time to dance and we danced real dances—no 'necking' set to jazz music, no kicking fox trots or acrobatic Charlestons. We waltzed to the witching strains of the Beautiful Blue Danube. We danced the Polka and the Schottish, and the galop. We wore low necks and short sleeves and 'trails,' and the dancing men wore white gloves or those who did not held a snowy handkerchief between their bare hands and the ladies' dainty dresses. No hot bare hands on naked backs in those days.

"The square dances held the most fun for the older crowd, and a good 'caller' was always a thing of joy. The night of this ball they had coaxed or bribed a cowboy to call a few sets and show the soldiers from Dixie just how it was done in the wild and wooly West. He wore 'chaps' and spurs, a red silk handkerchief around his neck, and he kept time with his big stetson hat.

"I wish I had the calls he called, most of them impromptu, I think. The first was: 'Git your partners for a Quadrille, Spit out your tobacco and everybody dance.' Once he called: 'Swing the other gal, swing her sweet! Paw dirt, doggies, stomp your feet.' This was mighty embarrassing to the uninitiated, as they did not know how to 'paw dirt' or 'stomp,' which, however, simply meant to do a sort of jig step and lift your feet high.

"Another call of his was: 'Ladies in the center, Gents round 'em run, Swing her rope, cowboy, and get yo' one!' He finished the set with: 'Swing an' march—first couple lead, Clear round the hall an' then stampede.' There was much laughing and cheering, for 'stampede' was a puzzler."

Naturally, few local dances had the grandeur of the Hays grand ball. As Gertrude Burlingame recalled about Topeka—still, in the 1860's, a small, sleepy town: "The only amusements of any kind or description were some little dancing parties gotten up by the Episcopal ladies, and we met in an old stone hall and the walls were so damp that the water ran in little streams. The seats were boards arranged around the room and as the ladies were so scarce, we were not permitted to be wall flowers, so we had lots of fun. We danced the cotillions and the Virginia reel and we had not heard at the time how dreadful they were and that we would certainly all go to perdition."

The year 1864 was a leap year, and to the women of Topeka it provided a good excuse for a party. It also provided a good excuse for an odd breach of Kansas propriety, when a woman named Ann showed up in a precarious state. As Gertrude Burlingame told it, "We had one woman among us, who kept a boarding house and had several little children. She was generous and good hearted as could be, but not quite as particular about the conventionalities of life as we wished. We rather hoped she would not want to come to the party and we would not mention it in her presence and hoped she would not know of it, but as we were making our final arrangements, in came Ann full of enthusiasm over the affair and said she would contribute a roasted turkey, etc. We felt pretty bad and could not say a word.

"The party came off and one of the first on the floor was Ann. She was dressed in a black silk dress, ruffled to the waist, and a black scarf knotted in front and looked very nice, but we watched her anxiously. She did not miss a set. At 12 o'clock, I had to go home and leave the others to serve the lunch, as I had left my sleeping infant daughter Hattie in Col. Holliday's care.

"When I got back, lunch had been served and the dancing was on and so was Ann. She went through that cotillion and started on another, when I noticed a commotion in the set in which she was dancing and Ann was hunting her husband. 'Where is Sam,' she went around asking and several men went to hunt him and found him dozing in a corner back of the stove.

"They got home safely and after Sam had fixed the fires he went for the doctor, but that little fellow did not wait for any doctor to introduce him to the world but came right along unceremoniously. (By the way, that little chap turned out to be the brightest, smartest boy you ever saw.) Mrs. Holliday, who went home with them, returning to the party in less than a half hour, told us of the arrival of the new citizen. We thought we would keep it to ourselves, but it got out among the men and soon they were giggling all over the hall."

Impromptu parties were always popular for an evening's entertainment. A dozen or more young people would often get together to plot a surprise visit to a neighbor's homestead. Packing baskets of food and drink, they climbed into their wagons and buggies and set off across the countryside.

"Surprise parties were frequent," explained Mary Lyon. "A wagon load or two of people would suddenly invade the house, of an evening. If the children were in bed, it took but a few minutes to hustle them out, take down the bed, and then ensued an evening of frolic, enlivened by the strains of the violin by an expert who was a blacksmith for every day; and perhaps he was accompanied by a young farmer as second. Although none were in evening dress, I am not sure they were not as happy as a present-day company in modern surroundings."

Catherine Cavender also remembered the surprise parties she attended. "We went 'Bob' sleighing and sometimes ice skating but the popular society fad was 'Surprise Parties.' The modus operandi was the young men met and planned the 'Surprise.' The girls filled big baskets with good things to eat and the crowd descended unannounced on the poor unfortunate victim—sometimes getting them out of bed—and, taking possession of the house, danced until morning. Uncle Jack Downing was a favorite victim, for he wielded a mighty sassy fiddle bow in those days.

"Once we surprised ourselves and rode over the prairie north of town in a big bobsled in blizzard weather, half the night hunting the folk we were to surprise. Mr. and Mrs. I. M. Yost, not long in Hays then, sent word from their farm 3 miles North of town to the 'boys' to come out and 'surprise' them, that they had plenty of turkey, mince pie, cake and coffee and to forget the baskets. We started out in a snow storm that turned into a blizzard before we got far. When we finally reached Yost's place, they had given us up and were going to bed, but lucky for us, there was a big light in the bay window."

On clear days, a horseback ride over the open prairie was a popular and congenial pastime. Friends visiting together in the afternoon would often mount their horses for a brisk jaunt across the countryside. Sometimes a picnic basket was packed for lunch along the way; other times the riders stopped only to pick wildflowers or to cool their feet in a nearby stream. The women, usually sitting sidesaddle, were as proficient at riding as the men and considered a fast gallop equally exhilarating.

"Our joy rides were horseback rides!" continued Catherine Cavender. "Wild dashes across the prairie, the wind painting our cheek with nature's red! Western women and girls were expert riders, and one of the best and most graceful riders of the day was Mrs. A. D. Gilkeson. I do not dare tell how the Grandmas of today used to 'cut-up' on horseback—you might suspect that Grandma was not exactly as shy and back-numberish as she would have you believe."

As Catherine Cavender noted, Annie Gilkeson was an exceptionally skillful rider. She had grown up on a farm outside Easton and, like most pioneer children, had learned to ride at an early age. One summer she participated in a riding contest at the local fair. Although she did not win first place, her ability, even at that early age, was well recognized.

"I had a part in the first fair held in Kansas," she wrote. "I have forgotten the year, but it was during the war and one of the judges was Colonel Moonlight. I was one of eight ladies who rode for the prize—a beautiful side saddle. One of the conditions of the contest was that, at a certain point, the ladies were to change horses. I rode a prize pony wearing a blue ribbon on his glossy black neck, and he was proud of the fact that he would not walk a step, but pranced all the time. When we came to the time for changing horses, not a woman would ride my horse.

"The prize was given to a Miss St. Clair, an easy, graceful rider whose well-trained mount rode it like a rocking chair. I was well satisfied with the verdict, not expecting to win the prize myself, as I had entered only to please a friend, and further, to show off the beauty of the pony. But not so the crowd, for immediately a clamor arose saying it was not just because conditions had not been met. In a very short time, a purse of six hundred dollars was raised and divided among the seven who had lost. So, it was proved that 'it does not always pay to win.' My share, I know, was seventy-five dollars."

On the prairie, dancing, riding and picnicking were by no means the only forms of amusement. Gamesmen hunted everything from ducks and geese to coyotes and buffalo, and occasionally women also tried their hands at shooting game for sport. There were winter sleigh rides across snowy fields, taffy pulls in warm kitchens, and group spelling bees in the local schoolhouse. Literary societies emerged and provided weekly forums for debates, recitations, singing and dialogues within every growing community. Amateur theatrical groups, made up of the local talent, presented plays in the courthouse or the schoolroom, performing everything from lively informal skits to Shakespearean tragedies.

"Those who have never lived in a new country," wrote one woman, "are inclined to think such a life is full of privations, with no pleasures mixed in, but there is a fascination about it and all can truthfully say they are happy, in good health, and well contented."

CHAPTER EIGHT

A Prairie Childhood

"When I was only a baby we came to Butler County among the earliest settlers. And it is there that my memory of pioneer days and ways centers. My memories must be childish memories for I grew up with that country and before I had reached maturity the country was bearing the fruits of pioneer sowing."

—MYRTLE LOBDELL FOGELBURG

CHILDREN WERE particularly valued in the frontier family, isolated as it was from distant relatives and past friends. With their easy laughter, the children brought humor to difficult times; with their energy, they brought lively companionship; with their developing strength, they brought helping hands to the family's labor. Altogether, they provided a comforting source of family continuity and security. "I recall when the last three babies were born," wrote one mother, "each time I thought, 'This is the nicest baby of all,' and from the way they were received into the family circle every one else would have said the same."

On the whole, the family tended to be large. A house full of six to twelve children was not uncommon, and the high rate of child mortality on the frontier encouraged many parents to compensate with additional children. On a practical level, each new pair of working hands helped the family achieve greater self-sufficiency.

For children of all ages, the daily work load was both physically demanding and time-consuming. For the younger ones, there were the daily chores of carrying water buckets, gathering buffalo chips and picking wild fruits. In later years they joined in the heavier work of plowing and planting, building fences and cabins, trapping small animals and helping about the house.

For the most part, child labor was divided according to the traditional roles of the sexes. While girls assisted their mothers with the regular household tasks, their brothers farmed the fields with their fathers. These working roles remained flexible, however. When the need arose, the girls, like their mothers, pitched in with the heavy farm work. Furthermore, during hard times sons and daughters alike often sought employment on neighboring homesteads or in nearby towns in order to provide the family with extra income.

As a child, Mary Alice Zimmerman regularly assisted her father with heavy farm chores. "I can well remember of the early-day struggles," she wrote. "The soil was virgin. It had to be broken, turned, stirred and taught to produce. With the simple means of the time, the process was slow, but the women bore their half of the load.

"I helped my father on the farm and learned to do the work pretty well, as I was strong for a girl. I soon preferred to have a team to myself when possible. I have always loved the great open out-of-doors, and I think that it was as much from choice as from necessity that I was much of the time out on the farm at work with father, as the younger girls could help mother. But I loved to work with mother and loved her way of making a home.

"Father sent me out one spring day to plant castor beans along the hedge to keep the moles away. He gave me about one gallon of seeds and a sharpened stick. As I look back now, I think it was to have been an all-day job; but, thanks to my ignorance, I found that I could press the stick quite deep into the wet soil, thus could put a lot of seeds in one hole, so was soon through. I never will forget the queer smile on his face when I returned with the empty bag."

On their family's McPherson County homestead, young Bessie Felton Wilson and her brother, Bernard, were put in charge of herding hogs. "One summer," recalled Bessie, "when my father had a bunch of twenty-five or thirty shoats and no corn to feed them, my brother and I herded them around over the farm wherever there was anything to be found that a hog could eat. After wheat harvest we herded them in the stubble field. How tired we were sometimes and how sore the stubble made our feet! We had several of the hogs names, and I used to make my brother believe that they were talking when they grunted, and I being able to understand their hog latin would interpret to him. When these hogs were marketed, we were rewarded for our labors by each being presented with a saddle father had ordered for us from Montgomery Ward & Co."

For the Mitchell family, much of the daily farm work was left up to an active and able-bodied team of six daughters. In looking back, Margaret Mitchell Womer vividly recalled those busy years on the family homestead.

"There were nine children in our family," she began, "six girls and three boys, and as the girls were older and my father not strong, the hard toil of the pioneer life fell to the lot of the girls. We used to set traps on the banks of the Republican and caught wolves, badgers, bobcats and skunks. Wild turkeys were very plentiful then and we sometimes used traps to catch them.

"We had some very interesting and thrilling experiences with some of the animals we caught. One day an older sister and I were out looking at our traps and noticed that a big bobcat that was caught had climbed a tree with the chain hanging to him. I sat and watched him while my sister went for a gun and shot him. Another time we killed a mother wolf and later caught her four little cubs that had fallen into a shallow well while trying to find her. One of my sisters was coming from an errand across the river, when she saw five big wolves chasing a wounded buffalo. They sat on one side of the path and watched her pass, but made no effort to harm her. We saw many large herds of buffalo as they came to the river to drink, and occasionally were able to shoot one.

"Our house was made of logs, and the girls all helped with the construction of it. The cave we made ourselves, and were justly proud of the work, for no one in our neighborhood had a better one.

"We made vinegar out of melon juice and tapped boxelder trees for sap to make syrup and it really was very good. We also kept a supply of skunk grease on hand in case of croup among the younger children. There were lots of fish in the river and my sister and I became quite expert in catching them.

"Sometimes there were unpleasant things to be done but we never thought of shirking them. We had a collie dog that was a great favorite of all the family, but as her family increased too rapidly, it was decided that she must be done away with. How to kill her was a grave problem with us girls. We thought we could not shoot her, so only one other method came to our minds. We took her to a bluff on the river, tied one end of a rope around her neck, and fastened the other end to a tree. Then we pushed her off and ran for home. The horror of the thing is still in my mind."

In the late 1850s, the homestead of the Gilkeson family became a wayside inn. Throughout her childhood years, young Annie Gilkeson undertook many of the daily household chores of cooking, cleaning, and managing the modest inn. She titled her memoir "Our House by the Side of the Road."

"It stood near a little town called Easton, close beside the road which was the main highway leading to the far West, twelve miles from Leavenworth, then the largest town in the territory. The house was a good one, considering the time and place. It was really two log houses joined together by boards. One house was two stories high, and the other was only one story. The distance between the two was sufficient to make a large room, which was used for an entrance. A small cabin was attached to the rear for a kitchen. . . .

"My father was not a farmer, but he had an ambition to see what he could do with a farm. All the knowledge he possessed on the subject was obtained from books, the 'Scientific American' being his chief textbook. We soon found, however, that the business of farming was of secondary importance compared to the form of work which we were compelled to engage in—compelled is the right word. With no thought or intention of keeping an Inn, we were obliged to do so.

"Very early in the spring, people began to travel westward to locate new homes. As our place happened to be a convenient stopping point for the first day's drive out from Leavenworth, and there was no hotel in Easton, they just settled down on us like the hordes of hungry grasshoppers which came later. So now commenced the martyrdom of my dear mother, which ended in the tragedy of her early death. She worked day and night to care for and feed these hungry people. I, then a child of eleven years, was her only assistance, as no other help could be obtained for love or money.

"One day, my mother went to town, leaving me in charge of the place. She expected to be away only during the noonday meal and thought I could put off anyone who might chance to come. All was quiet at the house. So, with my two small sisters, I went out nearby to gather wild strawberries, which grew in profusion. I was busy with the berries when I heard someone speak to me. Looking up, I saw a man. He said that he wanted something to eat; also, that at the house there were a number of others in the same condition. I told him my mother was away and that I could not serve them. He insisted that I could find something for them.

"So, I gathered up all I could find to eat in the house, and set it before them. I made for them, I remember, my first coffee. With much misgiving, in regard to its quality, I served it to them. But they all praised it, said it was fine. Never in all my life after did I get up a meal which received more praise and I felt more pride in. . . .

"We had only tallow candles for light, and one of my duties was to make them each week. The mold held one dozen and that was sufficient for the time. Another one of my easy duties, for mother would never allow me to do anything hard if she could help it, was to parch the green coffee. No ready-to-use coffee, done up in packages, was known in those days. Later, when I was older, I learned to milk cows and make butter. Father had a novel way of making it, gleaned from the 'Scientific American,' of course. He had made four heavy wire rings to cover the top of the kitchen stove. The pans of fresh milk were set on these and scalded. When it had cooled, this milk was then put in the ice box for the cream to rise. Then it was churned while perfectly sweet. So, the butter was sweet and good. But, oh, the bother and work for it!

"An interesting phase of our early-day housekeeping was its sleeping accommodations. We had but one large room to give to strangers, and it contained, I think, six beds. There being no room for partitions, both men and women had to do their undressing in view of each other. But I know how the women managed, for I have done it myself when away from home. They got into bed with all their clothes on. Then, with the covers pulled up, did all their undressing and also dressing under this shelter. But I have wondered since how such ladies as belonged to the Crosby family of Topeka enjoyed it, for I distinctly remember that two of them stayed with us over night. My memory of them is so vivid because of the impression they made on my youthful imagination by the wonderful gay wrappers they donned after removing their traveling dresses. I can even remember just how they were made, and oh, how I wished I had one like them!"

A prairie childhood meant long hours of work, but also hours of play—although in a world filled with poverty and privation children's toys were an unaccustomed luxury. Most pioneer youngsters did not have the familiar porcelain baby dolls, tin soldiers or wooden spinning tops. Instead they learned to stretch their imaginations and make do with the few possessions at hand. Strands of prairie grass were woven into toy crowns, berries were strung into necklaces, and old twigs were whittled into dolls and whistles. "We children," remembered Hannah Darrah, "enjoyed playing in the clay of the river bank. We became quite expert in fashioning dishes, dolls and whole herds of animals out of this clay, which we enjoyed quite as much as the children of today their squawking mama dolls."

Indoors, a trunk of old clothes or a cupboard of kitchenware always yielded its own special treasure trove. "One of the cherished memories of my childhood," mused Nellie Goss, "was the 'Old brown trunk' in the attic—when a child how I loved to rummage thru it. There were innumerable useless articles in it, but Mother had that little of something 'Of the Squirrel' for storage, that was prevalent in the majority of women. There were such things as charm strings, a jewelry box with bits of jewelry in it, a brown silk quilted baby bonnet, a blue and white checkered box that contained a slice of petrified wedding cake, an endless lot of knit lace and lace patterns, autograph albums and daguerreotype photos, etc."

On occasion, even an old potato, a corncob or a spool of thread was useful to pacify a teething baby or entertain an inquisitive toddler. The year 1864 was difficult for Gertrude Burlingame and her young family. Money was scarce, fresh food was hard to come by, and simple playtoys were beyond reach. "We had to change boarding houses in the spring," she explained, "and we got into one where they were not keeping boarders for their health. Everything eatable was very scarce. I was hungry most of the time, and one day a grocery man who had been to Leavenworth and returned brought home two sweet potatoes and his wife kept them on a fancy plate on her dressing table all the time. I had known her to give them to her six months old baby on the floor to play with. Playthings for babies were not thought of those days.

"I am afraid I forgot all about the ninth commandment, 'Thou shall not covet thy neighbor's house, his wife, his ox, or his sweet potatoes or anything that he hath.' Well, one day the sweet potatoes were missing. No one could tell what had become of them. I had looked at them so longingly, I was afraid they thought I had taken them, so I kept to my room.

"It was a week or ten days after their disappearance, when one morning I heard a commotion down at the end of the hall and all of the women of the house were gathered around something when the chamber maid came up to my door and announced they had found the sweet potatoes down a knot hole in the floor. None of them could get their hand down it, but they thought my hand was thin enough. *Thin*, why my whole body was nearly thin enough to get through. I reached down and brought up the potatoes and also long lost spools of thread, scissors, thimbles and many other things. That baby of mine walked all over the house when she was nine months old. She was a quiet kind of a child with big honest blue eyes and was made much of by the women of the house and given the run of their rooms and all the time she was feeding that hole, a baby trick, with everything she could get her hands on. But I assure you it was the only well fed thing about that house."

Small animals were usually plentiful on the prairie farm and delighted children then no less than they do today. "My very first memory," wrote Myrtle Lobdell Fogelburg, "is of chasing a pet duck about on a sunny hillside, the 'quack quack' with which he would elude my outstretched hands when I pursued him, and then the happy way he would come and settle himself in my lap or by my side at other times. I have thought of that duck many times in later years when I have seen a thing or person too urgently pursued.

"Another picture that stands out in my childish memory is of a family of playful kittens romping like squirrels over the branches of a fallen tree that had been brought from the wooded stream nearby for fuel."

Other small animals were not quite as winsome as ducks and kittens. As Clara M. Barber Hunt remembered: "In the pioneer days we were not bothered with rats, but mice were plentiful. I, being the youngest of the family, always asked father to get me a nickel's worth of candy when he was leaving for town. One time he asked me which I would rather have, the candy or a mouse-trap. I hesitated, for I knew we needed the mouse trap; but finally decided he should get it. When he came home and handed me the trap, I knew I would have to do without candy for some time, for the trap had cost fifteen cents. The trap worked all right and before we retired that evening we had caught twenty-four mice."

Among the special wonders of the new land, the Indians captured the imagination of many children. While some youngsters remained terrified of them, others viewed the Indians with unabashed fascination. They were openly curious about these people whose language, dress and mannerisms were so mysterious. It was not unusual that a child's inquisitiveness was met with the same interest on the part of peaceful tribesmen themselves.

The experience of one small boy in Jewell County exemplified the warmth and candor which many children displayed toward their Indian neighbors. Lillian Forrest tenderly described the incident:

"One afternoon as the summer was closing, Mrs. Clark went up the creek to visit her sister. Laddie Clark stayed at home with his father. He could amuse himself by the hour, and must have been a very attractive youngster. Whatever he heard he remembered, and could tell all about it.

"Early in the afternoon a band of so-called 'Noble Red Men,' arrayed in all the paraphernalia of savage life, suddenly came into the yard, and walked into the house. Why bother to knock at the door of any cabin located in the Indian country? Mr. Clark was amazed, but Laddie was delighted. Whatever Mr. Clark's motives or reasons were, he excused himself, and left his own house. And Laddie played the role of hospitality to the entire band of wild, gay-looking strangers.

"The Indians were greatly attracted to the little fellow, who began to show them everything in the house, even things packed away in boxes, and tell all about them. This is a top his Grandma gave him when they started away, and he showed them how to spin it, and they all laughed. This is a stocking his mother is knitting for him to wear when it gets cold. This is the best white shirt of his father's, and he had not had it on since last time at Grandpa's. Just one thing after the other, even to the use of the rolling pin. The Indians laughed, and sometimes said 'Huh.' Then Laddie tried to say it, and the Indians enjoyed the effort, one of them coaching him until he said it right. Laddie went on showing things, talking all the time, his curls bobbing around, eyes shining, as he kept glancing at all of them, but unconsciously, though wisely, most of the time at the leader.

"The afternoon slipped along and Laddie began on his colored pictures of religious scenes from the Bible, beloved by most children, and which he had permission always to see. First, there was Daniel in the Lion's Den, a favorite. He was such a good man that even the lions liked him and would not hurt him. Some Indian said 'Huh!' Then Laddie said it, and they all laughed. Then another favorite was Jesus blessing Little Children, and Laddie told all he had ever heard about it. Then he showed Jesus nailed to the Cross, and told how he loved everybody and died for everybody. The Indians looked intently at the picture, but did not laugh or say 'Huh!,' but all of a sudden left the house in a hurry, and went away as quickly as they came."

Not all new experiences were as carefree as little Laddie's with the Indians. Nettie Ferris recalled how she and her sister were left alone one day while their mother was teaching school and their father had to leave the farm suddenly:

"Father, while at work in the corn field, discovered that the cattle had broken fence and were missing. A storm was brewing, so he gave the little girls, aged about two or three years, instructions to keep the door closed and not to touch the fire. Then he departed in search of the cattle.

"Little Nettie and Minnie amused themselves by looking at pictures in the almanac, etc., until noon soon rolled around. There was still a very good wood fire in the little kitchen stove, and plenty to eat, such as it was, so the girls ate all they could find and thought they were having the time of their lives.

"Two more hours passed, three hours passed, the storm grew worse, no mother was there to tell them, 'Never mind, we are all right, it will let up by and by.' No father appeared.

"It was growing rather gloomy and lonesome, the fire was dying, and the heavy gusts of wind blew open the outer door. By the combined efforts of the children, it was repeatedly closed, all the chairs in the house (three in number) were placed against the door. They were as nothing against the heavy gusts of wind. All the wood from the wood box was placed in and about the chairs.

"The smaller girl cried, the other one wanted to but didn't dare, the room grew cold, the fire was out, every accessible coat, blanket and quilt was brought into use and finally, just at the end of the day, there appeared a wet, tired man bringing home the storm-driven cattle.

"After a short wait at the door until the sticks of wood could be removed and he finally gained admission and saw the plight of the poor little frightened tots and realized the lateness of the hour and how brave they had been, he cried for joy."

If storms came raging out of the sky to frighten children, out of the earth came another source of terror: rattlesnakes. Since one quick bite from a rattler could prove fatal, children of all ages were warned to keep a careful eye each step of the way.

"Rattlers were very numerous here in the early days," wrote Bessie Wilson. "Once when quite small, I crawled upon the roof of the cave to secure a board on which to place my mud pies. The board had been purposely laid there to cover a hole in the roof to keep out the rain. On reaching the board I sat down and turned it over. There coiled around the hole was a very large rattle snake. It raised its head about five or six inches and began lolling its long red tongue at me. I was too young to be frightened but called, 'Oh mamma! come and see the snake.' She came running, catching me by the arm and ruthlessly snatching me from my perilous position. By the time she had finished killing this snake with the garden hoe, she was ready to collapse."

Like the holiday season elsewhere, Christmas on the frontier was a joyous and festive occasion for children and grownups alike. Pioneer families, clinging to their sentimental customs, were determined to celebrate with what little they had. The traditional tree and handmade decorations added a touch of color to an otherwise stark cabin, and a simple gift was fashioned for each child from whatever materials were at hand.

Special holiday prayers and meals shared with friends and neighbors were often the highlight of the festivities. While the fields outdoors glistened with snow and ice, indoors blazing fires gave each small home a warm, hospitable glow. Long red stockings adorned the hearth, and the aroma of freshly made cakes, cookies and candies filled the house. "Christmas was a glad time for us," Nellie Goss recollected. "We were happy when it came and sorry when gone. In the late fall would come a barrel of canned fruits, preserves, jelly and the cans packed in dried apples, quinces, peaches, pears and cling peaches dried with the pits in them, and the contents were kept from us children and on Xmas eve we would hang up our stockings and in them was placed some of each kind of the dried fruits.

"In the barrel was also packed a pail of sorghum molasses for Mother to make the Xmas taffy and gingersnaps. Grandma did some hand work out of pretty flannel scraps, that was tucked in the barrel, made little flannel mittens and bound them with wool braid, ear muffs for the little boys, rag dolls and little quilts, etc., that was real Xmas. And Mother always shared with her neighbors, especially did the little folks enjoy the bread and jam (corn bread usually)."

Like children everywhere, pioneer youngsters anxiously awaited the arrival of Santa Claus. In contrast to the austerity and hardships in their lives, they treasured the few simple gifts tucked into their stockings and eagerly joined in the recitations of holiday poems and prayers and the singing of carols. Mary Rarick Rouse wrote: "We knew the Christmas story well and the boy Jesus whose birthday it was. As for gifts, if we ever had any they were homemade. No toys to buy if we wanted them, and nothing to buy with. Our stocking was always hung up, faith of childhood for Santa, an apple or popcorn ball or wooden doll or rag one, all homemade. We always found something and how happy we were."

Harriet Adams described the special jubilation and excitement she felt as a child in the 1870s:

"The Christmas which made the first lasting impression upon my mind, I think, must have been the one following my seventh birthday. I remember so distinctly the air of expectancy and secrecy which invaded the household. Sister Zu was quite active in fostering the spirit. She was an able entertainer, and furnished the stimulation necessary to make the approach of Christmas a very exciting event. Among our books was a volume of selected poems, some of which were illustrated. Zu often read to us from this, and before that Christmas this invaluable collection must have been consulted again and again, for between its covers, somewhere in the middle, was a fascinating picture of a jolly, white-bearded old man with a sleigh and reindeer, and oh! the undescribable delight of that little group as Zu read, ' 'Twas the night before Christmas, and all through the house not a creature was stirring, not even a mouse.' Then too, the moon and the weather must have fitted in more perfectly to the description, 'The moon on the breast of the new fallen snow, gave the luster of midnight to the objects below.' For, after dark I would peep out of the window, or out of the door to consider anxiously whether all conditions were favorable, the glistening expanse of snow deep enough to support that wondrous reindeer-drawn sleigh.

"Then as Christmas Eve approached I was filled with anxious questioning as to how St. Nick could get into our house, to fill our waiting stockings. There was no chimney down which he could slide safely, in fact I finally decided that it was an absolute impossibility for him to fit into the house through any chimney it possessed. My concern on this matter finally reached such a pitch that I took it up with Mother. I told her my fears, and she said he would most certainly be able to leave his gifts, for when no large chimney was provided, the parents would leave the door open a crack at least, so he could push his way in with no difficulty whatever. This was a most reasonable solution of the difficulty, and I was fully satisfied, and later events proved that my faith in her explanation was justified.

"No Christmas is ever quite complete without a tree and candles, and we little folk saw all the preparation of the tree. We were living but a short distance from the Little Blue River, and on the bluff nearest our home was a scattering growth of cedars. Father took us with him as he carried an axe and selected the tree, which he cut, and big brother helped carry it home. Then Father set it up securely in the center of the living room and found a piece of tin and made the candle holders, and fastened them to the tree. When that much was accomplished, it was time for the little folk to get to bed, for under no consideration would it be good form for any of the children to be awake when Santa would arrive.

"Christmas morning we were awake early, but it was an inviolate rule that the tree could not be seen until after breakfast was eaten. So we hurried through a perfunctory meal, then lined up outside the living room door, the least child ready to lead the grand march, while Father and Mother went in to remove the sheet with which it had been necessary to cover the tree to protect it from prying eyes, and to light the candles.

"When the door was opened we marched in and clear around the tree, taking in the beauty of the candles, and the tree festooned with strings of cranberries and popcorn and gay colored ribbons, while we looked for the gifts hidden in the branches and protruding from our stockings. Then there was the most delightful odor of scorching cedar, and Father would keep walking around and around the tree smothering every smoking stem and keeping the candles burning safely, while he and Mother distributed the gifts which Santa Claus had brought.

"I was blissfully happy, and I am sure my little brother George was too. There was nothing lacking to make it a perfect Christmas. I have long since forgotten what toys that magic tree bore, except one thing, and that was a Noah's Ark. To this day when Christmas shopping and I see a Noah's Ark among the other toys, I can picture two small children, a little girl and a smaller, sturdy little boy, side by side as they arranged twigs from the Christmas Cedar into rows or groups of trees and placed amongst them the animals which Noah had saved from extinction.

"In children the sense of comparative values is largely undeveloped, and I doubt very much if children of the present day, with the profusion of toys now attainable, derive any more joy from their expensive array than did we, with the less expensive and simpler ones which Santa Claus gave us."

Although hard work and austerity touched every frontier childhood, it was not only the difficulties which were remembered in later years. The tribulations were balanced by warm remembrances of playing along the creek beds, picking wildflowers, baking special wheatcakes or laughing at family celebrations. As one woman wrote, "What a blessing is the childish nature which clothes dull surroundings in fancy dress and drives dull cares away. The sand pile where we played after the red sun went down was transformed into moats and castles with just as much enjoyment as if the land, like Canaan, had been flowing with milk and honey."

CHAPTER NINE

Classrooms and Schoolmarms

"The miracle was that a love of 'learning' ever survived the rigors of school days then. But it did."

—VERA PEARSON

IN MANY WAYS, the history of the frontier reveals a pattern of ongoing transformations. Across Kansas, the barren plains were plowed into fertile fields, the tough sod was hewn into family cabins, and the endless stretches of prairie grass were fenced into rich pastures. In the course of changing the land, the people of the frontier themselves changed and grew. They became the architects not only of soddies and cabins, but of a new society.

This cycle of change also touched the lives of the first generation of pioneer children. In the beginning, the prairie wilderness offered the young few avenues for traditional learning. Hard work and deprivation seemed to be the land's own harsh instructors, and any child who desired schooling in the three R's found the prospects dim. Martha Hutchison, looking back on her own experience, wrote: "I was twelve years old, and there were not many advantages for a child of that age in a new country where there were no schools, no papers, or books, and whose parents could neither read nor write."

While most parents were not themselves well educated, they recognized that education was vital to the advancement of their families and the betterment of their communities, and soon an impromptu form of schooling was under way. If the mother was literate, it was invariably she who took on the responsibility of instructing the young, in the privacy of the family cabin. Despite the obvious lack of school supplies and reading materials, she taught the basic skills to a small circle of her own children and any neighboring youngsters. Often using the family Bible as a text, she taught them the alphabet and the rudiments of reading. "Mother found no time to read," recalled J. C. Ruppenthal. "But she guided and directed somewhat the children as they learned to read. Like her husband, she had learned to read and write English quite well without ever going to school to learn that language. Her mind was filled with the lore of the Bible as she had learned it when a child, with Mother Goose rimes, with both words and music of gospel hymns and popular songs, with the sayings of Poor Richard, and some German rimes and folklore."

In the cabin "classroom," the hard dirt floor usually served as the blackboard and a long pointed stick was used to scratch out letters and arithmetic tables. The children were made to memorize grammar rules and recite history dates, and spelling contests between siblings often helped pass the time. In the 1870s, Emily Biggs started the first neighborhood school in her own cramped dugout.

"Her children were growing up," explained her daughter, "and there were no schools. So she searched out her hoarded school books and her old school bell, made the versatile flour barrel into a teacher's desk; the goods box, dining table, kitchen table, shoe bench, general utility table became students' desks; and the small Guy and Stella, and frequently some neighbor's child, mastered the intricacies of the old blue-backed speller and the McGuffey series of readers with their wonderful hero tales—and a greater heroism was all around them.

"Many of the neighbor children got their first and almost their only schooling from Mrs. Biggs. She taught the simple rudiments of the three R's to a man who has since represented his county in the state legislature. A sheriff of Lincoln County learned to read beside her old cookstove by her buffalo tallow candles' light. One of the foremost district judges of the state is proud to count himself one of Mrs. Biggs' boys."

For most foundling communities, it was often several years before formal school districts were established and public funding was available for school support. And so the impetus to organize local schools was left up to the settlers themselves. The construction of a schoolhouse and the hiring of a teacher depended entirely upon the pooling of their own limited resources.

At first, the neighborhood schoolhouse was often no more than an abandoned dugout or sod cabin. A potbelly stove, with a load of cow chips stacked beside it, might fill a corner of the room, and a small slate blackboard might adorn the front wall.

"I was employed to teach a three months school on Oak Creek about four and one-half miles from Cora," noted Emma Handy. "The school building was a sod 'dugout,' about fourteen feet long with dirt floor, unplastered walls, two small windows in front, heated by a small fireplace about one yard across. It had neither blackboard, teacher's desk nor chair. The seats were small logs split and supported by pegs, and were placed at the sides of the room. I taught in five districts and in all there were no outbuildings, but some schools had teacher's desks and chairs, also blackboards and lights. The Cora school had a small frame building with floor and stove. I think at the time I was teaching, not more than three or four schools had floors."

Vera Pearson also described the starkness of those first classrooms. "They had a few bare benches, flat, without backs, and so far off the floor that little legs, dangling high in the air, would ache cruelly before a change of position was possible. An extra-brave or desperate pupil might lie down a bit to relieve the strain, but the season of relief would be short lived. No charts, no maps, no pictures, no books but a Speller. They would have 'numbers' later, but some of the little fellows would never get that far. The miracle was that a love of 'learning' ever survived the rigors of school days then. But it did, in some cases."

To compensate for the lack of textbooks and supplies, the students brought to school whatever materials they could find at home. With their dinner pails in hand, they trudged to class carrying their own miscellaneous books, slates, rulers, tablets or pencils. At times, the array of available books that could be brought to school made group readings or class assignments difficult. While some children were fortunate to have copies of *McGuffey's Readers*, *Youth's Companions*, spellers or dictionaries that had been transported from the East, others had only a tattered Bible or an outdated almanac for their reading lessons. Nevertheless, despite the disparities in both their supplies and their levels of work, the pupils came together in class for a time of learning away from their chores.

"I remember the first school I attended," exclaimed Roxana Rice, "a room crowded full of big boys and girls, noise and confusion with now and then a howl from some boy that was being whipped. I and my brother, with another boy, occupied a bench with no back near the stove. When the stove became too warm, we whirled and faced the other side. The boy with us wore a paddle fastened around his neck. On this paddle were pasted several letters of the alphabet and these were changed every day. How I envied that boy because his folks were making so much pains with him. The attention given him I coveted, though the letters he paraded I knew as well as I do today.

"I do not know how I learned to read. We had the English reader and the spelling book—Webster's great spelling book that saved the language of the country from being cut into little local dialects. My brother, older than myself, complained one day that his lesson was hard. Someone took the reader and read it to him. I thought it was very fine. To my surprise I could read it without a hitch."

Generally, the class structure was informal, even if the discipline was strict. The school terms were usually short, lasting only a few months at a time. Although most students were interested in their studies, they attended only as their farm chores and the weather permitted. The clanging of a sturdy iron bell that hung outside the schoolhouse door called the youngsters to class each morning. Arriving by foot or horseback, students of assorted ages and various grades took their seats together in the one room. The curriculum, usually ungraded, was left largely to the discretion of the teacher herself. Reading, writing, grammar and spelling always consumed a large portion of the class time, with the basic arithmetic skills in constant review. In addition, geography, history and geometry were taught when pertinent books, maps or globes could be obtained.

At this time, the teaching profession was open to both men and women who met the basic qualifications of a minimal education. In practice, however, it was women who filled the ranks of the profession. With salaries invariably low, most communities lacked the funds to attract many men. Women, on the other hand, lacked other professional opportunities and were eager to accept these positions. In fact, one early teacher maintained that "about two thirds of the women of Kansas have taught school."

Since public funds were initially insufficient to pay the teachers' salaries, the early community school was usually managed on a subscription basis. The local teacher taught for whatever salary she could get, with tuition ranging from one to two dollars a month per pupil.

Overland stage, c.1860.

Arriving by train.

An emigrant wagon train passing through Topeka, 1879.

A pioneer family poses with the covered wagon that brought them safely to Johnson County, Kansas.

A frontier couple newly arrived in Greenwood County. At first the family home was often no more than their wagon or some other temporary shelter.

A one-room log cabin near Humboldt, Kansas.

A dugout home in Norton County.

A Kansas "soddy," Decatur County.

A dugout interior, c.1905.

On the prairie, women wore dresses made of sturdy calico or gingham.

Harriet Elizabeth Adams remembered her mother's frontier homemaking in a world without conveniences.

Neighbors May Terry and Maggie Lee take time out from their chores to pose for a portrait. The year is 1870.

"Something very precious," wrote Mattie Huffman—the family plow.

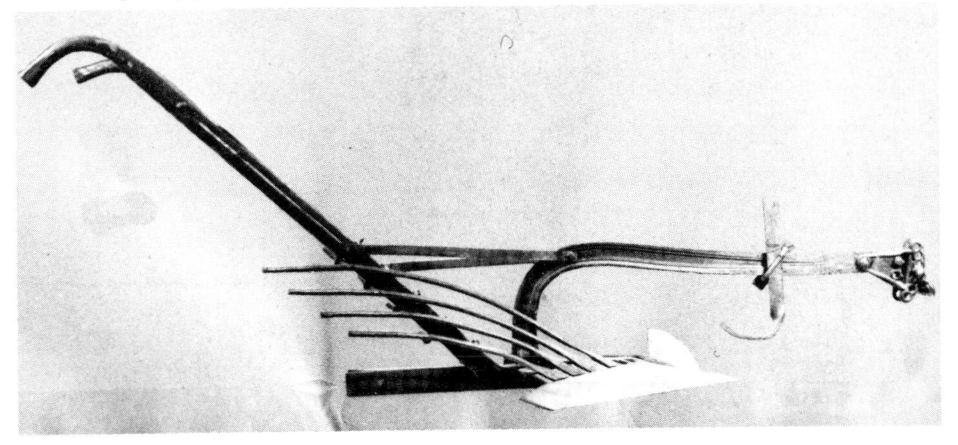

Frontier women often made their own yarns and cloth.

A Kansas washday.

Woman watching a boiling caldron.

A pioneer homestead with outbuildings. Settling miles apart from one another, pioneers faced the starkness of the wilderness alone. COURTESY OF JOANNA STRATTON.

Cattle in a blizzard on the plains. Illustration by Charles Graham is from Harper's Weekly, *1886.*

Anne Bingham remembered the isolation she felt as a young pioneer wife.

OPPOSITE

TOP
Fighting a prairie fire, as depicted in Harper's Weekly, *1874.*

MIDDLE
Illustration of a starving pioneer family in the aftermath of drought. From New York Illustrated News, *January 19, 1861.*

BOTTOM
A prairie windstorm illustrated in Harper's Weekly, *1874.*

A swarm of grasshoppers stopping a train. Illustration from Nebraska History Magazine.

A Kansas garden overrun by grasshoppers, 1874. "When they came down," wrote Mary Roberts, "they struck the ground so hard it sounded almost like hail."

A family of Pottawatomie Indians.

Chetopa, an Osage chief, paid an unexpected call on Hattie Wilson's family one day at suppertime.

Young women of the Cheyenne.

Two hundred thousand buffalo hides piled up in Dodge City. In twenty years' time, the American buffalo was virtually extinct.

Shooting buffalo on the line of the Kansas Pacific Railroad, as depicted in Leslie's Illustrated News, *June 3, 1871.*

An artist's representation of Sioux Indians preparing to attack.

"Custer's Demand." Artist: Charles Schreyvogel.

Sarah Jayne Oliver. Her daughter Kathryn recalled how her melodeon playing delighted family and friends.
COURTESY OF JOANNA STRATTON.

A summer picnic. "A gathering of Kansans was then, as now, a failure without a lunch," wrote Mary Lyon.

Celebrating the Fourth of July in South Haven, Kansas, 1889.

A German Lutheran wedding.

Masquerade party and dance, Englewood, Kansas.

A community outing in Clark County in the early 1890s.

Paying a social call in Sheridan County.

In order to supplement this subsistence salary, the teacher regularly "boarded around" at the homes of her students, residing for the longest period in those homes with the most children.

"When I received my first certificate to teach [in 1883]," remembered Katie McGee, "I was not yet sixteen years old, but as I received grades sufficient, I was allowed to begin my school on a permit. I taught my first term two miles from home, and received $15.00 a month and boarded around with the scholars. The second term was taught seven miles from home, and I received $20.00 and boarded around.

"Many and varied were the experiences of the teacher who had to board around—many places being three miles from the schoolhouse. Many times all I had to burn was green wood, and sometimes had to chop that myself."

Olive Owen also recounted her first experiences boarding around at Shawnee County homes in 1857. "To help out financially, as well as to do something for the country, it was decided that I might teach school. Although only fifteen, I was old for my age and had completed common school and had taken some work at the academy. . . .

"Then I went around the neighborhood and gathered the children for a subscription school. The parents couldn't afford to pay me much money, so I was supposed to board around as part of the remuneration. The greatest trial in this was that one family was a family of mulattoes. The father was a Frenchman and the mother a negro. I had to take my turn staying there for fear of offending them. As we had never seen negroes before we came to Kansas, I was naturally prejudiced. But my experience there was most pleasant. I was given a spare room; waited upon and treated like a queen, and fed upon the choicest of foods, for 'Black Ann,' as the woman was known, was a famous cook."

Belle McNair Logan worked for her room and board during her years first as a student and later as a teacher. It was in 1872 that her Kansas school years began. "That winter," she explained, "I attended my first term of school in Kansas, in Smith Center, working for my board at the A. J. Watson home. . . . I will tell you how I earned my board. I arose early each morning and got breakfast; we always had biscuits for breakfast, and beans and corn bread for dinner. Mrs. Watson was a cripple, unable to do anything, even to dress herself, but a good manager and could plan well which was a great help. After breakfast I washed the dishes and Hattie wiped them. I put the beans on before going to school and ran down at recess to make the corn bread. At noon finished the dinner, ate and ran back to school; after school made beds, washed the dinner dishes, then mopped, ironed or patched as was necessary, while on Saturday I did our washing.

"At the age of sixteen I received my first certificate to teach. I taught four years. My first two terms were in the Freaky district at $10.00 per month the first year, and $12.50 the second year. I boarded around and never wanted a place; every week it was 'Teacher, you will go home with us next week? We are expecting you,' and I think they did."

In time, these privately organized neighborhood schools were absorbed into public-school systems. In Kansas, the school system operated on the basis of separate rural districts established within each county. Under provisions of the state constitution, these rural districts, formed upon petitions by county tribunals, were intended to function independently.

In general, the residents of each district had control over the funding and organization of their local schools. Meeting annually, they determined the length of the school term, levied taxes or issued bonds for the school financing, and influenced the general teaching standards. Moreover, they elected their own district school board members and the overseeing county superintendent who managed the local schools.

In 1879, Sara Magrane Bissing and her family settled on a claim five miles south of Hays. Concerned at the absence of any school in her community, Sara herself undertook the organization of the first official school district in the area. "I went to town to see Dr. Gochenour, who was county superintendent at that time, and stated the case to him. He told me to take a petition and get the required number of signatures; then to come back to him and he would let me teach a three months term in order to draw the public money and start the school, which I was glad to do.

"Armed with my petition and carried by a good little bronco pony, I scoured the country for signers, which I readily got. Finally the school was established, but there was no school house, so mother said we could use one of our upstairs rooms. As teachers were not so plentiful then as now, nor quite so smart, I had no trouble landing the job, even though I had no certificate. As to the wages, I got the munificent sum of $20.00 per month and boarded myself and family. Let me tell you I was the proudest girl in Ellis County."

On a day-to-day basis, the administration of the district school system was carried out by a local school board, consisting of three elected members. It was the responsibility of the district board to hire qualified teachers, provide adequate school supplies, maintain the school facilities and file the required district reports. The board members, of course, were not always in agreement on these routine administrative decisions. In the town of Victory, the purchase of new school desks in 1878 sharply divided the three-man committee.

"In December," explained Bessie Wilson, "two members of the school board, after being interviewed by an agent, decided to purchase seats with desks for the school building. This was done despite the fact that almost every patron in the district, as well as the third member of the board, had expressed themselves at a called meeting as being opposed to buying at that time on account of lack of funds. When the seats arrived, these two men, with the aid of a friend or two, placed them in the school house after night. As soon as the third member found out what had been done, he and four or five of his faction went at night and took them out, piling them up on the school yard. Then the first bunch swore out an injunction against the second for one hundred and fifty dollars damage. The seats were again placed in the building, where they remained. The law of course protected the men who purchased the seats."

Nor, it seems, were the local school boards always receptive to an individual teacher's "progressive" ideas, In her first classroom, Lydia Murphy Toothaker of Johnson County was determined to teach geography, despite the objections of one member of the local school board. As she explained, "The members of the Board were John Morrison, John O'Roark and Christian Roberts. . . . Christian Roberts objected to the teaching of 'Joggerphy.' He explained between tobacco emissions, 'Miss Murphy, it wouldn't be so bad if it was just boys, but we think too much of the girls to have them spiled, their religion tooken away by teaching joggerphy.' Tactfully, I began by teaching the singing geography 'Augusta on the Kennebec, Maine, etc.' Christian was very fond of singing and before long he was lustily running the changes of the states and their capitals with his children. From that time on I taught geography without interruption, and no apparent corruption of morals or religion ensued."

These local school districts were not autonomous. Centralized on a county-by-county basis, they were managed, in large measure, by an overseeing county superintendent. Elected annually, the superintendent directed both the district boards and the local teachers on any matters regarding the operation of the schools. It was his responsibility to visit all the county schools on a regular basis to oversee the class instruction and curriculum. At his own discretion, he was able to review all prospective teachers by setting the prescribed standards, giving the qualifying examinations and issuing the necessary teaching certificates. In addition, the superintendent retained the authority to create and realign any school districts within his jurisdiction.

India Harris Simmons came to Kansas from Ohio to join her homesteading parents and was soon appointed as the first schoolteacher of the Prairie Range district of northwest Kearny County. The story of her first year shows that though a true school system was evolving, the circumstances in the local prairie schoolhouse were slow to improve.

"School opened in October of 1888 with nineteen pupils. Not wishing to postpone the opening of school until a suitable building could be secured, the patrons decided to use a dugout which had served as a dwelling for a pre-empter, who had 'proved up' and gone.

"The outlook, or speaking more exactly, the inlook, was not reassuring. The floor and walls were just plain dirt, not even adobe plaster, and the one window and the cellar type of doorway gave scant illumination. Plain benches without backs ran around three sides of the room. There were no blackboards or other school equipment. Decorating it, or improving it in any substantial way would take at least a little money which could not be spared by the district until more land was 'proved up' and made taxable.

"So, clean 'gunny bags,' a kind of coarse burlap bag, were ripped apart and fastened against the walls to keep the dirt away from the clothing. Use had somewhat packed and hardened the floor, which they cleared of loose dirt, and then laid down old rugs and pieces of carpet, on which the children's feet could rest. They cleaned the tiny four-paned window, at each side of which they hung a bright piece of cheap drapery, being careful not to obscure any of the precious light.

"A small wooden box, with a clean paper on top, held the water jug and the common drinking cup. A taller box, with a shelf inside and a pretty stand cover on it, served as the teacher's desk, and her chair was one of the home-made kind with a broad board nailed on slantingly for a back, quite common in the dugout homes. A little Topsy stove, on which the bachelor claim holder had baked his morning flap-jacks, was the final piece of furniture.

"When the little group had been called in, and nineteen happy expectant faces greeted her from the row of benches, the young teacher had a sense of misgiving as to her ability to change that crude little dirt-walled room into a hall of learning. Of course, she knew about Mark Hopkins and the log and the student making a University,* but Alas! That took a Mark Hopkins, and he wasn't present, but breathing a prayer that plain surroundings, like plain living, might be conducive to high thinking, she began the opening exercises which dedicated the lowly dwelling to its new high use.

"The nondescript supply of books which each pupil had brought from whatever state was 'back home' to him was placed on the bench by his side. Slates, which had to take the place of both blackboard and tablets, were of all sizes and descriptions, from Jimmy's tiny one with the red felt covered frame and pencil tied to it with a string, to Mary's big double one with the wide home-made frames fastened together with strong hinges and cut deep with initials and hearts. She had found it packed away among grandfather's books which he had used away back in Ohio. There were histories from Illinois, spellers and writing books from Iowa, readers from St. Louis city schools, and even some old blue-backed spellers, with their five-syllabled puzzlers.

"From this motley array the teacher made the assignments and arranged the classifications, depending entirely upon her own judgment. The pupils had been without school privileges long enough to be glad to have an opportunity to study, and their rapid progress showed they came, for the most part, from intelligent families. True, there was not a suspension globe for explaining mathematical geography, but an apple and a ball did very well. There was no case of the latest wall maps on rollers, but the large ones in the books answered the purpose when care was taken to hold them correctly.

"As for a library, well, the contribution from the homes, kept on the shelf of the teacher's box desk, made a good substitute. There were a whole year's numbers of Youth's Companion, whose stories, informational articles, pictures and puzzles furnished recreation for all ages. Volumes of the Chatterbox, Harper's Young People and a few books of the right sort, including some of Louisa May Alcott's, made a sufficient variety of literature for our needs. The books were

* Mark Hopkins (1802–87) was an American educator and moral philosopher. U.S. President James A. Garfield, his former student, was reputed to have said, "The ideal college is Mark Hopkins on one end of a log and a student on the other."

read aloud and the different characters were assumed by the pupils, who often 'played them out' as they called it, at recess time. We call it 'dramatization' now, and make it part of our daily program. But whatever the name, it surely helped to implant a deep and abiding love for good literature. . . .

"Towards spring, an unfinished frame building was secured at a bargain from a nearby townsite, and it was moved into the district, where it was permanently located and fitted up as much as possible for school purposes. No one could be secured at that time to plaster it, but the school took possession as soon as it was on its foundation, and they were so thankful for a floor, plenty of light, comfortable seats and desks, and a 'really truly' blackboard, that they didn't mind if the walls were as yet only lathed.

"There was very little passing on the roads at that time, and there was no need to have the windows even partly frescoed with soap or scouring powders, to keep pupils from looking out too much. It really was very lonely when lessons or games did not engage the attention of the pupils, and sometimes they, and the teacher as well, paused in their engrossing pursuit of knowledge to look through the open door at a speck of black on a distant swell of ground, hoping that it might chance to be a human being riding or driving their way, being disappointed later to see that it was no more than a clump of soap weeds which some mirage or some play of light or shadow had magnified and lifted into view.

"They had just one visitor that spring, the County Superintendent, Mr. Cyrus Russel, who descended upon them in his little open buggy, driving a white-maned sorrel horse—a familiar sight to the country school of this county for several years. A few days previous, to give variety to the playtime activities, they had visited a nearby gypsum bed, bringing back a goodly supply of the clay-like deposit. With no thought of manual art or visualized instruction, they had modeled the beautiful white material into flat maps and relief maps of the continents and into vases and plaques, decorated with flowers, and one ambitious girl had even attempted a bust of George Washington. They did not realize at the time that this work was the beginning of Manual Art in our rural schools, and it seemed to them a most important and disconcerting time for the school inspector to appear on the scene. However, he must have had the vision to see some educational value in their display, for he made a favorable report of the school and recommended the teacher to an excellent teaching position in the county seat for the next year.

"The next incident made an exciting break in their daily program. One afternoon the sky took on a peculiar coppery hue and to the southeast small clouds of dust kept rising above the swells and ridges that marked the horizon line, expanding and thinning until lost in the surrounding air, similar clouds constantly rising to take their places. At the recess period they stood watching this curious display of color and formation, when suddenly they saw a well-defined funnel-shaped cloud separate itself from the dusty mass and move rapidly in their direction. They were almost panic stricken when they saw it so near that it obscured from their view an old sod house that stood two miles to the southeast.

"There was a cyclone cellar under the school house, but no door had yet been made leading to it. They all ran into the house, where the teacher seized the kindling hatchet with the idea of chopping a hole in the floor or prying up some boards, when one of the white-faced children cried out from the doorway, 'It's done turned, teacher. It's going straight north.' And sure enough, in that freakish way that tornadoes have, it had shifted its course.

"The people in the district never grew tired of teasing the teacher about scaring away a tornado with a hatchet and said discipline ought to come easy to her after that.

"The last day of school came, and, considering the small number to take part, an elaborate program was prepared. The day might very appropriately have been called 'The Festival of the Cacti.' The older girls decided that the lathed walls did not make a very artistic background for their impromptu stage, so on the morning of the eventful day every pupil gathered quantities of wild flowers. The spaces between the lath were filled with the long-stemmed yellow Sweet William and wild pink geranium which grew in abundance on the fireguards surrounding the school house. The big, waxen golden blooms of the pear cactus were made into wreaths and, gayest of all, the pink blossoms of the cushion cactus were strung on cord and festooned across the front. Some were made into bright little garlands, which the little girls hung around their necks like a lace, and some had even twined them in their long smooth braids of hair.

"This charming picture greeted the parents and friends who arrived just before noon, bringing in their wagons and well-filled baskets for our first community dinner. How they did enjoy that dinner! One young bachelor said it was the first time he had enough cake since the last grange supper back in Illinois. An organ, loaned from a home six miles away, was an addition to the afternoon entertainment. Talented visitors from the neighborhood added solos and readings to the school program, and members of the school board made the regulation speeches. There were several excellent singers present who at the last gathered around the organ and led the audience in a most enjoyable Community Sing.

"Many profitable terms of school followed in this district, which gave the rudiments of education to several of our best teachers, but no more enjoyable term was ever taught than the one which had its beginnings in a dugout."

Eventually, the separate county systems were unified under the direction and authority of a State Board of Education. The qualifications of Kansas teachers were gradually standardized as statewide examinations and scholastic standards were instituted. Moreover, county normal schools were subsequently established to train and assist the rural teachers.

The transformation from early cabin teaching to a formal school system was a slow, haphazard process. Schooling evolved at an uneven pace from one part of Kansas to another, and even within each county there were discrepancies from district to district. During the 1880s, Lannie Frost Perigo was a teacher in Ellis County. Years later she recorded her experiences in its developing school system:

She taught "in a crude schoolhouse built by the men in the community, who quarried the rock from the banks along the Smokey River, dressed them and hauled them to the location they had chosen for the site of the schoolhouse. With only a few days help from a real stone mason, the schoolhouse was built. It was equipped with homemade desks and blackboards, a very few maps and a 'Globe' which gave this particular school quite the best reputation in many districts. Here I taught my first school.

"Not far away was a Russian village, Pfeifer, and from there came a number of Russian boys and girls to enroll with twenty Americans. I think the enrollment reached thirty-two before the close of the second month. This was a year of blizzards and deep snows, but the roads to the schoolhouse were always kept open by the patrons and very little time was lost because of these heavy storms. The parents were determined to give the children every advantage the times afforded. The Russian parents [were] just as enthusiastic as any American parent could possibly be. I had to teach the children from the Russian home English, a most interesting task because they were so eager to learn, so willing to work and so obedient.

"When my school closed, the school board from an adjoining district asked me to begin a school the next Monday in their district. Because I was young and enthusiastic and anxious to help the children in every way I could, I readily consented. The pupils who had been my pupils for the past six months were to be allowed to attend without tuition. I was a very trusting young person and made no inquiry about anything, just consented to begin teaching, signed my contract and on Sunday moved to my new boarding place.

"Monday morning, with five children of the family in a lumber wagon, the oldest boy, fourteen, driving a team of broncos, we drove four miles to the schoolhouse. When we stopped, I could scarcely believe my eyes. The schoolhouse was the crudest of dugouts. Only one window, no chimney, but a stove pipe lifting its rusty head a few inches above the plain board roof. Even before entering the room, about twelve by eighteen feet, I realized I had been hasty in not inquiring about some things. Then the pity of it all appealed to me and I threw myself into the work as earnestly as if the equipment was all that could be desired.

"To this little dugout schoolhouse came thirty-six boys and girls. Some from miles away. It was wonderful the eagerness they showed to gain an education, and was remarkable the earnestness the parents showed. There was no excuse allowed for any of their children to be absent from school, only for sickness and there was very little of that.

"When school had been in session a month, the members of the board came to me and asked me if I would be willing to teach every Saturday for the next five months so they could have an extra month of school in their District. This I consented to do. Not one boy was kept out of school to help with the work on the farms. Crops were heavy that year and they were really needed.

"This was the time of the very helpful County Normal and it meant so much to the teachers, for it brought them in contact with the best instructors that could be obtained and they in turn carried to the pupils the newest methods, and acquainted them with the best supplementary text books, text books being the great problem.

"I closed my school to attend the Normal, which was held in Hays.

I had taught thirteen months without a vacation and almost the same group of pupils. There was so little to work with but when we said good-bye that August day, it was with a promise that each pupil would keep up his study and be fitted to attend a graded school in the fall. These promises were kept by seven, four Russians and three Americans, who enrolled in the Hays public schools in September.

"In 1889 I taught my first term in the Hays public school. There were seven teachers employed then and it was considered an honor to be chosen as one of the seven. Of course, the equipment was some better than I had had in the country schools, but as compared with the present-day equipment it was very meager indeed.

"At the close of my first year in the Hays City School, the Superintendent of the Ellis School asked me to take the position of Eighth grade teacher. The Board offered me an advance in salary. I accepted and in September 1890 I began teaching in Ellis. There were four rooms and a half basement and five teachers. My enrollment was over eighty all that first year.

"For three years, we worked with this crowded condition and so little equipment, but we gave all of our energy, every ounce of it in service to the pupils in an effort to make up for the lack of equipment. One of the boys who worked under these difficulties and conquered them, conquered greater things in later life and became noted in the world of finance—Walter R. Chrysler, known now throughout the world as the manufacturer of the Chrysler Cars. At the close of my three years in Ellis, I was offered an advanced salary to return to Hays, which I did.

"Looking back over those early days, we think the Israelites were not the only people required to 'make brick without straw.' "

For the frontier teacher, life on the job was far from easy. Many young women were unhappy at their posts, and many, teaching for only a few years, were simply biding time until they married. But there were also those whose fierce love of teaching helped them withstand the difficulties. As one schoolmarm proclaimed, "I'm thankful God gave me friends and opened the way for me to get into work for which I was fitted and took delight in. I consider teaching an eternity job. Who can tell how far-reaching may be the ideals implanted in the heart and mind of a little child?"

CHAPTER TEN

The Frontier Church

"How grateful we are to God, who guided our steps to this wonderful country of the brave and the free, and who has helped and guided us through the struggles and vicissitudes of the pioneer days. May his rich blessings rest on the coming generations as it was rested on the pioneers."

—Christine Hokanson

FROM THE OUTSET, the settlers' strong religious beliefs offered a spiritual respite from the daily hardships of wilderness living. With simple but unswerving faith, they turned to their ministers and to God for the strength and guidance to carry them through difficult times. "How [is it] the pioneers preserved their cheerfulness?" asked Lilla Day Monroe. "You cannot say that they imbibed it from each other, they were too far apart. You cannot lay it to the simple fact that they were acquiring homes, because, as compared to what they had left when they came to Kansas, the huts and dugouts had to be glorified by idealism if they were to be called real houses. No, there seems to be only one source of their cheerfulness, of the sublime courage, of their indomitable determination to conquer and to surmount all difficulties—and that was their simple faith in God. They were not bothered by creeds and dogmas. They took the solace of religion as they breathed the pure air of the prairies. They bothered not about the chemical properties of the air that invigorated them.

They were not superstitious, not fanatical, but held fast to the promises of the Father, and their first efforts after getting located were to establish places of worship and schools for their children."

Religion also served as a link with the traditions of their past lives. As we have seen, for most people the move westward brought abrupt and utter changes in every sphere of their lives. Yet their religious beliefs remained unchanged and provided them with a measure of reassurance in the new land. Moreover, the continuing spirit of faith became an important bond between generations, for, as one settler wrote, "We tried to teach our children to love God and his work. Husband and I have worked in different lines, always keeping our home as Godlike as we could."

Even on their first evening in Kansas, the family of Nutter and Nancy Murphy gathered together for their nightly worship. As daughter Lydia recalled, they drove into Shawnee, Kansas, a town of one thousand, on October 21, 1859. "Father visited the parsonage the first place. The minister went with him to find a house, but not a vacant one was to be had. A large ramshackle place looked vacant, but was occupied in the back by its owner, an Arkansas man and family. The front rooms were filled with whiskey barrels. These rooms we rented and the minister helped father roll the barrels to the cellar.

"That night the family Bible rested in the center of the room. We gathered around the table, seated on boxes and improvised chairs while the usual evening family prayers were held after the reading of a chapter of the Scriptures. During the fifty years of his Kansas citizenship, this morning and evening scripture reading and prayer was not once omitted in my father's house."

For these settlers, religion not only served to stabilize their own individual lives, but fostered, against the prairie distances, a firm sense of community. The very sharing of their common beliefs was a strong social catalyst on the frontier. "There was no church," mused Effie Thompson, "but the scattered families would gather at one of the homes to have Sunday School and hear an occasional circuiteer. They knew the hardships of frontier life. They felt the pangs of loneliness; but bravery, sacrifice, courage and true companionship with Jesus Christ made them rich in experiences of neighborly helpfulness."

At this time, the Kansas population was predominantly Protestant. Although some groups of Catholics, Jews, Quakers and Orthodox did settle in various parts of the state, they were greatly outnumbered by

Methodists, Presbyterians, Lutherans, Episcopalians and Baptists. As their communities became more populated, neighboring families joined together in small informal congregations. Bonded by their faith in Christ, these neighborhood groups were not usually divided along denominational lines, but met as mixed Protestant unions.

Crossing the rutted roads that separated their homesteads, the families gathered each Sunday in any convenient place, often using the cramped quarters of a sod cabin or the spreading shade of a nearby tree. "There were no school houses nor churches," remembered Harriet Woodin Comstock, "so religious services were held around at the homes, mostly at our house, as it was larger than common. It had been the custom to stay for dinner, many coming several miles."

These neighborhood services were usually kept simple. When, as was often the case, there was no qualified preacher to guide them, individual members would lead the group in worship. The meeting often began with the reading of a passage of the Scriptures. Special prayers were recited as the neighbors clasped hands, and favorite hymns were sung to the pitch of a harmonica, a fiddle or possibly a piano. Lillian Van Natta Smith recalled that in the small community of Wilmington an abandoned log cabin served as the neighborhood church and schoolhouse. "All the neighbors gathered there on the Sabbath for Sunday School and church. Mother had a good voice, so also had my Father and they were chosen to start all the songs. We had no musical instrument of any kind, just an old-style tuning fork owned by L. W. Bush, a teacher of music. He would strike the tone, and all begin to sing. I remember how happy they all seemed."

In 1860, the Monticello township was a sparsely populated community lying twenty miles west of Kansas City. For the Murphys, both devout Methodists, the absence of regular church services seemed unbearable. As a result, they secured the services of a Methodist minister and their own home for Sunday worship, welcoming neighbors of all denominations. In continuing her memoirs, Lydia Murphy Toothaker recalled:

"This new home of Nutter Webb Murphy and Nancy Stephenson Murphy, both Virginia born, became the center of the social and religious life of the community. Here the first religious services in Monticello township were held. Mother was endearingly called Aunt Polly by the growing community and so remained until her death.

"Father and Mother were ardent Methodists and missed their beloved class meetings and Sunday services. The nearest Methodist meetings were at Olathe, ten miles away, but there was no church in Olathe, these meetings being held in Hays Hall, an unpainted unplastered building. This body were Methodist Church, South. Our family was too strong abolitionist to thoroughly enjoy meeting with these southern sympathizers. Presbyterian services were held at De Soto, some six or seven miles west of us. The Rev. William Smith was the minister and became a life long friend of our family. Even these staunch Presbyterians did not fill our religious needs. Because Baldwin City, through Baker University, just established, became the mecca of Kansas Methodists, one fine fall morning Father mounted faithful Tomp and rode to Baldwin thirty miles away with a request for a minister for our neighborhood.

"Arrangements were made for services every two weeks at our house. Saturday afternoon and evening was the day selected. Irrespective of former religious affiliations, these new settlers came bringing all the family. There were the Bonneys, former Baptists, the Corliss, Unitarians, the MacDouglass of Episcopal stock, the Plummers who in Kentucky had never attended a Methodist meeting. Sister Ella was given the duty of keeping the babies as quiet as possible upstairs. Brother Emmett entertained the young children with games in the yard, while the older children and I were allowed to be a part of the meeting.

"What fervent Amens arose during the sermon. The walls of the house fairly shook with the Methodist hymns 'lined' by Douglass MacDougall, who lost his life in the war. There was fervor if not melody in:

How sad by state our nature is
Our sin how deep it stains
And Satan binds our captive souls
Fast in his slavish chains.

I can hear the roar of:

Let every mortal ear attend
And every heart rejoice
The trumpet of the gospel sounds
With an inviting voice.

"For some years the meetings were held in our home, later being changed to Sunday. When the Lone Elm School house was built, we met there and years later the Monticello Methodist Episcopal Church came into being. These meetings were social as well as religious and were the only break from the hard toil of the empire-building, home-making pioneers, except an occasional quilting, sheep-shearing or sorghum-making gathering."

As in Monticello Township, community congregations gradually found more spacious facilities for their weekly services. In the absence of a town church, such familiar sites as the local schoolhouse, court-room, stable, community store or railroad depot often echoed with the sounds of Sunday worshipers. In Smith Center, wrote Cordelia McDowell, "Meetings were held wherever convenient, sometimes in a carpenter shop, with Mother Earth for a floor, and shavings and carpenter tools for ornaments."

When the Stephen Osborn family first moved to Wakeeney in 1879, the townspeople gathered at the local drugstore for Sunday-morning worship. "How well I remember the first church services we attended in Wakeeney," wrote Mrs. Osborn. "The services were held in one part of the drugstore, each person attending taking his chair. There were perhaps fifteen or twenty in the congregation.

"Later church services were held in the new school house. My brother, A. L. McCreary, who lived south of the railroad, had a small organ which was taken to the school house each Saturday, drawn there by an ox team; on Monday morning it was returned to the McCreary home. Mr. McCreary filled the post of organist as well as that of tenor in the choir.

"When the Union Pacific R. R. Co. built a new stone station, their old frame station was moved to the east part of town to be used for Union church services. The Railroad Co. presented the church with an engine bell which was hung in the small belfrey of the church and called the people to church each Sunday morning. Services were held in this building until each denomination was able to build its own church."

In early Hays, a union of mixed denominations met in an old courthouse for weekly worship. There Catherine Cavender, the daughter of an Army officer stationed at the fort nearby, attended her first service in the summer of 1877.

"It was a simple, beautiful service," she explained, "no gilded trappings, no blazing candles, sweet odor of flowers or tang of incense. Just the dusty old court room, but the presence of God was there with the few gathered together in His name. Some of those sun-browned men and women and little children had driven miles across the prairie to be there. There were town folks and soldiers and ranchers and cowboys.

"We sat on long hard benches. There was a little melodeon or small organ, and a choir sang the morning hymn. The sermon, according to a little diary of mine, was from the 105th Psalm, 42, 43, and 44th verses. The theme was that the prairie might be made to blossom like the rose. I do not remember that sermon, I was so taken up with the people around me. From the little organ came a short prelude, and a woman's voice, clear and sweet with deep, cello notes, pealed out in sacred melody. It was the voice of Miss Mollie Montgomery, later on the wife of Senator Hill P. Wilson.

"Hays has many beautiful churches today and the people tread different paths to 'meeting' now. 'Each of the rivers of righteousness,' Confucius says, 'flows into the lake of Heaven.' And those old union meetings bound hearts together with bonds no religious dogmas can sever."

In earlier years, the family cabins and public buildings were adequate for the small frontier congregation. In time, however, a more accommodating and permanent facility was needed. Local parishioners, anxious to build their own church building, gradually assembled whatever funds and materials they could. Toward this goal, the congregation solicited contributions from both its own members and others in the area. Special fairs, raffles and picnics were organized to promote the new church, and the women worked together through their ladies' sewing circles to raise money. Occasionally, national church organizations even gave some assistance to the struggling congregations.

Money itself, however, was a notoriously scarce commodity on the frontier. When the needed funds fell short, the congregation relied heavily on contributions in kind. Local families donated whatever timber, nails and tools they had. The men worked together to build the church structure, and the women culled from trunks and corners any curtains or furniture that could be spared.

In Kansas, most early churches were austere structures built mainly of log, brick, sod or limestone. Limited in size, they were marked by a simplicity of both architectural design and interior furnishings. Long backless benches, made by hand, served as pews. Plain tables were remade into altars, and simple pulpits were often fashioned from any extra planks of wood. No matter how crude it was, the parishioners remained justly proud of the one-room chapels they could finally call their own.

In October of 1867, the cornerstone of Smith Center's first church was laid. It wasn't long, however, before the congregation's meager funds dwindled and construction came to a stop. "A critical time in the history of the church occurred," remembered parishioner Cordelia McDowell. "The day arrived when a workman's lien was to be placed upon the four walls of the church building. Would it be sold at auction? Who would pay enough for it, even to clear the indebtedness? No one wanted such an unfinished building. Must it be sold? And would we have to begin all over again for a church? Finally a Good Samaritan appeared, bought all the indebtedness and saved the building for a church.

"December came and our church still was unfinished—delayed on account of the lack of funds. A meeting was called and it was agreed that, providing the Presbyterians and Methodists would do what they could consistently to help us finish the church, the Trustees would guarantee to them the use of the church for one-half the time for five years from the time it was completed and occupied. Everything now looked promising for a speedy fulfillment of our wishes.

"The whole community became interested and on Christmas Eve, 1877, we enjoyed our first meeting in the church. A community Christmas tree was brought from the banks of the Solomon River and when placed in the church extended from the floor to the roof. You will note I stated, 'to the roof,' not the ceiling, as the church had no ceiling at that time. However, the church was not dedicated until the spring of 1878. The amount of money necessary was raised, and the church was dedicated, 'Out of debt.' Having no safety deposit vault, we slept with our little collection for each day under our pillow with a pistol at hand."

The early settlers of Ottawa County had even more difficulty erecting their first community church. Lavina Gates Chapman, a stalwart Presbyterian, believed the Lord Himself may have had a hand in those difficulties! She recounted: "The first Presbyterian Church was built at Lindsey, and they received as many contributions from the Methodists as from the Presbyterians. They got the church enclosed and the Methodists were to have every alternate sabbath. They needed more money to furnish the building, so they nailed boards to the windows and decided to raise what was needed by giving a dance and had all in readiness when I told them I would pray to the Lord to blow the building down rather than to dedicate it with a dance. Oh, the burden that was in me that day, and it was as beautiful a day as I ever saw, but just before night there came up a storm and laid the building down to the ground.

"So they wanted us to give more money. Well, they got the building up again and, of course, would still have their dances now in spite of the elements. Another beautiful day and the cooking and preparations were all done. Of course a few do not amount to much, but we could talk to God and he had said, 'Whatsoever you ask it shall be, do we ask in faith, believing,' and I asked that the building might be blown to the four winds.

"Oh, such a beautiful day as it had been. All was in readiness and I said, 'Lord, Lord, will you let them dedicate it with a dance?' Just before dark a storm came and some of the church went east, some north, some west and some south, the ground where the church had stood was swept as clean as if it had been swept and they never got the pieces together again. Houses were moved off their foundations and the next morning it was a sad little town. The pieces that were found were collected together and sold to the highest bidder. Brother Cooper who lives on Pipe Creek has some of the boards in his house now. A piece of one of those boards would be a relic to me."

From the outset, women often assumed the leading role in all aspects of church work. Together, they worked to organize the local congregation, plan its weekly meetings and teach the Sunday Bible classes. If the congregation wanted an organ or the pews had to be replaced or the church roof needed fixing, it was usually the women who arranged special fund drives or raised money through bake sales and sewing circles.

"We had no organ at our church," remembered Minnie Campbell, "and no money to get one. My mother agreed to see there was an organ there, and she started a subscription paper. In a few days there was a good organ in the church and it was paid for. Also another time after our church had been newly papered, no one liked the altar, and the man said he would put something there that would be much nicer if they could raise the money. My mother said, 'You fix the altar, and we'll see you get the money.' And today when I see this beautiful altar, I always think of the Mother who wanted her church to be as beautiful as her home."

In addition, women were the most active participants in the philanthropic and missionary work sponsored by their congregations. Always responsive to the plight of those needier than themselves, they organized special women's groups to provide whatever money, food or clothing supplies they could muster.

"Mother joined the Lutheran Church," continued Minnie Campbell, "and her life proved she had consecrated it to Christian service. She served in almost all of the offices of the church. . . . During hard times when no crops were raised, she was always at the head of some organization aiding the poor. One time I remember so well a family lived near us who had no stockings or shoes and were forced to run around on the snow in their bare feet. My mother went to town and asked for old socks and stockings and asked for contributions to buy shoes for these children. She spent many, many evenings fixing those old socks for these children and today those children are holding good positions and are honored wherever they go.

"She and Mother Bickerdyke spent many hours planning for the poor and the sick and the needy, and it was an every-day occurrence to see them with an old horse and buggy distributing things to those in need, especially to the old soldiers and their dear ones. Her hands were never idle. She was always thinking of some kind deed she could do."

Finding an ordained and experienced minister to lead them was another pressing problem for the frontier congregation. Although the early settlers managed by themselves at first, they were anxious to find a preacher to deliver Sunday services, perform baptisms, officiate at weddings and administer funeral rites. Since full-time ministers were hard to come by, many congregations depended entirely on the services of itinerant preachers who traveled from one community to the next.

The most efficient system of these "circuit riders" was organized by the Methodist Church. From the outset, the church had divided the area into formal districts, each controlled by a presiding elder. Under his authority, a district was further divided into a number of "circuits," each of which was assigned its own minister or circuit rider. This itinerant preacher was awarded a handful of "appointments," separate congregations which he served on a regular rotating basis.

Once assigned to a specific circuit, the itinerant preacher was expected to provide his own transportation, usually journeying by horseback from one community to the next. With his saddlebag at his side, he traveled throughout the year to attend to the settlers' spiritual needs. In return, he relied on their hospitality for room and board along the way.

Unfortunately, the circuit rider's arduous efforts were rarely well rewarded. Each congregation was responsible for collecting his salary from its membership, and few settlers had the extra cash to subsidize a preacher. Instead, they usually resorted to paying him in kind with donations of any fresh crops, flour, hay, meat or dry goods they could spare.

According to Mary Keller, the early congregation at Marion often had difficulty raising any remuneration when the preacher made his rounds. "In the early years it was no easy task to keep a preacher. Collecting the salary was very different from the present time. I have had to help get it by taking a team and farm wagon and riding over the sparsely settled country and gathering up meat, corn meal, some flour, chickens, eggs, sorghum molasses and anything that people could spare. For there was but little money."

The itinerant life of the circuit rider was a difficult one for his family as well. During the 1860s, Reverend John Woodburn, a Methodist minister, served the Nemaha County circuit. On the road for several days each week, he left his young wife to care for their home and growing family by herself. Their daughter, May Woodburn Crane, remembered:

"Father was a circuit rider in those early days, preaching in log school houses in Nemaha County for a number of years and later in Washington and Jackson Counties. At first he rode horseback to his different charges and later made the trips in a spring wagon which he bought. He would leave home usually on Saturday and be gone sometimes for several days. During these absences from home he would visit at the homes of his parishioners and when he returned he would bring with him the donations which he had received. I well remember how we children waited to see what Father would bring home.

"In those days money was very scarce and the itinerant preacher received very little of it indeed. Father would bring home such things as potatoes, turnips, onions, meat, chickens, sacks of cornmeal, and sometimes even discarded clothing and old toys. I remember some dolls which were sent to us children. They were old and worn, but they were the only ones we had and very dear to us. There were always extra donations at Christmas time. The people who came to church would tell Father when they had something to give, and when he got ready to come home he would drive around and collect the things.

"Mother was a remarkably good manager—the circuit rider's wife had to be. Often Father would bring home more than we could use of some things and not nearly enough of others. We children were sometimes critical of the things he brought, especially the clothing. Some of it we thought was not good enough to be made over and we wanted to use it for dressing up in our play. But this Mother would never allow. She always preserved a sweet spirit about the donations. She insisted that the things we received were gifts and should be taken thankfully and never spoken of with levity.

"Even at best the donations were not enough to keep the preacher's family. Father helped support his family by working as a carpenter and stone mason. He built the log house in which we lived. It consisted at first of one large room with fireplace, which was living room, dining room and kitchen in one, and a loft which was for a bedroom. As the family increased a lean-to was added for bed room.

"There were eleven children in all, seven boys and four girls. But even with this large family there was always room for the guest beneath our roof. Our home was used as a sort of hotel or wayside inn for friends and for strangers coming into the country. And with all the hard work and the privations of the new country, Mother kept her sweetness and her poise and dignity. She had a keen sense of humor which helped her over many drab places in life."

In each prairie town, the anticipation of the circuit rider's Sunday visit became a special community event. As the arrangements were finalized for the visit, neighboring families often vied for the privilege of entertaining the guest preacher. At home, the cabin floors were scrubbed clean, fresh linens were laid out and special meals were planned. In town, the local church or schoolhouse was cleaned and readied for the Sabbath meeting. For the women, the preceding Saturday was a particularly busy day spent cooking fresh hams, roasts and breads for Sunday supper. Green coffee was parched for the expected festivities, fresh butter was churned and special cakes and cookies were baked. Harriet Walter recalled the air of expectancy that filled one household:

"Has the old preparation for the Sabbath disappeared? It was the custom in the Pioneer Days to get everything ready for Sunday dinner and the coming week that was possible.

"In Ernest Clarke's house all was excitement, for Brother Craft, the Baptist Preacher, would be at the School house Saturday afternoon for the monthly covenant meeting. Mary Clarke carefully set her sponge for the white bread Friday evening. It was well wrapped and set in a warm place to rise. Saturday morning it was mixed up before breakfast because the smartest housewives got their bread baked by noon. It should rise to twice its bulk twice at least and then the rolls and loaves were moulded and allowed to rise to the right height and degree of lightness before baking. It must be just right. A rich golden brown, and maybe the Boston brown bread was steaming too. Of course, there were cakes to be baked and beans and rice pudding if there were no pies.

"Fashion changes with cake as in other things. Mary knew nothing of Angel or Devils food cakes, but a Cream layer was a favorite. Made in three layers and as light as a feather. Laid up with a cream filling. You used a plenty of the rich 'Gooey' mixture between layers and then, 'Oh, Boy!' as your grandchild would say, it was good. For special occasions you made a large marble cake and baked it in the skillet in one large loaf, dropping first a spoonful of white, then yellow and then black cake dough in the skillet, till all was used. The black was colored with cloves, cinnamon and alspice.

"That wasn't enough, though—the cooky jar must be kept well filled. There were the white cookies which fairly melted in your mouth. The ginger snaps to eat with milk or coffee or maybe a soft gingerbread. I can taste that gingerbread yet. Truly a dish for the gods. Pies, of course, dried peach or apple or green tomato, or if she wished a one-crust pie there were vinegar, cream, custard or pumpkin. If the dried fruit were used it was first soaked over night then stewed and sweetened. If you never ate one you don't know what you've missed.

"There must be meat too. In summer the ham was boiled for slicing or the chicken was baked or made ready to fry. In winter the large beef or pork roast was cooked to a turn. Then Mary felt that with some vegetables and a 'spread'—eggbutter, pumpkin, or apple butter—she could await with pleasure Brother Craft's visit. She did hope Sister Craft would feel that she could come too, and as she mused of her love for her master, her pastor, and wife, she scrubbed the kitchen to shining cleanliness. The little Clarkes shared in the scrubbing too.

"It seems to me there should be a turning back to the Preparation Day, a relaxing, a closing up of the business, a shutting of the machinery and a viewing of God's love through His beauties all around us."

In a world where leisure was a luxury, the Sunday festivities provided a welcome break from the week's work. Reserved as a day of rest and relaxation, the Sabbath afforded a family the special opportunity to visit with neighbors after the morning services and enjoy the day's activities. Community picnics were spent mingling with friends and meeting the newcomers, and Sunday suppers were a time for exchanging news and viewpoints. In the quiet of the evening, the family gathered alone to read from the Scriptures, play music, or enjoy long talks by the fireside.

"No one need talk to me of 'Puritan' Sundays—long and tedious treaded," wrote Katherine Elspeth Oliver. "We 'kept' Sunday. It was a day quite different from other days—a superior day—a day full of delightfully 'different' things. In lieu of play, the long drive to 'town,' church and Sunday school and a picnic lunch eaten in the wagon on the way home were compensating pleasures.

"In the afternoon, mother read and read to us in her beautiful intelligent voice—Sunday things and the Youth Companion which our parents considered good enough for every day in the week, and we had 'Sunday games' most engrossing. Father read too from the Bible—the solemn things from the Prophets and Proverbs and from Revelations—things that, like mother's music, swept us within strange and solemn portals from which we drew back in wonder and awe. Mother read us the brighter things—the Psalms.

"Always just at Sunset it seems to me (the unparalleled sunsets of the Kansas prairies, we sitting out on the high upstairs porch) mother used to read us the 'Shepherd Psalm.' I always remember it so. And as the last splendid promise, read in my mother's calm reassured voice, was concluded, 'Oh the sunset—see—the sunset!' someone would acclaim and its sudden glory sweeping through the kindled cloud portals seemed a visible affirmation of all that had moved our hearts and imaginations this day concerning the things of the Unseen."

PART FOUR

CHAPTER ELEVEN

The Frontier Town

"Years went by, towns sprang up and our horizon broadened more and more."

—MYRTLE LOBDELL FOGELBURG

IN THE BEGINNING, the frontier town was often only a solitary cluster of ramshackle buildings jutting from a sea of prairie grass. Its main street was little more than a wide grassy path, well rutted by horse hoofs and wagon wheels. By the curb, warped planks of timber were nailed together as storefront sidewalks, while crooked tree limbs and old wooden posts served as hitching rails. Rows of plain frame buildings housed the town's residents and businesses. Here and there, a hand-painted sign nailed out front identified the general store, the land office, the livery stable or the post office. The hotel, with its wide veranda, and the saloon, with its swinging doors, dominated the center of town. Nearby was the public well, the church and the stage depot. As the town grew and additional streets were laid out, other buildings were erected and new stores opened for business.

In Kansas, the early towns seemed to sprout as quickly as there were people to fill them. By law, a new town could be officially established provided that 320 acres of land would be reserved as the townsite when it was occupied. Speculators and businessmen, anticipating profitable investments, staked out the requisite number of acres and compelled settlers to preempt adjacent quarter sections. Often securing up to a thousand acres at a time, they divided the future townsite into lots and shares to be sold to prospective residents and businesses.

Once the townsite was laid out, the town promoters planned advertising campaigns to draw people to the area. Town lots were given away to attract such necessary business establishments as a hotel, a livery stable, a saloon or a general store. Advertisements were placed in Eastern newspapers, and town agents were stationed at river landings and border towns to fuel the promotional campaign. As a further boost, the town often staged special celebrations to welcome newcomers and auction off remaining lots.

All too often, however, the frontier town straddled the uncertain line between boom and bust. Pioneer families and merchants were easily lured to a growing town, but at any sudden turn of events they were just as likely to pull up stakes and move on again. If a nearby trail changed direction or the stage line shifted its route, the local businesses often closed and moved to more promising areas. The extension of the railroad farther westward, taking settlers and businesses to rival communities, was particularly damaging to a struggling town. Moreover, adverse weather conditions, poor crop yields and fluctuating land prices were liable to deter new immigration and inhibit further growth.

A town's selection as the county seat of government was always pivotal to its future prospects. By law, the local seat was designated through countywide elections. In one county after another, bitter contests took place between rival townships. All were convinced that the acquisition of the county seat would bring jobs, trade, vitality and steady growth to their towns.

When the election was over, the loss of the county seat to a rival community sometimes destroyed a town altogether. In Woodson County, the seat was moved several times before Yates Center was finally selected. Elizabeth Currie remembered the confusion: "I do not know who were responsible for what happened, but the county seat began moving. First to Kalida, near the center of the county, a small burg of a few houses, a school house, a blacksmith shop, a hotel, a store. It did not stay there long . . . but it moved to Defiance, a still smaller place composed of two or three farmhouses. How the men from Defiance got it moved there I never knew. There were threats and quarreling all the time.

"Finally, Abner Yates of Illinois, who owned a large tract of land in the center of the county, offered the citizens of Woodson County a square mile of his land for a county seat if they would name the town for him. It was voted on, and decided. Yates Center became the county seat August 12, 1875. Mr. Yates came here soon after, and lived in the town till his death.

"Not only were the buildings moved from Defiance, but all of Kalida was moved except the schoolhouse, and the home of James Davidson and Mr. Ray. My husband had a yoke of Texas oxen and was hired to supervise the moving, and he helped till the last house was moved to Yates Center. Kalida and Defiance are dreams of the past."

Similarly, the fight for the county seat of Graham County sharply divided its growing communities. After several years of controversy, Hill City eventually triumphed over the town of Gettysburg. Mary Gettys Lockard recalled that victory—a bitter one for her—and the rise and fall of her own town of Gettysburg.

"In the fall of 1878, my father decided to start a new town in the then unorganized county of Graham. The place he selected as the sight for his new metropolis was on the north side of the South Solomon near where the old freight road crossed the river. He had camped more than one hundred nights near this place during the previous years and had fallen in love with the spot. He plotted his town and gave it the name of Gettysburg, and fondly dreamed of it as the flourishing future county seat.

"He built a large stone house which was opened as the first hotel. He either built or assisted in building a number of other houses, both residence and business. The new town grew and seemed to flourish until within a year it had thirty buildings, and a hundred population. But alas! It was not to be the county seat, nor destined to be a thriving city.

"N. C. Terrill had settled four miles southeast on the south side of the river. He started a town and named it Millbrook, though there was no brook nor any prospect of a mill. The site was high and dry. They could not find water, though they bored to a depth of about 400 feet. They had to give it up and moved the town down nearer the river. There was plenty of merriment in those furious days over the proposition made by some wag, probably a Gettysburg sympathizer in the county seat fight, to cut that four hundred foot hole up into shorter lengths and sell it for post poles.

"In the meantime W. R. Hill came and started the town of Hill City, four miles east of us, and on the same side of the river. Mr. Pomeroy, a millionaire from Atchison, became interested in Hill City, and Col. Chapman of Council Bluffs, Iowa, together with M. Heaton, a banker of Norton, bought the town of Millbrook. The county seat war was hotly waged for two or three years, but the odds were too great, and Gettysburg lost out, Hill City being the final victor. So it came about that my father in 1882, broken in health and purse, moved back to the old place in Norton County."

In 1867, the city of Hays was formally established on a site near Fort Hays. The Kansas Pacific Railroad reached the new town in October of that year, and it soon brought a stream of farmers, businessmen, cowboys and soldiers. Within a year, the town had expanded to a population of one thousand and had begun to acquire the attending variety of stores, hotels, saloons and stables.

Josephine Middlekauf moved to Hays the same year it was established. She was a child and remembered the town with a child's eye for detail. "Hays even then was quite the place," she wrote, "as it had absorbed the little town of Rome that had been on a site about a mile west of Hays. It being the terminus of the railroad, the round house, the turn table and all of the other buildings that go to make a railroad town were located just east of the Schwaller Lumber Yard.

"In my mind's eye, I can see Old North Main Street in all its former glory: from east to west from Chestnut street were the Capless and Ryan Outfitting Store, the 'Leavenworth Restaurant,' Dalton's Saloon and Faro House, 'Hound Kelley's Saloon,' the office of M. E. Joyce, our first justice of the Peace, a jewelry store, Mrs. Gowdy's little sod hut, Ed Godard's saloon and Dance Hall, Tommy Drumm's saloon, Kate Coffee's saloon, Mose Walter's Saloon, R. W. Evans' Grocery Store and Post Office, Sol Cohen's Clothing Store, Paddy Welch's Saloon and gambling house, the Perty Hotel, M. J. R. Treat's Candy and Peanut Stand, Cy Godard's Saloon and Dance Hall and in the corner 'Nigger White's' barber shop; and all the saloons were not on the North Main Street either. It was conceded that there were at least seventy-five places where one could quench his thirst with liquor all the way from 'whiskey straight' at twenty-five cents a drink to 'Madam Cliquot' at five dollars a pint.

"Fort Street was likewise built from Normal Avenue north as far as the courthouse square; true, most of the buildings were of flimsy construction and were taken down and put up again wherever the railroad made its next stop. Tents and dugouts were also numerous and while all was 'hustle and bustle and go' and thousands of feet tramped the streets they were still paved with buffalo sod."

Ten years later, young Catherine Cavender arrived with her family in the still prospering city of Hays. If Catherine was nurturing the idea that the West would offer her strange new adventures, then her first minutes in Hays were not disappointing:

"One beautiful mid-June day our troop train pulled into Hays City. The Hays part seemed all right but there was something wrong with the rest of the name. To me City meant tall buildings, great Churches, big theaters and 'hoss Cars.' Here was a little prairie town sleeping in the June sunshine!

"After all these years I see it as I saw it then! One wide street about a block in length; down the center, dividing it into a north and south main street, were the tracks of the U.P.R.R. with a little red station and long platform. On the north side was a huddle of stores, saloons, boarding houses, more saloons and dance halls, a big stone drugstore, a barber shop and the best hotel west of Salina, The York House. On the south side were more saloons, a jewelry store, a photograph gallery, two big stores, the post office, and a newspaper office.

"That June morning when our troop train pulled into Hays City, we waited on the station platform, as the ambulances that were to convey us over to Fort Hays had not yet arrived. We were somewhat disappointed of many things we had expected to see but were deeply interested in the long rails with the cowponies tied to them, in the broad hats and the jingling spurs, and the funny one-story, square-front buildings. You can see just such prairie towns pictured in the 'movies' today.

"We were on the extreme West end of the platform when suddenly there was a pistol shot on the North side—a woman in a low-neck, short-skirted dress rushed screaming through the swinging door of a saloon, a man rushed out after her firing his pistol at her feet. She ran down the bumpy old board sidewalk and into the open door of Mrs. Bay, the first-class dressmaker of the town. When the man saw she had reached sanctuary with a respectable woman, he went to a long rail, untied his pony and rode away, firing his other six guns and whooping in glee as he dashed past Fitzpatrick's old corner. We were wall-eyed with the wonder of it all, until a railroad man explained that it was only a drunken cowboy having a joke and shooting at the sidewalk to see her run."

The local hotel or boardinghouse was an important asset to any town that hoped to attract new residents and businesses. Although the accommodations were by no means luxurious, the hotel was always a popular gathering place for newcomers and townsmen alike. The guests varied from day to day. Sometimes, women emigrants, with their children in tow, stopped to rest before journeying onward. Land speculators and traveling merchants often boarded there while surveying the area.

In Cottonwood Falls, the James Nichols family served a variety of guests in their hotel, the Doolittle House. As G. S. Nichols wrote, "[Mother] soon found herself planning meals and menus and presiding over tables where were seen men of many degrees and stations in life. Prominent here was the cowboy in boots and spurs with his hair growing down to his shoulders. Here was the ranchman, the farmer, the prospective land buyer, the land agent, some suspected cattle rustlers who were finally captured, convicted and sent to the penitentiary. There were also the phrenologist, the merchant, the doctor, the lawyer, the 'Judge' and the minister. A gang of stone cutters that worked in the large stone quarry near by helped to give a variety to the patrons of the place."

For the most part, the guest rooms were small and cramped, furnished with only the bare necessities. A rickety bedstead, with a straw-filled mattress and a stiff pillow, usually took up most of the room. A washstand stood in one corner, with a water basin and pitcher to serve the guest's needs. Sometimes an armchair or a small chest of drawers was included as well. On the whole, the rooms were less than comfortable. Lit only by dim kerosene lamps, they were invariably dark and musty. Moreover, the ever-present bedbugs usually caused further discomfort. Nevertheless, the accommodations proved satisfactory to most guests weary from their travel.

The hotels usually provided board as well as room. At noon, the dinner bell called the guests to lunch served in the downstairs dining room. Most meals were kept simple, with dishes of plain cornbread, roasted meats or boiled potatoes. Afterward the guests might retire to the parlor for coffee or gather on the veranda to discuss politics and share reminiscences.

For the innkeeper, the frontier hotel was not always profitable. Permanent help was hard to keep, food prices were usually high, and business fluctuated with the town's unsteady growth. In the 1870s, Dr. Allen White and his wife, Mary, operated a hotel—in somewhat atypical fashion—in the town of El Dorado. Their son, William Allen White, the renowned journalist, later described his mother's impatience with the founding, and the floundering, of the family business:

"El Dorado in that day was a tough town. . . . My mother stood it but she disliked it. The shooting and drinking and sporting around were not what she had bargained for in life when she spent ten years getting a college education when most women were having their love affairs and babies. . . .

"My father, who had been a country doctor and a country merchant and had always dabbled in real estate and made money easily and so had a light opinion of it, decided that he would be a gentleman farmer. He bought a big farm, built a log house on it with a big fire place and all the foolish trappings of a pioneer farmer's place in the early part of the last century—the kind of place in which he was born and reared. He could as well have had a decent board and plastered house with fairly comfortable appointments. But no—he wanted to reproduce the good old days.

"I was only a child then, but I remember what an awful family row started over that fake farm adventure. My mother could get no hired help to go to the farm, and the loft was full of hired men, for my father in his fifties couldn't farm. He even built me a trundle bed to go under the big leg bed and that made work, and when my mother blew up—well, we moved back to town and the men had a great joke on my father. Men were supposed to run their own homes in those days, but not men who married my mother. She was, as I say, what is called a captain.

"When we got back to town my father, who was one of those hospitable expansive souls, was forever inviting people in to stay with him. He built a very large house for the seventies, ten rooms, and kept it full of company. This also was not to my mother's liking, and I remember she was always telling him we were going to the poorhouse with so much company.

"So what did he do, but open a hotel; and certainly there was a mad woman. She loved to cook but she had to have the best and he had to have the best, and that meant thick beefsteak and rare roast beef and throwing away everything but the breasts from the prairie chickens, and real buckwheat cakes that you stir and leave on the reservoir of the stove to rise over night, to serve with real maple syrup in the morning, and all for $2.00 a day.

"The help wouldn't stay, and mother had all the work to do. She saw we were losing money—and little my father cared, for he would swank around the front porch in his nankeens, his white vest and his white suspenders, talking politics, while my mother used to sweat in the kitchen and complain that we were headed straight for the poorhouse. . . .

"Then one day she blew up again and the hotel closed. She was right. But it broke my father's heart. Keeping hotel and losing money at it, so that he could not accuse himself of capitalizing his hospitality, was the one proud period of his life."

Undoubtedly, the general store was the most frequented establishment of the frontier town. At first, a single store usually met the community's needs, stocking everything from quinine and calico to hand tools and breaking plows. Occupying a cramped Main Street storefront, it was invariably the center of the town's business life, the place where homesteaders came from miles around to purchase their supplies and sell their crops. For the pioneer woman, a shopping trip to the town general store offered a heartening change from her isolation and daily chores.

"Well, we will go marketing," exclaimed Gertrude Burlingame. "It is full fifty years ago. This is Craigue's and Morn's grocery store, the best in Topeka. They are getting in their winter supplies. On the counter are baskets of eggs—three dozen for a quarter. Big jars of butter brought in by the farmers, quite soft—no ice in those days—12½ TO 15 cents a pound and two grades. Baskets of chunks of maple sugar from the East. We made our own maple syrup, dried apples and peaches. We used a great many dried apples during the winter. Cheese from New York, a bucket of hulled corn hominy, over these was a mosquito netting, a protection from the flies—flies pretty thick.

"On the floor, barrels of flour, two grades, white and middlings, or shorts sometimes called, and meal very coarse, buckwheat flour—the kind that makes a man want someone to scratch his back. A barrel of apples from Missouri, sacks of potatoes, turnips, cabbage, pumpkins and long-neck squashes. And back of those were barrels of New Orleans molasses, vinegar, salt pork with a big stone on top to keep the pork under the brine, salt, sugar three grades, fine white 20 pounds for a dollar, light brown, and very dark, just as we have now.

"Kits of mackerel 2 grades, the big fat ones and then the smaller ones. I don't remember the price but they were cheap and were used extensively. Around that part of the store hung up the cod fish, whole, salted and dried and hung up by tail. Also hung up around were hams, shoulders, and slabs of breakfast bacon, and strings of red peppers, and then fresh meats. They must have been very cheap as they gave us all the pigs feet and beef liver, and occasionally a hog's head for hogshead cheese and a basket of good meaty spare ribs for 10 cents. Kegs of lard.

"Back of the counter, on the shelf, were large boxes of the big square soda crackers, crocks of honey, coffee—green Rio and Mocha (we had to parch and grind it)—tea, black and Japan in large cans, starch in bulk, bottles of catsup, cayenne, and soda and cream of tartar instead of baking powder. Big glass jars of striped candy. Some spice and rice.

"And still farther back were kept some things for the country trade. The farmer's wife was fond of exchanging eggs and butter for things that would help out in the kitchen. And there were plain white dishes, steel knives and forks and pewter spoons, and jars for pickles, and milk crocks, pans, wooden tubs, pails and brooms (and the most conspicuous pieces among the crockery were the ones we put under the bed). And for the farmers, hoes, rakes, spades, ropes and some kegs of nails and I should have said before the tobacco was much in evidence both for smoking and chewing.

"Butter! I took mine home and hung it in the well, which was my refrigerator and a good one. Crackers, stacks of them, large and small, white and clay colored and cheap. Mackerel, my father bought a keg every fall. We would freshen two or three at a time and dry and broil over the coals for breakfast two or three times a week. In very cold weather we sometimes had oysters, and we were having lots of game those days, sometimes venison or buffalo steak. Plenty of quail and prairie chickens and ducks in the right season. Codfish, we (our family, I mean) had not got to eating codfish yet. My father, who was a Southerner, said they were the food for blue bellied Yankees.

"In those early days all the well-to-do people had their own pork barrels. I had a pair of newly-weds who had come out from Boston, but the man had been married before and had a large picture of his first wife. The bride told me that after they were married he brought that picture in and hung it up and said to her, 'We will always keep Stella's memory fresh in our home'; and she said a few days after, a waggish friend of hers was looking at the picture, and she told him what her husband had said, and he laughed and said, 'Gosh, this will be over the pork barrel before the winter is over.'

"I believe all I have mentioned were staple articles. You see they were all necessary foods but everything was cheaper than now and everybody in Kansas was poorer than now. But the grocery man seemed to thrive all right. Both Craigue and Morn were able to get good homes and live well."

In larger towns, the general-merchandise store was eventually supplemented by more specialized establishments. Pharmacists opened drugstores, tailors started clothing shops, blacksmiths forged, and enterprising butchers provided their own fresh cuts of meat. But whether general or not, the store was not simply a place of business. On shopping days, the store was crowded with homesteaders buying provisions and townspeople stopping by to relax. Customers who had traveled any distance clustered near the stove, warming their hands and talking together. Women paused to exchange advice and compare purchases, while children sidled in to buy sticks of peppermint, maple sugar, pencils or bits of ribbon.

Mail days in particular brought a steady stream of customers hoping to receive long-awaited letters. In most communities, general stores and other stores served as makeshift post offices until permanent facilities could be secured. When the weekly mailbags arrived, local residents were already waiting in line at the rear counter. "Mail was precious to the early settlers," explained Jessie Stratford, "news from the 'folks back home' was eagerly awaited. Persons walked or rode horseback from the far edges of the county—frequently as far as 40 miles for their mail in those days."

Women regularly served as postmistresses and mail clerks in these early storefront offices. For the most part, their work was tiresome, their hours were unpredictable and their salaries were meager. "[Grandmother] became post mistress of El Dorado in 1871," continued Jessie Stratford, "accepting the office when J. W. Kellogg declared if some one did not take the office he would 'throw it into the street.' The postmaster's salary was then $24.00 a year. The office was in the drug store . . . Mail arrived on Thursdays and Saturdays of each week and [Mother] recalls that many bitterly cold winter mornings she and her mother arose when the stage arrived at two o'clock A.M. and distributed mail by the light of a coal oil lamp."

Sara Bissing, a clerk in the Hays post office, sometimes found her duties equally inconvenient. "The postoffice," she remembered, "was then in the rear of Courtney's Book Store. I never could decide whether the postoffice was a drawing card for the book store or vice versa, but there was usually a good patronage at Courtney's.

"Sister Ella went into the postoffice as assistant under Uncle Joe Wilson. I got into the postoffice work also. I stayed with Uncle Joe for about a year and a half, during which time we were busy and worked hard all the time. There were no eight-hour days then. If trains were late, we stayed on the job. Unless it broke a date for a dance or a surprise party, we thought it all right.

"During the winter of 1885 and 1886 we had a severe blizzard and heavy snow that stopped all railroad travel for about ten days, as nearly as I can recall. Of course no mail came in during that time. The first train came in January 12, 1886, the day sister Alice was married to Ed Glennon. You can imagine our feelings, knowing we had that mail to take care of and a wedding on hand, but we went at it.

"Uncle Joe thought he could help, but we thought otherwise. He was trying to distribute, while we were throwing bundles of papers on the floor near the boxes to be convenient for us later. Of course in our hurry a bundle would whack him on the foot or shins until he acted as though he were dancing the Highland fling. That was one way we mixed fun with work but we finally got through in time for the 'big doin's,' and danced until near morning."

From the start, the local newspaper was an active voice in the life and politics of every frontier town. Across the plains, newspapers were started as soon as townsites could be plotted and populated. It took little more than an enterprising editor and a simple hand-operated press to churn out the weekly tabloids which advertised the community, recorded its history and promoted its interests. In fact, the first newspaper was in operation less than four months after the opening of the Kansas Territory. In Leavenworth, the *Kansas Weekly Herald* published its first issue on September 15, 1854; it was followed by Kickapoo's paper, the *Kansas Pioneer*, two months later. By the time Kansas achieved statehood in 1861, more than one hundred newspapers had already been published, and by 1889 there were 733 weekly papers in operation.

At first, the community newspaper often was simply a mouthpiece for town promoters and local speculators. The early issues were filled with notices advertising vacant lots or new businesses, along with articles extolling the virtues of the growing community. But once the town's development was well under way, the paper invariably focused on political crusades of the day. Few frontier papers were independent of political parties or community factions. Usually the editors were highly opinionated and partisan and used their papers as pulpits to espouse their own views and interests. Flamboyant in style, their writing was often vituperative and their objectivity questionable.

As towns grew and controversies deepened, rival newspapers often appeared. Economically, most frontier towns could support only one paper. As the journals vied for advertisers and subscribers, their editors fueled the fires of competition with scathing editorials. Catherine Cavender recalled the feisty exchanges between the editors of the two Hays papers.

"The Hays City of that day," she explained, "with a main street one block long, had two good newspapers. The *Hays City Sentinel*, with Father Montgomery as editor and his gifted son, Frank, noted in later years for his clever work with the *Kansas City Times*, as assistant editor, reporter, type setter, and office boy. The other paper was *The Ellis County Star*. The editor was J. H. Downing, one of the wittiest men who ever wielded a vitriolic pen.

"The bouts between those two papers, when politics ran high, were attuned to make the fur fly. What Uncle Jack Downing had to say in his witty, cutting way, and how Frank Montgomery with his keen, lance-like style, would answer were the events of greatest interest."

In many towns, women assisted with the weekly publications. Working in the back rooms, they helped edit articles, set type and work the presses to get the tabloids out on time. In Hays, Ella West Downing, wife of the local editor, was a mainstay in the production of *The Ellis County Star*.

"Mrs. Downing had become one of the 'pioneer women' of Western Kansas," wrote her biographer, "and all of the thrills and hardships of that group became a part of her life. . . . Mrs. Downing recalls that often when things went wrong at the office both she and Mr. Downing, the baby bundled in a basket on the press boards, worked until far into the night with a Washington hand press to get the paper out in time for the mail. She set type, folded papers and did a thousand and one things incident to the publishing of a weekly newspaper in those days, days that were full of toil and excitement."

In the early years, every frontier community had its share of trouble with raucous gunmen, gamblers and rustlers. From time to time, roving outlaws broke into local banks, held up passing locomotives or robbed stagecoach passengers. Drunken cowboys occasionally disturbed the peace, cattle thieves rustled grazing herds, and claim jumpers swindled unsuspecting homesteaders.

Like other towns in the 1880s, Medicine Lodge often had difficulty maintaining law and order. "Medicine Lodge was a typical frontier town," wrote Mary Saunders Rouse. "One rainy morning at nine o'clock four men rode up to the bank, three of whom went inside. The fourth held the horses. They killed the president and the cashier; when the shooting began, the citizens ran to the hardware store for guns and to the livery stable for horses. The robbers were never out of sight of the posse, and were cornered in the hills and brought back to town. That night the citizens took them from the jail and hanged three in the courthouse yard, the fourth was shot as he tried to escape."

Justice on the frontier was not dispensed in any systematic or regulated manner. Although many towns hired sheriffs to police their communities, jails and courthouses were not built until later years. In the meantime, makeshift jails were set up in empty storerooms, back offices and livery stables where suspected criminals could be shackled and guarded. But security was lax and guards were easily bribed, so escapes were not uncommon.

In Burlingame, the cabin home of J. H. and Mary Polley served as an early community jail. As one Polley daughter recalled, the arrangement was anything but successful:

"Along in the '60s Father was elected Deputy Sheriff under William Cozine. There being no jail at that time Father kept the prisoners in our home. A man named Bates was arrested for burglary and was awaiting trial. He was kept at our house. Father kept him handcuffed, shackled, and chained to the wall when guarded by Mother.

"One day Mother wanted to go with Father about ten miles away where Father had to serve some papers. Abe Polley, my grandfather, offered to stay and guard [the prisoner] if Father would not hand-cuff him or chain him to the wall. Grandfather was very sympathetic. Father left a gun to use if necessary. Grandfather became interested in a book and Bates in some manner got the gun. A scuffle followed. Bates bit Grandfather's thumb off. The gun was broken in two, Grandfather getting the stalk and the piece with the hammers on and Bates the part with the caps on. Grandfather did not think he could shoot with that part. But Bates took a rock and hit the caps, shooting Grandfather. Grandfather lived three weeks.

"Bates went to the wood pile and chopped his shackles in two and escaped. Father started to hunt for him that night. . . .

"Bates was arrested and put in jail in Olathe. He was taken to Burlingame, where he was tried and convicted of murder and sentenced to be hanged by Judge Watson. The courthouse was being built. A gallows was fixed and the platform on which he stood was knocked from under him. This was the first legal hanging in Kansas. It was in 1866."

At times, vigilante committees seemed to be the most effective deterrent to the general lawlessness of the day. Distressed by inadequate policing efforts and insufficient jail facilities, townspeople often took matters into their own hands by organizing posses to track down suspected horse thieves, bank robbers or outlaws. Armed with ropes and rifles, they set off across the countryside to carry out their own brand of justice. When a suspect was finally apprehended, the angry mob rarely waited to give him a fair hearing or lead him back to jail. Instead, the captive met his final judgment by hanging from the limb of the nearest tree.

In many ways, horse rustling was regarded as the most serious and contemptible crime of all. Since horses were indispensable for a family's livelihood and transportation, they were very often the only possessions of any real value. As a result, horse thieves were likely to arouse strong community vengeance. Mary Lamb Shelden, who worked in El Dorado's hotel, vividly recalled the terrifying events of 1870:

"Like all new countries, Kansas, and especially this part of it, had to deal with the tough element, the forerunner of civilization, one might say. Here the horse-thief organization infested the country and had to be combated by another organization, the anti-horsethief, or vigilantes association. The horse-thief element had worked itself pretty well into politics, at least to the extent that the sheriff and constables were interested and failed to arrest or prosecute anyone charged with the crime. Convictions by process of law became impossible. This condition apparently was the justification for the drastic measures taken later on to exterminate the outlaws. Whether the end justified the means some to this day have grave doubts, but on the principle that desperate diseases require desperate remedies, after the loss of many horses—about the only asset the early settler had—the vigilantes hung five and shot three of the most active men in the gangs.

"The first of these tragedies occurred in November, 1870. A man by the name of Crawford came from Illinois with his family, driving three teams [of horses]. They took claims between Douglass and Wichita. In one night, all three teams were stolen. A day or so before, Jack Corbin, who posed as a government detective, had accosted the newcomer, who was riding a mule to town, claiming it was a government mule. He knocked Mr. Crawford off of the mule and took it to Wichita, where later the sons found it.

"A few days later, Mr. Crawford was in the Douglass house where the election was held and recognized the man who took his mule as one of the voters. He learned his name. That night, Jack Corbin was hung and two brothers, George and Louis Booth, were shot. Later in the night, Big Jim Smith, supposed to be the ring leader of them all, was shot as he was on his way to the Booth home. It was said that Corbin confessed and implicated the others.

"The night of the election, I remember very well that Jim Smith, all booted and spurred and armed with his two 'six-shooters,' ate his supper at the hotel. There was quite a rush in the dining room, because of the election, and I was helping serve. It fell to my lot to wait upon Smith. He had been drinking but was civil enough in his behaviour. I over-heard him mutter to himself, 'They are after me—they are after me.' I, of course, did not know what was on his mind until later. He was a powerfully built man. He always rode a mule into and out of town at a 'lope' which was the prevailing gait for riding. The mule was shot from under him and his own body riddled with bullets on the banks of the Little Walnut just north of Douglass.

"About midnight, the stage-coach came in bringing mail and passengers. The driver, with teeth chattering, told us he saw a dead man on the river bank as he crossed. This gruesome news at that hour of the night set my teeth chattering, too. It was part of my job to get up in the night and help my brother 'change' the mail and look after any passengers who might come in. After the old coach and driver had rattled on, I went back to bed but not to sleep. My teeth wouldn't let me until I got into bed with my brother and his wife.

"These lynchings might have ended the trouble had not other men who were interested in receiving and secreting stolen stock tried to work up vengeance on the supposed vigilantes. The prosecution of prominent citizens brought matters to a crisis in December when four arrests were made for complicity in horse stealing. These men were James Quimby and his clerk, Michael Dray, Mr. Morris, a druggist, and his son. Great excitement prevailed. Reports were thick that the horse-thief bands were coming to liberate the prisoners, burn the town and murder the citizens. The town filled up with men from the surrounding country, all heavily armed, to stand guard over the prisoners and town. Every man wore a brace of pistols, a knife and carried a shot-gun. I think there were about two hundred of them all told.

"It was a busy time for the hotel folk, as they had the job of feeding these men and, with the limited equipment and shortage of help, it was quite a task. It gave one a thrill, or a chill as the case might be, to see the men march into the dining room stacking their guns as they came. This condition remained about four days, when the prisoners were taken to the Big Walnut about a mile south of Douglass and hanged to trees.

"I personally do not know anything about what evidence was had against these men. It was certainly a deplorable act whether they were innocent or guilty. I afterward knew Mrs. Quimby and children well; the children were pupils of mine and I was especially fond of them. Mrs. Quimby was a refined, quiet woman and perfectly devoted to her family. But never could she quite get away from the shadow of this terrible tragedy."

In the eyes of its children, a prairie town had its own special kind of excitement. There was romping at Sunday socials, clapping at holiday parades, and joining in at community dances. There was listening to the angry speeches in the county-seat fight and to the stumping for school-board elections. On occasion, there were the mysteries to be fathomed in the traveling sideshow and the alluring wares of the itinerant peddler. And while town children may not have had small farm animals to play with, the prairie town also had its share of "creatures great and small."

"I think my sister and I were the first young children here," wrote Josephine Middlekauf, continuing her memoir of Hays. "At any rate I can't recall seeing any others the first two or three days; then a Mrs.

Vandewater came with her small son Walter and daughter Hattie from St. Louis. They were real city people. There wasn't anything in town too good for us youngsters; all kinds of pets were given us, dogs, gophers, prairie dogs, eagles and, in the Spring, young antelopes and buffalo calves, which we fed, loved and cared for until midsummer heat, when they sickened and died.

"Fred Kruger was one of the few who raised a buffalo from calf to buffalo meat and he was quite the pet. [The buffalo] made regular trips to the settler store at the fort, where the soldiers would give him a bucket of beer and he would put on the most comical 'drunk' you can imagine, with an entire change of program each time for the amusement of all the spectators, then lie down and sleep it off and come 'moseying home' as meek as humans on the morning after and sorry for it. As he got older he became dangerous and was killed.

"Cats were unknown the first few months in Hays, so a Mr. Benjamin wrote a friend in Leavenworth to send him a couple. His friend gathered up fifty or sixty cats, crated them and sent them out C.O.D. Mr. Benjamin paid the expenses and sold the cats at a good profit, so the joke was not on him after all.

"One of the things of never ceasing interest to us youngsters was the Othero & Sellers 'Bull Trains.' They had as many thrills as a circus. One may wonder how anyone could see anything fascinating in a Mexican Bull Train. I can see them now and remember the thrills we children got. There were eight or ten yoke of oxen, with their wide spreading horns, yoked to a big covered wagon with two trail wagons chained to that end driven by a Mexican with his fanciful clothes and bright-hued handkerchief and wide-brimmed sombrero. Take one group like that after another for a mile or more in length until it looked like a great colorful serpent winding its way slowly and gracefully over the hills back of the fort and I am free to confess, even after all the years that have passed over my head since, I still like to picture it and I can almost taste the little pine nuts that we would have to shell a quart to get a 'toothful,' that was part of their freight from Mexico.

"Another thing of equal interest to us and grown-ups was to watch the Concord Stages drawn by some of the most beautiful horses in the world 'swing out' for Denver and wonder if the passengers would reach their destination or be scalped a few miles out.

"The coming of the Seventh Cavalry with General Custer in command was another big time for us. In March or April of '69, after being out all winter running down a band of Indians who had two women, a Mrs. Morgan and a Miss White, captives, the Seventh Cavalry came here to camp and to draw a six months' pay. The poor fellows had been out all winter with scarcely enough clothing and on half rations.

"After tents were pitched and camp made, Custer, for their loyalty and faithfulness, gave them two weeks off duty to do as they pleased. What they 'pleased' was to come to town and eat and drink; they cleared the town of food and almost of drink. Every evening Custer would send up two dozen or more six-mule teams hitched to big army wagons and have all the drunks put in, two or three deep, and hauled back to camp to sober up and let them do the same thing next day if they wanted to.

"In the meantime, we had a real, sure enough circus advertised as the 'best ever' and it surely must have been as one has never thrilled like it since. 'Wild Bill' afterwards married the owner of it, Madam Lake."

The prairie town was the mainstay of frontier society—a marketplace, a meeting place, a crossroads for interstate commerce and communication. Though women sometimes found it a rough and lawless place, they also loved the town for its hubbub and vitality. Those who labored on the family homestead went to town not only to shop but to join in church activities, sewing circles and literary societies where news was shared and confidences exchanged in a warm community of women. Those who lived in town often ran general stores, managed hotels, worked as dressmakers or served as postmistresses. Women united to organize the town library and support its expansion. In time, a number of women stepped forward to express their views at political rallies, and, as we shall see, a stalwart minority later embarked on temperance crusades and began the campaign for woman suffrage. Those women who lived more obscurely still had the pleasure of watching a raw town of dirt paths and shanties grow into a real metropolis. As Josephine Middlekauf wrote: "After sixty years of pioneering in Hays, I could write volumes telling of its growth and progress, more often under adverse conditions than favorable ones. . . . suffice to say I have found it all interesting and worth while and feel I have been singularly privileged to have seen it develop from the raw materials into the almost finished product in comfortable homes, churches, schools, paved streets, trees, fruits and flowers."

CHAPTER TWELVE

The Cow Town

"The town was full of cowboys. On summer evenings we could hear the loud voices in the saloons and the tinkle of the piano in the dance hall. There were many saloons in our little town and no woman ventured on the streets at night."

—ELIZA JENNY PARENT

TO THE POPULAR MIND, no picture of the Kansas frontier would seem complete without the images of swaggering cowboys and thundering cattle drives. Likewise, the Kansas cattle town, with its saloons, card sharks, dance-hall girls and sharpshooting town marshal, is part of the American myth. Historically, many such wild and notorious characters did enliven a number of Kansas towns, but their glory was relatively short-lived. The cattle-driving era occupied only a brief segment of the state's history and was confined to certain parts of western Kansas at that. From roughly 1866 to 1886, the Texas cattle trade brought between five and seven million head of longhorns to the Kansas markets and poured millions of dollars in revenue into the frontier economy. At the end of this period, however, local ranches, with their herds quietly grazing in enclosed pastures, were all that remained of the great cattle trade.

For the most part, women played an incidental role in the cattle trade. The cattle drive north from Texas was grueling even for men, and only the hardiest and most experienced were hired for the journey. Women were simply not welcome on the trail.

At the end of the exhausting drive, however, female entertainment was heartily pursued by the travel-worn herders. Along with the gamblers, speculators and outlaws that swarmed into the booming cattle towns, a transient female population of barmaids, prostitutes and dance-hall girls was lured by the prospect of money and excitement.

These women were regarded as unsavory, however, and were shunned by the home-building women who came to inhabit and civilize the frontier. Most pioneer women disdained any association with the cattle drovers and the fringe elements of the town's population. As homesteaders, women often felt threatened by the huge stampeding cattle herds which ate their grasses and trampled their crops. As townspeople, they resented the violent antics of drunken cowboys and gun-slinging outlaws. As mothers, they deplored the immorality of the town saloons and dance halls as a corruption of their children and their communities.

In many ways, the Kansas cattle trade developed out of both need and convenience. In the 1860s there was a severe shortage of cattle in most Eastern states, where stocks had been sorely depleted during the Civil War. In Texas, on the other hand, vast herds of wild longhorns roamed the southern ranges. It seemed only logical that this cheap and abundant supply of cattle should be transported eastward to meet the nation's rising demand for beef and leather goods. At this time, however, the railroad had not yet reached Texas, and the neighboring Southern states were only beginning to recover from the devastation of the war. The extension of the transcontinental railroad into Kansas provided a practical solution to this transportation problem. Texas herds driven north to Kansas railheads could be easily shipped onward to Eastern markets.

Until 1867, a quarantine against Texas longhorns had existed in Kansas due to the frequent outbreaks of Texas fever. Although the Texas cattle themselves were immune to the deadly disease, they carried the tick, which often dropped to the ground and infected other breeds of cattle. In 1861, the first state legislature passed a strict ordinance prohibiting the entry of Texas longhorns across state borders during the warm months of the year. As one woman wrote, "Texas cattle could not come into the state unless they were dipped to kill the ticks on them. I read recently that Oklahoma was now mostly free from ticks; it has certainly been a long hard fight for stock men there. Many good cattle have died from Texas fever carried by ticks." By 1867, however, it was clear that sizable profits could be made if Texas herds were driven to Kansas railheads. As a result, the quarantine regulation was modified to permit Texas cattle in those areas west of the sixth principal meridian and south of the center line of the state.

Abilene was the first center of the Kansas cattle trade. In the spring of 1867, Joseph McCoy, a Chicago entrepreneur, came to Kansas to investigate possible markets. Traveling westward, he selected the tiny village of Abilene as his headquarters. Then the western terminus of the railroad, Abilene was unsettled, but its water supply was abundant and the surrounding grasslands were lush. Having secured a favorable contract with the railroad, McCoy soon began the work of transforming the sleepy prairie town into a teeming trade center. By the summer's end, the railroad depot, the stockyards, the barns and the shipping offices were completed and the requisite hotels and saloons were underway. Town promoters were sent south to Texas to attract herds and drovers to the area, and by September the town was ready for business.

On September 5, 1867, the first shipment of cattle—twenty carloads in all—was sent from Abilene to Chicago, and by the year's end roughly 35,000 head of cattle had passed through the town. The following year, a strong advertising campaign waged by McCoy in Texas brought twice as many cattle to Abilene, and by 1869 the town boomed with an annual shipment of 175,000 head of Texas longhorns.

It was in 1871 that Florence Bingham first visited the roisterous town of Abilene. "As the train came in sight of the town," she recalled, "a lonesome feeling I shall never forget came over me. The country and town looked so different from the East where every farm had its wood lot, and I had never seen a prairie before. I was almost terrified with fear of what we would find in this wild western country which was settled with cow boys, long horns and such men as Wild Bill. . . .

"We built a little home on a ten-acre tract on Buckeye about a mile north of the railroad. Mr. Bingham bought me a big rangy Texas pony; fortunately I was well used to riding, as Mr. Custer had taught me very early in life to be a good horsewoman.* My pony was a swift

* General George A. Custer was married to Elizabeth Bacon Custer, a first cousin of Florence Bingham.

traveler and I enjoyed many a fine ride over the vast prairie north of us where the antelope and other wild animals roamed. Because of the long-horned Texas cattle it was not safe for anyone to walk except near the stores. Usually two women walked together on the streets and were never molested if they behaved themselves. I always rode down town evenings to come home with Mr. Bingham. . . .

"We used to watch the cattle 'round ups' which was not as cruel as one would suppose, for the cow boys knew how to throw the cattle without injuring them. About as many men and horses got hurt as wild long horns did.

"One morning a man was found murdered along the railroad tracks. The men suspicioned another man and that evening they searched him and found part of the murdered man's clothing and his money, so they forthwith took this man to the creek a little northwest of our house and hung him to a beam of the old mill. My husband did not tell me anything about it. The school was on the south side and the next morning, much to my surprise, the school children came running past our house, all excited. They were going to see the man who was still hanging at the mill. They seemed to think it quite a lark and swung him back and forth by his toes. I could have seen him from my front gate, but I certainly did not want to.

"It was necessary that quick punishment be inflicted upon the criminal those days, but I preferred Wild Bill's way of doing it. Wild Bill was one of the finest-looking men you ever saw on horseback and always a perfect gentleman as far as we were concerned. He always shot to kill but suppose he did—he never killed anyone that did not deserve killing. . . .

"In the fall of '71, about October, Wild Bill left. The Union Pacific Railroad had been extended to Ellsworth and much of the cattle trade followed it."

Other cattle towns followed in the wake of Abilene's sudden trade boom. As the railroad gradually extended westward, the new railheads established their own shipping yards and flourished for a short time until a new market developed elsewhere. By 1871, Ellsworth had already usurped much of Abilene's cattle business, with nearly two thousand carloads of cattle traded. A few years later, Ellsworth was in turn surpassed by the towns of Newton, Wichita, Caldwell and Dodge City.

Similarly, the town of Hunnewell enjoyed a brief boom in cattle trading. On June 16, 1880, a branch of the Atchison, Topeka and

Santa Fe Railroad reached Hunnewell, and that same day the town's first building was erected. Other buildings were hastily constructed, and the town grew rapidly throughout the summer. A railroad station was completed by July, and huge stockyards were built at a cost of some $7,000 to facilitate the anticipated cattle trade. Mattie Huffman, who lived nearby at the time, reminisced:

"At the time Hunnewell grew up was the cowboy epoch for that part of Kansas. When they took a notion to shoot up a town, it was well for the residents to stay inside to avoid being hit by stray bullets. As a usual thing there was no loss of life; however, I remember once during Hunnewell's first summer that a dining-room girl looked out the door to see how many were in town, and was shot.

"My home was between Hunnewell and Caldwell. When the officers made it uncomfortable for the cow-boys in one town they would go to the other. Sometimes as they passed our place their clothes would be almost torn off and they would be riding like the wind. They often stopped at our well for drinking water. They became tamer in a few years."

Over a twenty-year span, millions of longhorns were driven to these Kansas towns along three major cattle trails. The Chisholm Trail was the most popular route of travel. It followed an earlier path laid out by an Indian trader, Jesse Chisholm, between his Wichita trading post and the Oklahoma Indian Territory. Six hundred miles in length, this trail stretched from San Antonio to the central Kansas towns of Abilene, Ellsworth, Newton and Wichita. The Shawnee Trail lay east of the Chisholm Trail and extended to Baxter Springs in the southeastern corner of Kansas. Dodge City to the west was the terminus of another popular route, the Western Trail.

Most Texas herds were driven north along these trails during the spring months when roadside pastures were lush and nearby watering holes were well filled. The drive itself lasted anywhere from forty days to five months, with the cattle traveling at an average pace of ten to fifteen miles per day. The driving herd usually consisted of two thousand head or more of cattle. Trotting side by side in small clusters, they often strung out for a mile or two in length. At times, the scene was one of bedlam as the steers were moved along at a fast pace. The Texas longhorns themselves were large, rangy animals with long legs and wide-spreading horns. Headstrong and powerful, these rugged cattle were known for their strength and stamina. On the move, they kicked up clouds of dust and pounded the ground with a thundering din. Angry steers bellowed and their horns collided and clacked loudly as the mounted cowhands shouted orders and cracked their whips.

Generally, a crew of ten to fifteen hands was hired to drive the herd to the Kansas markets. These men were carefully selected for their physical stamina, their riding skills and their courage. For most herds, there was at least one cowboy for every two hundred head of cattle. The most experienced and skillful herders always rode in front of the herd to set the pace and guide the cattle along the path. Other cowboys were positioned alongside to make sure that any straying cattle were kept in line. Less experienced hands rode at the rear of the herd to prod along the stragglers.

A retinue of assistants and supply wagons always accompanied the punchers and the longhorns on their way north. The trail boss was the foreman of every cattle outfit. Aggressive, quick and resourceful, he mapped out the route of travel, managed the crew and handled the financial transactions. The cook usually ranked second in command. From day to day he served the cowboys, cooking their meals, preparing their bedrolls, cleaning their clothes and treating their wounds. It was his responsibility to oversee the chuck wagon, the major supply wagon which served as the cowboys' home throughout the long journey. In addition, several horse herders were hired to complete the traveling outfit. A full stock of saddle horses was needed to keep up the rugged pace, and at least five or six horses per cowboy were supplied for the trip.

At dusk, after the long day's drive, the weary cattle were rounded up in the smallest space possible and bedded down for the night. While several cowboys stood guard over the resting herd, the others retired to the campfire for food and relaxation. Afterward they spread out their bedrolls on the hard earth and slept under the prairie sky.

Nights along the trail were not always restful, however. A distant clap of thunder, the crack of a pistol or the sight of a prowling coyote was liable to frighten the herd and start a stampede. The sleeping cowboys had to be ready to mount their horses at a moment's notice. Grabbing their guns and lariats, they raced after those steers leading the melee and prodded them together in a circle. As the riders surrounded the herd, the frantic cattle were gradually forced into a tighter and tighter circle. When they were finally calmed, the cowboys lulled them to sleep with soothing chants and quiet songs. At daybreak, the herd was recounted, stray cattle were rounded up and the long march to market resumed.

In the summer of 1870, Mattie Huffman's family bought one thousand head of longhorns that had been driven from Texas to the Abilene stockyards. From there the Huffmans herded the cattle north to Leavenworth. Mattie Huffman, fifteen years old at the time, helped to cook and clean for the busy herders.

"I shall now get into 'north of 36' history,"* she wrote. "This is the period my brother likes so much because he was in the excitement of buying and herding. He went with Father and several other men to Abilene, to buy cattle in the summer of 1870. They bought quite a string of cattle, about a thousand head. (I believe cattle men call it a 'string.') The Texas cattle were so wild that it was difficult to hold them anywhere. Several men had to be with them day and night. They could not be brought into Leavenworth County until after frost on account of Texas fever regulations.

"They were holding them for this reason not far from Abilene, beside a small grove where the men had their camp, when the thriller happened. It was one night while all the men were asleep except my brother, then about twelve years old, and his cousin, who were watching the herd. A cow came up to the salt-barrel near the camp; in taking a nibble of salt she in some way got a sack fastened on to her horns. Of course she went mad with fear and spread terror among the entire bunch by dashing among them. A stampede was on in no time. All the sleeping men came to life and climbed trees reflexively, expecting the cattle to trample their camp. Fortunately they chose a circular route instead, missing the camp by a narrow margin. It took about a week to get all the cattle together again. They would come upon them gathered in small bunches.

* Mattie Huffman is referring to *North of 36,* a novel (1923) by Emerson Hough. Hough (1857–1923) was a popular Western novelist who combined sentimental romance with Western themes. *North of 36*, one of his most famous novels, was a fictional account of a trail drive from Texas to Abilene, Kansas. Of the 36th parallel, Hough wrote: "Once upon a time the immortal gods . . . cast down upon the surface of the earth their great chessboard. . . . They traced a wandering and wavering line between the tall grass of the prairies and the bunch grass of the plains. It lay somewhere near what men afterwards came to call the one-hundredth meridian. Across this line at right angles they put down yet another indefinite line to finish off their board. Since they knew nothing of geography or mathematics or politics, they did not call this line the parallel of thirty-six north. . . . Had they gone one degree further north they would have established the south line of a land called by men the state of Kansas."

"It was the custom to drive the cattle for a full day when they were once started, as it was no easy task to check them and they seemed to have no respect for the dinner hour; so naturally the men could not have either. Father tells it that after the cattle had torn up a great share of the scattered fencing between Abilene and Topeka, they stopped them just outside the city limits on one Saturday night. On Sunday morning they passed through Topeka with fear and trembling lest the cattle get excited and ruin the town as a consequence. A. F. Ashby, an exceptional horseman, led the herd through at such a rapid pace that they did little damage. He also exhibited exceptional strategy in leading them across the bridge at Topeka. A bridge was such a foreign spectacle to them that they would go jumping along at a high speed.

"Finally the men got the cattle as far as the unclaimed land (a portion of the Caw reserve) which was only four miles from our home. They held the cattle here while each man picked out his. During the time this was being done, the men worked in shifts; and so naturally ate in shifts also. This is where my part in the 'North of 36' history comes in. I was then fifteen years old and spent practically all my time for a season getting the numerous breakfasts and as many suppers for the herders.

"The portion of cattle we kept were by no means disposed of after all this. At any time of night as they roamed about through timbered pastures, some unexpected noise such as the breaking of a twig might frighten them on one of their mad races. When we would hear the horns cracking together, Father would get up and go out and sing to them until they were quiet. This bunch of cattle was finally fattened down on Stranger creek where there was plenty of corn, and eventually in the late spring, they were shipped out from Leavenworth. The profit from this herd was considerable for those days, and we felt quite rich until the panic came on the following year."

For the homesteaders who lived along the cattle trails, the passing herds and cowboys brought mixed blessings. Many families welcomed the opportunity to sell their crops and produce to those outfits low on supplies. Others encouraged the herders to bed the cattle on their lands for the night, hoping to obtain a year's supply of cow chips by morning. Some settlers merely enjoyed the sudden excitement as the longhorns and the cowboys thundered past them.

Pauline Floeder Wickham grew up on a farm six miles southwest of

Wichita. The Wichita cattle trade thrived during the early 1870s, and Texas herds on their way to market frequently passed the family homestead. Although only a child at the time, Pauline recalled the hospitality extended to the weary cowboys:

"Some of the early settlers had trouble with the cowboys. We found them to be very kind and courteous in their primitive way. Some of them were creatures of feeling and quite a large degree of refinement, for many of them had come from homes in the East and later married [and] settled down.

"As it was necessary for them, as a rule, to drink from the same ponds, pools and buffalo wallows that the cattle drank from, they certainly appreciated a chance to get a drink of cool well water, and they frequently called for that purpose. We were always pleased to furnish them a glass which was an improvement on drinking out of their hat or boots, or getting down and drinking like a horse. They always seemed very appreciative and thanked us very profusely."

Over the years, however, many homesteaders strenuously objected to the driving herds which stormed over their lands. As it was, the Kansas farmer had more than enough problems with erratic weather conditions, inadequate water supplies, and grasshopper infestations. The sight of a thousand stampeding longhorns trampling their crops and devouring their grasses was infuriating. Moreover, there was always the lingering fear that these Southern herds would cause an outbreak of Texas fever among their own livestock.

Despite their objections, the homesteaders had no effective defenses or recourse against the intruding animals. There was no policing of the long trails, and a shotgun was all but useless against a cattle invasion. Fencing off their fields and pastures was not an easy solution, either. Supplies of stone and wood were limited in Kansas, and the whipping wind made fencing all the more difficult. It was not until the widespread marketing of barbed wire in the early 1880s that farmers were finally able to cordon off their lands and protect their crops.

Jennie Marcy lived on a farm near Baldwin City. Although there were no cattle trails nearby, a herd of Texas longhorns driven north by a neighbor brought unexpected excitement on one summer day. "It was a balmy day in early June; neither too hot nor too cool. The men folks at the little farm house had gone to town. Why were the men always away when terrible things happened! It was then that the coyotes were more neighborly, or the Indians were following the trails from the Reservations to the Territory, or the prairie grass mysteriously caught fire.

"The writer sat before the window that particular morning, working her feet 'like a house o' fire' treading the little old Grovner-Baker sewing machine, an ancient low-armed contraption, but still 'the latest improved model'—oh yes, a little larger than a coffee-mill and a trifle higher than a milking stool. Suddenly, a queer, sonorous, rumbling sound reached the ear and in a jiffy I was out of doors and readily saw with my own two eyes that something was about to happen, for down the road not far from the little prairie home were a thousand cattle, more or less. Ugly strangers they were, 'with big heads, little eyes, long legs and crooked thighs,' and horns a rod long from tip to tip.

"Where was old Pete, the recognized 'holy terror' of a watch dog? Yes, there he was in the shade of the lean-to kitchen. He was peacefully snoring, never dreaming of the excitement in store. With a loud snap of my fingers, I succeeded in arousing the two-faced canine. It is true he looked that way, for his face was half black and half white, giving him a never-to-be-forgotten peculiar vicious and villainous expression, this big bulldog of ours. We, together, sneaked cautiously around the off side of the house, where I pointed out the strange intruders. Then as I clapped my hands sharply and yelled, 'Sic 'em! Sic 'em!,' he bounded off immediately for active duty. But instead of facing the enemy as I had planned, he reconnoitered a bit, then rushed directly around the moving mass to the rear, displaying his ivory teeth and the utter lack of one single grey matter in his huge cranium. However, he snapped spitefully at the very heels of the long-horns until bedlam seemed turned loose. The fence boards snapped with a crash and pieces were hurtled here and there in every direction, while the three and four year olds rushed like winds over the forty-acre enclosure. I told Pete in plain English just what I thought of him, and clinched the statement by shutting him in the barn to calmly meditate over his past sin, if possible. And he found not a single morsel of complimentary food for thought, either.

"But what had happened? My dear Mother had passed through the narrow opening between the high stone walls to 'view the landscape o'er' and to behold our newly thrust-upon cattle possessions. But horrors! An ugly, lank, vicious bovine spied her and plunged at the precious form. However, providentially Mother saw the situation at a glance and like an athelete darted through the opening and crouched behind the stone wall, while the infuriated beast was suddenly called to a halt and shamefully returned to the herd to tell what he had not accomplished.

"I threw the bridle-rein over the kitchen door knob, and simply flew to my mother's side and found her completely swooned away from sheer fright. I alone on the quarter section and not a house in sight! I rushed to the well for cool water with which I bathed her forehead and lips, and very soon I helped her into the house and to the couch.

"By this time I had become desperate, ready to perform any reckless act regardless of the surrounding danger. I quickly mounted my pony and hurried my course through the deep, narrow ravine and stealthily climbed the hillside, where I completely surprised these Texas emigrants from the rear. And like the imprisoned Pete, I now fully understood that he too was desperately afraid of those sharp long horns. When I had time I meant to apologize to the poor dog. I made my approach on the repulsive intruders like a Kansas cyclone and with a savage shrill war-whoop, like a band of Comanche warriors, I really succeeded in scaring the whole bunch of animals. If I had only possessed a bloody tomahawk, I would have thrown it at the very first fellow that batted an eye at me.

"But unfortunately, they rushed to the broken-down fence and there stubbornly planted themselves with a 'thus far and no farther' attitude. They simply would not cross the bar. They milled around like the old-time political warhorses up in Copeland County during the sessions of the legislature. Three times these unwelcome foreigners from the South swung off over the hill and dale, and three times I rounded them up and returned the unruly bunch to the place by which they entered. As I sat there on my wiry little pony, I wondered why the good Lord armed the semi-wild cattle with those long head weapons, while the poor, though rich, glossy, silky, long-haired thoroughbred Galloways are minus the semblance of even the horny button to press when the antagonistic bovine combat is on. These thoughts flashed through my mind, but what was I to do next? I had reached the limit where a feller needs a friend.

"Joy! Joy! Over the hills, slowly approaching, was a good Samaritan from the lowlands, who readily took in the situation and hastened to my assistance. He came hurriedly though quietly to my side and beheld at close range just what I was trying to accomplish. Then, while I circled and crowded to the very wall these animals, he talked encouragingly to them with his crooning, 'So Bossie! So Bossie!' and with extended arms pointed out to them the way they should go, but to no avail. It seemed a hopeless case. They simply would not move one step nearer the goal.

"This thing was growing mighty monotonous and desperately exasperating to the very limit. We were worn to a complete frazzle. The good Samaritan was visibly losing his patience (and I, too) and finally he exploded with such a terrific volley of oaths as I never, never heard before. He was an accomplished linguist, for he spoke in every tongue under the sun; and right there and then I crowned him post-master of languages. He swore like a trooper. The sulphureous fumes poured forth through the opening in this heavily bewhiskered physiognomy until the man, young girl and those brutes nearly suffocated.

"Finally, the biggest, most stubborn mogul, the ringleader of this invading army, quietly stepped over the debris and meandered innocently and knowingly southward on the main highway. One by one, like sheep, the rest followed, and I tagged along on my pony. Fast, then faster, I hurried them along. The thud of their hoofs, accompanied by the clicking tattoo of meeting horns, was a sign that I at least had the enemy on the run. I hastened them along until I succeeded in getting them to trot, then busily canter, and in a fine gallop, I rushed them on to the banks of the clear sparkling waters of the beautiful Wakarusa, where I sent them heartlessly, relentlessly pell-mell down the steep bank into the 'sea,' to be drowned and be forever washed from the face of the earth.

"Weary, though conscience-free, pony and I cantered back home, where I found my good friend perched upon a fence post smoking his old cob pipe and religiously guarding the wrecked fences and ruined young crops. As the writer approached, he said, 'Young lady, I was born in Boston, the intellectual hub of the universe.' 'Yes,' I meekly replied, for I had heard that self-same statement time and time again, for invariably he introduced himself in that particular self-satisfied manner. 'And it is nigh on to fifteen years since I came to this God-forsaken country, and one thing I have learned in these fifteen years is the undisputed fact, Miss, that you cannot drive cattle without swearing at them.' I could not, dare not, deny the statement when I had just witnessed a perfect and complete demonstration so recently of his splendid ability to start that bunch of heathenish quadrupeds. But I did think that he was mighty slow in learning his lesson, for I caught the trick in five minutes, no more, no less.

"What was poor me to do now? Would I be a total failure as an amateur 'cowgirl'? And I, one of my father's 'boys' in this new country, and this was my very own white pony, given to me for the express purpose of watching the fences, that no stray stock 'break through and steal' our meager crops. I knew nothing of the thrill of horseback riding, until less than a year after my arrival west, when the scenes of this story were realized, for I had been reared in one of our Eastern cities, and tenderly mothered under strict Methodistic wings. 'Swear not at all' was in the curriculum and was a major part of my parental training.

"The day after this most thrilling incident the writer learned the cause of this day's chaotic disturbance and destruction. One of our neighbors down on the bottoms had been down to Texas, where he rounded up and smuggled through the borders (all unbeknown'st to me, of course) this marauding bunch of 'Lone Stars,' fifty-four in all!"

After many strenuous weeks on the trail, the long drive to Kansas finally drew to a close. As the herd neared its destination, the trail boss rode ahead to locate temporary grazing grounds. Open fields with plentiful water supplies, thick grasses and easy access to town provided the most desirable location. The campsite was then pitched along a nearby stream or watering hole, the wagons were unloaded, and the herd was set out to pasture.

Since grazing cattle required considerably less work than driving them, a number of cowboys were usually dismissed at this time. The others were retained to watch over the grazing herd and assist with its final sale. Often, one or two cowboys were sent to town to replenish the supplies and gather news of other herds or potential buyers. Back at camp, life seemed particularly dull and routine after the excitement of the long drive. During the day, the cattle were allowed to roam freely while the attending cowboys kept a quiet but careful watch. At dusk, the herd was rounded up and bedded near the campsite, to be guarded by a night shift.

When it was time to sell the fattened cattle, the herd drover set off to make the arrangements in town. At the Kansas railheads, most Texas longhorns were sold to buyers who herded them onto railroad cars and shipped them eastward. Some drovers, however, chose to ship their herds themselves for later sale in the eastern markets. In addition, there were usually Kansas buyers in town who purchased cattle for their own western ranches.

Offered for sale in whole or in part, the herd was generally sold by the head. Once the sale was arranged, the cattle were quickly counted and readied for delivery. Counting the cattle was a slow, tedious task in itself. Usually, several cowboys, mounted on horseback, faced one another several feet apart and did the counting while the other hands forced groups of cattle to walk single file between them.

After the longhorns were prodded to town, delivered to the buyers and loaded onto railroad cars, the cowboys finally received their wages and a long-awaited vacation. Often earning twenty-five to forty dollars a month for their work, the men set off to enjoy themselves in town. The first stop was usually the barbershop, where the dusty trail hands received a good bath, a shave and a haircut. The general store was next for a fresh change of clothes. Attired in new leather boots, wide-brimmed Stetsons and bright bandanas, the cowboys were ready to relax. "Dressed in gala attire," recalled one observer, "they wore high-heeled boots with large clanking spurs of various hues, shirts that bloused freely with no hint of suspenders, large colored handkerchiefs knotted loosely around their necks and large-brimmed stetson hats. Some showed the influence of their Spanish neighbors and wore large brightly colored sashes."

At the height of the trading season, the cattle town vibrated with constant activity and high-spending excitement. Inevitably, large numbers of speculators, gamblers, prostitutes and gunmen swarmed into the area. The town streets were lined with bustling barrooms, brothels, dance halls, gambling houses and variety theaters which catered to the herders' needs and whims. "The festive cowboy on pleasure bent," explained Mabel McNeice, "demanded saloons, dance-houses and gambling dens and these accordingly sprang up to meet the demand. The quiet little village of a few months before became a 'red-hot town' with a street designated as 'Red-Hot Street.' "

Looking back on the early days of Olathe, Mrs. Walter Mason proclaimed, "Few people can picture a frontier, prairie town as it was in the '70s. The struggling outlines of the village were separated from the boundless prairie by a frail three-board fence built to protect the town lots and the gardens from the town cows and the Texas herds which fed on the grasses of the boundless prairie up to the edge of the village. Herds of hundreds of Texas long horns were driven by the little village, feeding over the prairies and drinking from the clear streams, as they came from Texas to be marketed at Kansas City. Red-shirted cow boys, six shooters flapping on their hips as their cattle ponies whirled after stragglers from the herd, the rider cracking the huge plaited whip like pistol shots ran the unruly steer back into the herd. The place teemed with saloons. Ribald language floated out between their swinging doors, and ruffians poured into the streets mad with liquor, flourishing weapons and struggling in a whiskey-crazed tumult."

For women, the violence and lawlessness of the cattle town was particularly frightening. Although most women could handle a gun, they were usually unprepared to dodge stray bullets or fend off drunken cowboys. Frances Poor wrote: "In the latter part of November, 1870, we were sent to Abilene to be night operators during the Texas Cattle Drive to the place. It was then a very small, rough, pioneer town; quite often a person would be shot down in the night, carried away and no one could learn anything about it. I suffered more real terror the few weeks we lived there than in all the rest of my western life."

When Minnie Lawless first moved to Wano in 1886, it was also a tough, turbulent cattle town. "Wano was simply a gathering place or trading post for the ranch men and cowboys," she wrote. "The very first night, about midnight we were awakened by shooting and shouting, but were too frightened to leave our rooms. In the morning we learned that there had been a big roundup and the cowboys had gotten into a terrible row down at the 'Dewdrop,' a saloon and gambling place in the town. One man had been shot but not killed. That morning a cowboy called 'Bum' rode his pony 'Babe' into the store and with his revolver drawn, ordered the clerk to give 'Babe' all the candy she wanted. Needless to say, the clerk obeyed."

Despite Minnie's fear on that terrifying night, she also recalled that, by day at least, cowboys could demonstrate another side to their natures: "There was a schoolhouse built in Wano that spring and a Sunday School organized. Services were held occasionally as itinerant preachers passed through. Many times I have seen the little school house entirely surrounded by cowboys mounted, their horses' heads close up to the open windows. They listened respectfully and were liberal when the 'Hat was passed.' "

Alma Waterman of the town of Lakin on the far-western plains also acknowledged that most cowboys she met "were men who conducted themselves as gentlemen and from whom I never heard an oath." But one night in 1880 a particularly rowdy bunch of cowboys caused a frightening commotion.

"We moved into the upper rooms of the new depot [my husband, J. H. Waterman, being the Santa Fe agent at this place], and it was there that we experienced one of the most thrilling events of our life. Some cowboys had attended a funeral at Deerfield and to cheer themselves up had taken a drink, and as they came into Lakin, the passenger train stood on the track waiting for orders. They rode their horses up on the platform, and as the train pulled out, they broke the glass in the window and put a few shots into the lower part of the cars. It happened that Vice President Coolidge's* car was on the train, and as soon as the word reached Dodge City, a train was sent out with the Sheriff and 40 to 50 men, all armed with rifles, shotguns and revolvers.

"They captured two of the men at the saloon in town, the other man tried to get away on his horse—they shot the horse, and he got into Chapman's dugout, but they kept shooting until he put out a white flag of surrender. The three cowboys and the telegraph operator, who had been celebrating with them, were handcuffed—taken to Dodge—tried and convicted, serving a short sentence in the penitentiary. So their fun ended in disaster."

By the mid-1880s, the long cattle drives to the Kansas railheads gradually ended. As increasing numbers of homesteaders settled the western plains of Kansas, fenced fields and thriving communities blocked the trails and limited access to open grazing grounds. Several severe winter blizzards annihilated many herds, and declining prices crippled the cattle market. Furthermore, the construction of the railroad across the Texas borders made the long cumbersome drives unnecessary. Finally, the westward extension of the official quarantine line against the Texas cattle eliminated many Kansas cattle towns and eventually ended the drives altogether in 1884.

The demise of the drives, however, did not destroy the Kansas cattle industry. Throughout the 1870s, ranchers had grazed huge cattle herds on the open, unsettled ranges of western Kansas. As homesteaders gradually settled these grasslands, the traditional animosity between the farmer and the cowboy resurfaced. While the homesteaders struggled to protect their fields and crops, the cattlemen demanded the continuing use of a free and open range. Anna Gray wrote: "We found that the cattle men who grazed their herds on the

* Alma Waterman was referring to P. Jefferson Coolidge, who was actually president of the Santa Fe Railroad from May 1880 until August 1881.

prairie were not pleased at the coming of so many settlers. They were known to have driven some of the settlers' cattle with theirs when they took them to market. We had a few head of cows but had no trouble as we treated [the cattlemen] well and sometimes they would come and ask shelter from the rain. [They] also bought meals from us and paid."

With the erection of barbed-wire fences and the sophistication of farming methods, however, the western grasslands were gradually enclosed. As the cattlemen themselves were forced to fence their pastures, large ranches were established with their own herds of cattle and crews of cowboys. In time, the beef animals were upgraded, stock-breeding methods were improved, and a thriving "closed-range" industry developed.

For many women, the confinement of the cattle industry to private pastures added new responsibilities to their working lives. While women were not permitted on the trail, their assistance was needed on the family ranch. When the help fell short, women often set off on horseback to locate stray cattle, mend broken fences and inspect watering holes. Moreover, they helped treat wounded steers, tend the new yearlings and milk the dairy cows.

Like other women, Fannie Holsinger spent long strenuous hours working on her family's ranch. One year, a particular angry cow proved too difficult to handle. As she explained, "One of our neighbors, an Indian, finding the white settlers too thick for his liking, decided to move to Oklahoma and sold his stock at public auction. We bought a cow with a fine record. That cow nearly ended my Kansas career before it was well started.

"I went to the pasture to find her new calf. She found me instead and chased me out and over the fence. I felt nervous when it was time to milk, so my husband drove her into a small rail pen and stood guard over me. He could not milk, as he had a crippled right arm, a Civil War legacy. I had just remarked the wonderful flow of milk, my husband turned a moment, and as he turned back he saw me in the air where the angry cow had tossed me. I fell across her neck and was again tossed, then fell in the fence corner a limp rag.

"My husband sprang forward and gripped the horns. The brute shook off and tossed him, but less successfully. One horn caught a trouser's leg and ripped it to the top, but he lit on his feet. Disdaining him, the crazed creature ran to where I lay. I was only conscious enough to see her drop to her knees, to hear the maddened breathing and to see again those terrible horns trying to goar me through—then blackness. My husband dragged me from under the vicious head, and literally threw me over the fence, then clubbed furiously before he could get over himself.

"They thought I was dead. I escaped with bruises the full length of my body. As long as that cow lived if she caught sight of me in the yard she would cross the pasture and stand with her head over the fence till I disappeared in the house. From my husband she would run. If ever an animal was insane she was. She died a few weeks later in agony with what was called 'mad itch.'

"The Police News, a New York publication which was the yellow journal of that day, got the story and illustrated it. The full-page picture showed a regular movie hero tossing a sleeping beauty over a high board fence with impressive buildings in the background. 'Must have put on your Sunday clothes to milk,' sniffed my friends."

Fannie Holsinger's bout with the crazed cow is, in a way, emblematic of the decades of the Kansas cattle drives. Kansas herself was butted and bruised by hordes of dull, indifferent beasts; they trampled her fields and went on wild stampedes which must have seemed like massive fits of pique. It was a harsh and rowdy era, but its memory has been colored by time into an era of thrilling cowboy pranks and flashy dance-hall girls. Like the glamorized picture of Fanny in *The Police News*, the legend wears its Sunday best.

CHAPTER THIRTEEN

The Immigrant Community

Victoria

"Out in the 'short grass country' of western Kansas, when the pioneer days of the early seventies are mentioned, we think of covered wagons, meager homestead fare, parched fields, sunbonneted women who dared hardships, and bronzed, square-jawed Yankee men, who wrote history with the plow.

Then of those towns—outposts of civilization, yet filled to the brim with such humanity as knew no law or civilization. There were many of them—Abilene, Dodge, Hays—frontier cowboy towns where history was written with the gun—and written quickly. . . .

But close your eyes on this rough hard history of the plains, forget the roughneck cowboys . . . , the saloon brawls, the death-dealing gunmen who fattened Boot Hill, and that floating and often broken brushwood washed out of the main stream of American civilization into pioneer outposts. Forget time and distance—let yourself be transported to a spot in Kansas, twelve miles southeast of Hays, along the Union Pacific Railway. . . .

Open your eyes on Victoria, with all that name implies of British culture and traditions. It was 1872, and Victoria, Kansas, was a bit of old England transplanted in full bloom to the raw prairies of the middle west."

—MARY CARRICK HAVEMANN

IN THE EARLY 1870s, the village of Victoria was an oasis of gentility on the barren land of central Kansas. Populated by British aristocrats and gentry, it was a community of great wealth, high culture and lavish traditions. While other pioneers packed their wagons with old clothes, tin utensils and wooden tools, the Victoria colonists filled their steamer trunks with sterling and gold, silk and satin, porcelain and crystal. Instead of struggling to wrest a livelihood from the arid earth, these Englishmen enjoyed the pleasures of cricket games, fox hunts, banquets and soirees. It was a community where leisure took precedence over work, where wealth mitigated privations and where social etiquette was as important as physical stamina.

Actually, Victoria was only one of a number of foreign communities. As was true of other states, Kansas was settled by a steady stream of foreign immigrants throughout the 1870s and 1880s. In those years, many thousands of disgruntled Europeans left their homelands to escape from destitution, religious persecution, political tyranny or military conscription. With dreams of prosperity and adventure, they fled to America and the shores of opportunity.

Since most of the Europeans were farmers by occupation, the open prairies, with their rich grasses and fertile soils, were particularly enticing. While some were influenced by correspondence received from relatives and friends already in Kansas, others were solicited by state agents, town sponsors and railroad promoters. In 1864 the Kansas state legislature established a special bureau of immigration. Under its auspices, special agents were hired to tour parts of Europe and promote direct immigration. Their efforts were bolstered by the activities of immigration companies headquartered in Chicago and New York.

It was during this period that the Kansas railroad companies also assumed a major role in the promotion of foreign immigration. In previous years, the federal government had granted these companies vast tracts of land to facilitate the rapid construction of statewide railroad lines. Once the tracks were laid and the railroad was in operation, the companies became anxious to sell their surplus lands. In order to attract buyers, they sent agents abroad to advertise inexpensive tracts of land in Kansas and to offer special low transportation and freight rates to prospective purchasers.

Although most of the immigrants arrived in small family groups, there were a number of large colonies which migrated to Kansas. In the late 1860s, the organization of various emigration aid societies, particularly the First Swedish Agricultural and Galesburg Colonization Companies, brought the first sizable influx of Swedish settlers. Populating the Smoky Hill Valley, they established thriving communities at Lindsborg, Freemont and Salemsborg. In 1869, two hundred Scottish families made their homes together at Scotch Plains near the northern border. In the next few years, large colonies of German-Russian immigrants arrived. The Mennonites came first in 1874 and were soon followed by the German-Russian Catholics who founded the towns of Catherine, Herzog, and Munjor. At the same time, three large British communities were established at Wakefield, Victoria and Runnymede. In addition, there were scattered enclaves of French, Bohemian, Norwegian, Dutch and Danish families.

In the case of Victoria, Sir George Grant, a wealthy London silk merchant, was the driving force behind the settlement. Intrigued by the reports of America's untrammeled grasslands, he toured the Great Plains in the spring of 1872. Toward the end of his journey, Grant passed through Fort Hays and traveled eastward across Ellis County. There the sight of endless, rolling prairies, dappled with colorful flowers and grazing buffalo, held him spellbound.

Enamored with his discovery, Grant vowed to return with a contingent of his fellow Englishmen. After negotiating with the Kansas Pacific Railroad, he purchased fifty thousand acres of land in eastern Ellis County and began organizing the Victoria colony. In the spring of 1873, the sons and daughters of many of England's most noble families set sail for the American frontier.

"On April 1, 1873," recorded Jane Hardie Philip, "the Steamship Alabama sailed down the Clyde from Glasgow, with a number of passengers bound for Kansas. There were also a good supply of fine horses, cattle and sheep on board. She encountered some very rough weather, was disabled a part of the time, and was finally stranded on a sandbar at the mouth of the Mississippi. May 17 the first of the new colony landed at Victoria.

"Most all of the settlers preempted a quarter section; also homesteaded 80 acres besides buying railroad land from Mr. Grant. On their arrival they found no house for miles, with the exception of the Section House, and a fine depot built more for the accommodations of settlers than for the company's use. They only reserved a small room as ticket office and one as a freight room, the rest of the building being used as a sort of a hotel. There were twelve bedrooms upstairs that the settlers could use and they all had the use of the kitchen, where they could cook their own meals—a very necessary arrangement. But soon two and three roomed houses began to be dotted all over the prairie where every one was welcome to the best the house afforded."

In the coming years, more than two hundred Englishmen, as well as a number of Scottish and Irish immigrants, settled on Grant's prairie purchase. True to their heritage, these colonists homesteaded with a dazzling flair of their own. Delicate French satins and fine English tweeds were as common in Victoria as calico and denim. Victoria homes were decorated with fine furniture, oil portraits and family heirlooms, Victoria tables with lace tablecloths, sterling flatware and bone china. Victoria roads were traveled by horse-drawn carriages.

"Whole families came," noted Mary Carrick Havemann, "bringing their traditions, gold candlesticks and linens. But many were younger, unmarried sons of wealthy or titled parents. They came adorned in top hats, their pockets full of money, and the assurance of a quarterly allowance following them. Country gentlemen in England sent sheep, horses and cattle—the best the realm afforded—to stock the ranches of their sons in America."

The Englishmen of Victoria were just as unwilling to abandon their social customs as they were to forgo their luxuries. In keeping with their traditions, the morning's affairs often included formal fox hunts. In proper hunting attire, men and women alike mounted their horses and galloped after packs of yelping foxhounds. If a fox could not be found for the hunt, cottontail rabbits or coyotes usually sufficed. As one participant claimed, "That the 'Fox' was a li'l old coyote did not lessen the sport."

"On many a crisp fall morning," continued Mary Carrick Havemann, "Victoria was astir at dawn. Hounds held in leash were restless, horses tied to riding blocks whinnied and champed their bits. Riders were galloping in from surrounding farms and ranches—riders arrayed in riding britches and scarlet hunting jackets. The women's costumes were green and almost swept the ground. They sat on their horses gracefully, for English riding masters had taught them to ride. Many of the gentlemen's negligible hunting saddles were imported.

"There was banter and gaiety. For Sir George often had guests from London or New York at his manor and they had to be entertained. And what more fitting amusement for these sons of Britain than riding to the chase over an infinite billowing prairie? The majority of them were more at home in the chase than behind the plow, anyway.

"What did they chase? Rabbits, hundreds of them, coyotes by the score; antelopes and buffaloes—not so many, but keener sport when found. Not only were these animals chased but they were captured, too, for the hunting hounds and shire horses, like the Victorians themselves, were of England thoroughbred. And at least one spot in Kansas was merry England then—when the chase was on."

For the colonists, a day's social engagements regularly took precedence over household chores and farm work. In the afternoon the men might gather for games of cricket, while their wives visited over tea and crumpets. In the evenings there were often formal banquets, grand balls or holiday soirees. "The English gave wonderful entertainment," recalled Catherine Cavender, "dinners with long tables, laden with baked buffalo, antelope and quail, mince pies, plum puddings and tipsy cake, and after the dinner a dance that lasted till morning and there were Lords and Lairds to dance with, too!"

Sir George's villa, a two-story stone manor house, was a frequent setting for candlelight dinners and holiday dances. Grant himself was a veteran entertainer, and his lavish affairs were always the highlights of the social season. "Mr. Grant, the founder of the Colony," remembered Jane Hardie Philip, "always had visitors from New York and other eastern states, and when he gave parties, everyone was fed on the fat of the land, some times it was not very fat but everyone had good appetites and good digestion."

In the Carrick home, the family piano brought from England provided musical entertainment at evening parties and afternoon weddings. "Mrs. Carrick's piano," explained Mary Carrick Havemann, "was imported from Scotland and set the pace for many a gay party and dance. For English hospitality was lavish. Not only were the old world friends and relatives entertained, but friends from New York came to visit; and famous American officers and their ladies from old Fort Hays tripped on into the wee small hours.

"But Mrs. Carrick played for more solemn occasions also. Just after a revival had swept through a neighboring pioneer settlement, she was invited to the Wilds' home to play for a daughter's wedding. Inquiring about the bride's choice of music, she was informed that the book was opened at what Sally wanted played. Investigating, she found a hymn book on the organ, propped open at 'Nearer My God to Thee.' Relating the incident later, Mrs. Carrick said, 'You may be sure I closed the book, and played something quick and devilish.' "

In spite of all the gaiety, Victoria settlers were certainly not free from the encroaching hardships of pioneer life. "Life was not always merry," admitted one woman. "Even with plenty of money it was pioneering."

Ben Davidson, one of the first of Victoria's settlers, reported a disaster for each of Victoria's first three years: a prairie fire, a grasshopper plague and the costly failure of a great sheep-raising enterprise. And, like other frontier communities, Victoria had its share of trouble with horse thieves and cattle rustlers. The colonists had stocked their ranches with the finest breeds of draft horses, English rams and short-horned cattle. Inevitably, these prized animals became a target for knowledgeable rustlers.

"These young Victoria 'Bloods' had some very fine horses," remembered Jane Hardie Philip, "a great temptation to horse thieves. One morning several were missing. Sheriff Ramsey came from Hays, chose George Philip as his deputy, they rode among the Smoky Hills until about 2 P.M. and seeing no signs of the horse thieves decided to give up the chase and go home, Ramsey to Hays and Philip to Victoria. The sheriff had no sooner disappeared than the horse thieves came up out of a draw a short distance ahead of Philip with the command 'throw up your hands.' They took Philip's horse and revolver, giving him their pack horse to ride home, where the boys had a good deal of fun at his expense.

"The following summer Sheriff Ramsey was shot by a horse thief and at the same instant he shot his man, both dying almost instantly. When Mrs. Ramsey heard the news she gave a shriek and was taken to the insane asylum in Topeka, where she died a few days later. There is a fitting monument to the memory of Alexander Ramsey in the Hays cemetary. No braver man ever lived."

To men unskilled at farming, the tough sod and the arid climate proved to be formidable adversaries. While many learned to handle a plow successfully, others continued to rely on personal wealth and cattle stocks for their livelihood. As Jane Hardie Philip explained, "The colony was composed principally of gentlemen's sons who had been taught no occupation but sent out with their pockets full of money, which they spent freely, knowing that in due time another remittance would arrive."

For the bachelors, housekeeping chores only created further exasperation. Inexperienced in cooking, some men even imported special canned goods for their convenience. "The R.R. conductors used to say," continued Jane Hardie Philip, "there were more canned goods unloaded at Victoria than at any other stations along the road. It was so much easier for these young bachelors to open cans than to stand over a stove."

Pioneer life was not any easier for the English ladies who had once relied on maids and butlers. Yet although they were untrained in the ways of cooking, cleaning and sewing, they persevered to adapt to the new conditions confronting them. "In the section house," recalled Jane Hardie Philip, "was a kind, motherly Irish-woman, Mrs. Norton, who will never be forgotten by these women, many of whom never did their own house-work and had no idea how to rough it on the prairie. She showed them how to make bread; also to use the slim provisions the new country afforded to the best advantage."

When sickness or tragedy befell them, the life in this faraway land seemed all the more difficult. Jane Hardie Philip, continuing her memoirs, described the plight of one Victoria family. "Mr. and Mrs. Seth from Glasgow, with five grown sons and daughters, contracted fever coming up the Mississippi, and died shortly after their arrival here, except the father and one son. They had been accustomed to every luxury and came out to a hastily constructed shanty or dugout, where they could scarcely procure the bare necessities of life, far less any comforts. There were no screen doors and windows to keep out the swarms of flies, mosquitoes, and bugs of every description that infested the prairie; no ice to cool the fevered brow, nor even nourishing food so necessary to an invalid, although the neighbors did all they could, for with all these discomforts, there were never a happier or more unselfish people, always ready to share whatever they had."

Within the space of a few years, it was apparent that the Victoria colonists were ill-suited to the ongoing rigors of the open range. Their spirits flagged with each passing season. In time, poor crop yields, meager water supplies, grasshopper infestations and winter storms depleted their resources and weakened their stamina. One by one, they abandoned their early dreams, packed their belongings and returned to England.

By 1876, only a handful of the original colonists remained. Sir George Grant himself refused to leave the village he had worked so hard to build. After his death in 1878, however, the Victoria community quietly dissolved. "Those who stayed moved to Hays," recalled Mary Carrick Havemann, "leaving the old village deserted. The houses were moved away, and even the old church was deserted, and finally torn down." Yet even though the British settlement itself had faded from the prairie, Mary Havemann affirmed that its spirit and gentility continued to endure throughout the coming years.

"Music, books, and magazines came from England, fashion plates and rare prints from Weldon's. For never once did those colonists forget their traditions of culture—nor the Queen for whom their colony was named. There were prints of Queen Victoria, life like and beautiful. These are still reverently cherished in the large houses in Hays, where the sons and daughters of the colonists now live. There are life-size portraits of bonneted ladies and bearded gentlemen from the five generations back. There are hand-spun linens, table cloths long enough to deck tables at which medieval lords and all their retainers might feast. There are priceless handed-down pieces of pottery, copper tea kettles with queer spouts and handles, pipes with long curved stems hang on the walls or are smoked by broad-shouldered old gentlemen with stubby King George beards.

"None of the old colonists remain at Victoria. But when they came to Hays, the Victorian spirit came with them, and this old world heritage still pervades the homes of their children. Little boys sit cross-legged on furry buffalo rugs while they listen wide eyed to their grandfathers talk of the early times in America, and of the earlier times in England.

"Traditions and culture are not products of one generation. But they last. And if these Victorian colonists were spendthrifts, if they were ignorant of the pioneer methods of farming, if they were kept by the folk at home, and if they did neglect the bread-and-butter side of life—their contribution to this section of the Melting Pot are inestimable. With the harder, more practical qualities of other settlers, this little band of gentlemen's sons and daughters welded its gift of culture."

PART FIVE

CHAPTER FOURTEEN

The Wounds of War

"A caravan of ox-drawn wagons slowly wended its way through wooded roads and prairie trails from Hannibal, Missouri, to Big Springs, Kansas, in the early winter of 1854.

In the hearts of the pioneers who were traveling in those covered wagons was the same spirit which prompted the pilgrims of the May Flower to seek a land of freedom. The State they were leaving was avowedly a slave state, and these people were hoping that in the Territory to which they were going they would find a home of freedom. Freedom for thought, speech, action and slaves.

They had no vision of the terrible strife, tragedies, privations and suffering which they were to endure, with fortitude, courage, loyalty, sustained by a deep abiding love for home and state, in order to establish that freedom. They could not visualize that before that dream came true there would frequently be:

At bedtime, a happy family group—Father, Mother and Children gathered around the fireside. In the morning, a sad fatherless, husbandless home.

In the evening, horses housed and resting for the work of the following day. In the morning only empty stalls.

In the evening, a cozy log cabin with the cheery glow of candles at the windows and a peaceful family within. In the morning, a hopeless mass of blackened ruins."

—IDA KOCH LANE

IN THE OPENING YEARS of its settlement, Kansas was a political powder keg. The slavery controversy, which had already divided the rest of the nation, burned across this territory with all the fervor and malice of a prairie fire. Emotions flared and tensions increased as the early pioneers became embroiled in the bitter battle between slavery and freedom. In these times, hostility and violence became a familiar part of life as opposing gangs of abolitionists and proslavery fighters spread terror throughout the countryside. Only the final stamp of statehood in 1861 could dampen the smoldering antagonisms and bring the peace of freedom to this land.

The Kansas Territory had been wracked by political dissension from the beginning. In opening the plains to white settlement, the Kansas-Nebraska Act of 1854 had provided that the inhabitants of both Kansas and Nebraska would be allowed to decide for themselves whether slavery or freedom was to rule their land. At the outset, it was clear that the Nebraska Territory to the north of Kansas would become a free state. The fate of Kansas, however, remained uncertain. As a whole, the Southern slave states had supported popular sovereignty with the belief that the Kansas Territory, bordered by the slave state of Missouri, would be easily wooed to the Southern cause. But the fiery abolitionists of the North were determined to stop the spread of slavery at all costs, and they were well prepared to take their battle to Kansas.

With the passage of the Kansas-Nebraska Act, the fight for Kansas began. Desperate to win the territory to their separate causes, partisan groups from both sides of the slavery controversy promptly urged their supporters to settle the area. Proslavery Missourians, aroused by the rhetoric of Senator David Atchison, led the way across the Kansas border and established the towns of Leavenworth and Atchison. The Northern abolitionists quickly followed. Aided by the financial and ideological support of the New England Emigrant Aid Company, they congregated in the vicinity of Lawrence and Topeka. Pitted against each other, the factions steeled themselves with the strength of their moral convictions and political aspirations.

At first, the fight for Kansas was primarily centered in the political arena. With increasing blocs of voters behind them, the proslavery and abolitionist antagonists both turned to the ballot box to further their cause. Under the direction of appointed Governor Andrew H. Reeder, the first territorial legislature was elected to office on March 30, 1855. In order to control the ballots, Missouri activists crossed into Kansas in such substantial numbers that the proslavery candidates easily dominated both branches of this first legislature. Convening at Shawnee Mission in the summer, the legislative assembly readily adopted the Missouri slave code for the protection of slavery in Kansas.

For the antislavery settlers, however, the political battle had only begun. Convinced that the proslavery victory was the result of obvious fraud at the polls, they adamantly refused to recognize the Shawnee Mission legislature and its "bogus" legal code. Rallying at Big Springs in September, 1855, the abolitionists organized the Free-State Party and prepared to establish a provisional state government of their own. By drafting a separate state constitution and conducting special elections, they subsequently selected their own territorial legislature, governor and Congressional delegation. Although this partisan government did not receive official recognition or aid from the federal government, it did add further fire to the Free-State cause.

With two separate governments in operation, the territory was wracked by increased confusion and disorder. As money and ammunition poured into Kansas from sympathizers in both the North and the South, the settlers' hostilities quickly erupted into violence and bloodshed. Organized gangs of proslavery and abolitionist marauders terrorized the countryside; towns were raided, coaches plundered and farms ravaged. Worse yet, partisan homesteaders found their families viciously intimidated, their homes deliberately burned and their associates killed or incarcerated.

Settlers on both sides of the controversy suffered a share of the depredations and tragedies. While proslavery "ruffians" sacked Lawrence and massacred antislavery sympathizers along the Marais des Cygnes River, Free-State desperadoes ravaged the Southern towns of Franklin and Pottawatomie.

"The Border Ruffian War started in 1856," recalled Mary Darrah, "and the community in which we lived was settled mostly by a proslavery element. On account of the strife many of them left their new homes and went back to Missouri. Those were heart rending days for my young mother. Many times my mother answered the door when, if my father had gone, he would have been instantly shot down. He was ordered time and again to leave the place inside of twenty-four hours.

"He was taken prisoner, but a good friend, although not in sympathy with the politics of the family, interceded for him. For days he stayed hidden in brush among the hills, and gradually made his way to Fort Leavenworth. During those two weeks my mother knew not whether he was dead or alive. The only way in which she could receive any communication with the outside world was to send her two small sons to the Ruffian Camp near by. They were jeered at and came home crying after being told that some of them would come and scalp their daddy, but through it all my mother's courage never wavered."

As dedicated abolitionists, Franklin and Harriet Adams and their family became the frequent targets of the enmity and vengeance of proslavery factions. Settling in a small cabin on the outskirts of Leavenworth, they lived in constant dread of discovery and reprisal. One of the eight Adams children later recounted the frightening events of one summer night in 1856:

"My grandfather, Joseph Adams, who was in the upper part of the house, and lying awake, heard the approach of horsemen. He gave the alarm and all lights were immediately extinguished, and everyone became very quiet. A few minutes later the horsemen were very close at hand. In the darkness and shade of trees they had lost the tracks leading to the house. They rode back and forth for some time but a few hundred yards from the house, where all the adults were up listening to the tramping of the horses and low muttering talk and curses of a drunken band. Finally, convinced that they had lost the way, they rode off.

"My uncle, Henry J. Adams, was very sick at the time and scarcely able to sit up. However, both father and Uncle Henry left the home on foot during the night and started toward Fort Leavenworth as was safe, when they saw a teamster hauling sacks of lime to the Fort. Father hailed him, and they helped Uncle Henry onto the loads of sacks, where he could lie covered by the tarpaulin which protected the lime from rain. He was taken safely to the Fort and Father reentered the woods and found his way to Lawrence where the Free-State men were gathering.

"About eleven o'clock the same morning the ruffians returned, and this time easily found the house, riding up and demanding to see my Father and Uncle. My Grandfather and Mother, holding up her baby daughter, met them, while the children retreated into the house in terror of the drunken group of ten or twelve horsemen. When the ruffians found that the men had escaped, they entered and searched the house for valuables and firearms.

"My cousin Louise often told how terribly frightened she and her sisters were and how amazed at mother when she remonstrated with the men for rumaging thru her wardrobe and bureau and messing up the house. They feared the men might hurt her.

"It was three days before the household heard whether the young men had escaped their hunters or not. At last a messenger brought mother a penciled note from father, written on a small piece of paper, telling of his whereabouts and his brother's safety. This scrap of paper is folded away in a tiny purple velvet purse with a few other treasures which managed to survive the two devastating fires which destroyed one home during her lifetime and one a few years later."

Sometime after that harrowing week, the Adamses moved to Atchison, where "the proslavery agitation continued bitterly. Father, having the courage of his convictions, received much unwelcome attention. . . . One incident growing out of this political issue made a story which came to us children thru outsiders, and which mother skillfully evaded when we questioned her. She was at home and father in town when some friend brought her the story that a man was hunting father with a gun and had sworn to kill him on sight. Mother took a pistol and immediately set out on a hunting expedition of her own. She did not meet the man, tho a number of their friends were aware of her quest, and I imagine father felt a bit sensitive at the suggestion that he might be unable to protect himself."

During these troublesome times, relatively few Southern emigrants brought slaves to Kansas. Both the high cost of transporting them and the volatile political situation prevented any large-scale importation. Nevertheless, a number of Southern zealots were determined to prove that slavery was feasible outside the South. These slaveholders were not simply motivated by profit per se, but brought their chattel with them to promote their proslavery propaganda. As a result, most slaves were treated relatively kindly in Kansas and did little hard labor. According to estimated figures, two hundred to three hundred slaves resided in Kansas by 1857.

"It seems strange to me now, as I look back," wrote Annie Gilkeson, "why the people of the South were so determined in bringing their slaves into Kansas, knowing, as they must have, the fight that was going on to keep them out. But they persisted even up to the time that Kansas was admitted to the Union as a free state.

"The man who built the first hotel in Easton was a fine gentleman from Kentucky. With his family, he brought one colored woman, who was a very fine cook and so useful in his hotel. He gave her freedom, but she would not leave the family who had always been so good to her.

"Another case of bringing slaves into Kansas I know of was quite different and savors of the irony of Fate. The man who had sold my father his farm and whose wife had left him because of the hardships of a few months, afterward built a sawmill on the banks of the thickly wooded stream. Tiring of this business, he tried to sell.

"Came another man from the South, bringing two Negro girls, one seven and the other eleven years old. Looking for an investment, he came across the man who wanted to sell his mill. He evidently was a man of some vision and could see in the spirit manifested by the early settlers that they might win out in the fight for Kansas freedom, and he had better get something for his property.

"So, he proposed to the mill owner that he exchange the mill for the girls. The man, being very anxious to sell, agreed to the bargain. So it came about that the man who had battled for Kansas freedom himself became a slave owner. To get money for his mill, he must sell the girls, and this he had to do. He took them to the slave market at Platt City. One girl sold for seven and the other for four-hundred dollars. It was a severe joke on the free state man, which he did not much relish."

As tensions over the controversy increased, the number of Kansas slaves gradually decreased. The continuing civil strife in the area compelled most slaveholders to return their slaves to the safety of the South. Moreover, calculated attempts by Kansas abolitionists to forcibly free local slaves discouraged any further importation. In fact, by 1860 only two slaves reportedly remained in Kansas.

Determined to undermine the slavery system, dedicated abolitionists had organized a clandestine transportation network to send fugitive slaves to freedom in Canada and the North. Extending through fourteen Northern states, the great Underground Railroad brought thousands of slaves to their "promised land."

In Kansas, the abolitionists quietly operated their own liberty line through those counties supporting their cause. Although the Fugitive Slave Act of 1850 had provided for the vigorous prosecution of anyone caught harboring or aiding runaway slaves, most Free-State communities gave their support and assistance to the underground line. Usually transported by night, the refugees were carefully passed from one secret hiding place to another in a slow trek northward.

Recalling her family's participation in the Underground Railroad, Olive Packard Owen wrote: "I was married when I was sixteen to William Owen, who had come to Kansas a year earlier than our family. My husband was also a strong abolitionist, and with my father and mother, established what was known as one of the stations of the Underground Railroad. Here, John Brown stopped with slaves that he was piloting through to freedom in the North.

"The last time he came, he had sixteen slaves and was traveling with them in a covered wagon. They arrived after dark. John Brown came to the door to inquire if there was anyone there except our family. On finding there was not, he drove the wagon into some brush back of the house, and slept there a few hours, starting off again before day-light. Before they left, my mother and I got up and cooked their breakfast which consisted mostly of corn bread. I remember they all sat down at a long table with John Brown at the head. A little colored baby had been born on the way, and they had christened him John Brown.

"It was on this trip that John Brown with his slaves was overtaken near Holton by some slave holders, and held them prisoners until he sent back to Topeka for help. Several men went to help him, and succeeded in sending the slave holders back home. It was related by the slave holders themselves, that before releasing them, John Brown forced them at the point of a gun to kneel and say a prayer."

By the summer of 1856, John Brown had become a legendary figure to the abolitionist cause. Fired by a passionate hatred for slavery, Brown was perhaps the most audacious and dauntless of all the Free-State fighters. Although he spent only three years in the territory, he commanded some of the most savage attacks on the proslavery settlements and managed to free a considerable number of Missouri slaves as well. With his dogged fanaticism, "Old Brown of Osawatomie" became a celebrated hero to the abolitionists. But his relentless ferocity and zeal also made him the most widely hated and hunted enemy of the proslavery antagonists.

As tensions mounted in the summer of 1856, the warring factions, well armed and organized, fought fire with fire. The battle at Osawatomie was but one incident in a long series of armed confrontations. At this time, Osawatomie was a small thriving community located about one mile from the confluence of the Pottawatomie and Marais des Cygnes Rivers. Populated primarily by Free-State sympathizers, the village had gained prominence as the home of the five sons of John Brown. Because of their fervent convictions, the Brown brothers were an obvious target for the vengeance of the so-called border ruffians. To protect his sons and fight for the Free-State cause, John Brown left his New York home for Kansas in 1855, well supplied with both ammunition and determination.

In retaliation against Brown and his followers, some four hundred Missouri rebels gathered along Bull Creek and marched toward Osawatomie on August 30. In the early hours of the morning, an advance scouting party, led by the Reverend Martin White, silently crept toward the village. As they neared Osawatomie, the party encountered young Fred Brown, who innocently bid them hello. Without warning or provocation, White shot him dead. The battle of Osawatomie had begun.

Shortly thereafter, the rest of the proslavery forces, under the command of General John Reid, descended upon the village. Well fortified with muskets and a cannon, they easily overpowered the abolitionists and quickly set about to destroy their stronghold.

It happened that Emma Adair, a niece of John Brown, had moved to Osawatomie with her family in the spring of 1855. At the time of the battle, the family's cabin harbored a sick family from Boston by the name of Babb. Emma's father, Reverend Samuel Adair, was holding Mr. Babb's gold watch in trust for money he had advanced to him. When the hostilities started, nine-year-old Emma sped down to the river bank behind the cabin and hid the valuable watch beneath the roots of an old stump until the danger had passed. Years later, she related the harrowing events at Osawatomie:

"Fred Brown, the son of John Brown, with a number of young men rode down from Lawrence the evening of August 29th with messages from General Lane to Captain Brown. They spent the night at the cabins of near neighbors, Morgan, Crondite and John Carr. We had not been able to send or receive any mail from the east for several weeks since our mail carrier and stage driver had been taken prisoner at Westport. Fred Brown told my father that if he could write letters, he would take them back with him to Lawrence and try to send them to our friends in the east by way of Nebraska.

"We were awakened the next morning by firing and the sound of horses' feet going rapidly past our cabin. My father hastened out with his cousin David Garrison who had been sleeping in the north part of the cabin. They soon discovered the body of Fred Brown lying in the road to the south east of our house. . . .

"So Fred Brown was their first victim on the day of the battle of August 30, 1856. One of the young men, the one who slept with him that night, told afterwards that Fred said he would get up early, feed their horses, go over to Uncle Adair's for breakfast and the letters, and be ready to start on their return to Lawrence. As he came into the road the men riding from the direction of the town came up. They afterwards reported as a good joke the conversation that passed between them. Fred thinking they were friends said, 'Good morning boys. Are you going to Lawrence today? It seems to me I ought to know you.' One of the scouts, called Martin White or old preacher White, replied, 'I know you,' and fired a shot into his heart.

"When my father and Garrison discovered the body of Fred, my father ran back to our house, saddled and bridled our horse and started my thirteen year old brother to town to warn the people. David Garrison ran across the prairie to the Carr house to give the alarm there, and then came back to meet my father to try to decide what to do. My father climbed up on the stake and rider fence in front of our house. From there he saw the main army approaching from the west. Afterwards, he often spoke of the striking effect as the rising sun reflected from their gleaming bayonets and guns.

"As my father stood looking he said, 'It won't do to remain here,' and he got down and turned and ran back into the house. David Garrison started to run again across the prairie to join his friends there, and in so doing, exposed himself to view. A detachment was immediately sent after him and he was killed.

"One of the other young men, Mr. Cutter of Lawrence, was also sighted and fired upon and left for dead. He was seriously wounded and lay helpless all that winter at the home of John Everett. About one half mile west of our house, a detachment from the main body of the enemy stopped at the Fuller home and there took Bainridge Fuller, the first prisoner captured that day.

"At a cabin owned by a brother of our well known Susan B. Anthony, the men were just preparing breakfast when the word came of Fred Brown's murder and of the approach of the enemy. Captain Brown immediately called his men together, and they came into town. He gathered as many more men from the village as he could."

Alarmed by the rapid approach of the enemy troops, John Brown hastily assembled a small but fearless band of some forty Osawatomie settlers. At first, the group was prepared to defend the town from within the community blockhouse. However, once informed that Reid's men were armed with a cannon, the villagers abandoned this plan and quickly retreated to the banks of the Marais des Cygnes River.

Hidden in the thicket of the river bank, the Free-State forces separated into three groups. Brown, with seventeen followers, kept to the right, while Dr. W. W. Updegraff directed ten men in the center and Captain Cline led fourteen fighters to the left. With the enemy rebels passing less than six hundred yards away, these men anxiously prepared to fight for their homes and their lives.

"When they had approached to within rifle shot," continued Emma Adair, "the firing began. Our men, from the shelter of the underbrush, had a good opportunity to annoy them. So effective were our men's shots that the north branch of their line was thrown in great disorder, and it was some time before they rallied and again advanced. The enemy had a cannon with them and the firing of that, the screams of the wounded, the shouts of the leaders and the rifle shots could all be plainly heard from our house, and made an impression on my mind never to be forgotten.

"The ammunition of the Free State forces became exhausted and they at last were forced to retire across the river. George Partridge was killed while crossing the river. Theron Powers, a sick man, was also killed. Spencer Brown, son of C. C. Brown, was taken prisoner, as were also Charles Keyser and Robert Reynolds. These two had become separated from the others when the order to retreat was given.

"Charles Keyser was shot soon after the army went into camp and his body was never recovered, but his name is on the monument at Osawatomie. Mr. Reynolds, with the other prisoners, H. K. Thomas, Mr. Moyer, Bainridge Fuller and Spencer Brown, were sent down the Missouri River. One other man, a Mr. Williams, a Missourian against whom the ruffians had a spite, was beaten to death, Two men, Dr. W. W. Updegraff and Daniel Collis, were seriously wounded.

"The enemy then marched on the town, plundering and burning all the houses but three, or about 35 or 40 in all. Two of these escaped by the residents putting out white flags, showing their sympathy with the enemy. The third was set on fire, but citizens, coming back after the departure of the murderers, were able to put out the blaze before it was completely destroyed. One of the prisoners, Bainridge Fuller, was tied so near to a burning store that he was severely burned, and it was many months before he recovered from his injuries.

"After taking every horse and wagon they could find and loading them with stolen goods and their own dead and wounded, they left town by the same route over which they came. They stopped at the home of C. C. Brown, the first house west of town, and plundered and burned it. C. C. Brown had a fine piano, the first and only one in the vicinity. This the ruffians tried desperately to load, but they abandoned the project and it was burned with the other contents of the house.

"Our cabin was the first one on the main road to escape being burned, which my father attributed to our having given refuge to a family from Boston, a Mr. Babb, his wife and three children, several of whom were quite sick. The father, Mr. Babb, was very sick, but my mother and Mrs. Babb insisted on his trying to get out of the house. He protested that he would be killed anyway, but between them they got him to his feet and out of the house and into the brush north of the cabin.

"When the enemy came they placed their cannon directly in front of our home. The men surrounded the house and many crowded inside. The screams of the terrified children were no doubt disconcerting, for after making sure there were no men about they exclaimed, 'Oh well, we will not kill women and children but if we get hold of any men, we'll put this over their heads mighty quick,' and they shook out a rope. They then departed, taking with them a number of head of cows and calves.

"All that day, the body of Fred Brown had lain in the burning sun by the roadside. Settlers living south of the Pottawatomie had watched the burning of the town from the high hills and when they saw that the enemy had departed, they hastened in to help gather up the wounded and the dead.

"Fred Brown's body was brought into the north part of our cabin. Someone reported that David Garrison was lying dead in a deep ravine some distance to the southeast. By this time, it was night and the wolves were howling terribly. My father said no time was to be lost, so he and my brother went in search of the body. An old man who lived in the neighborhood consented to go with them on the condition that my father go first and carry the lantern. They were fortunate in finding the body undisturbed by the wolves, and it was brought to the cabin and placed beside that of Fred Brown.

"Their funeral, with that of those who were killed in town, was held the following afternoon. All of the bodies, except Mr. Williams, were placed in the same grave on the high ground to the southwest of town. Afterwards, they were removed to a lot given for the purpose by Charles Foster, and here a few years later in 1877 on the anniversary of the battle of August 30, the monument to their memory and to the memory of John Brown was dedicated."

Although sporadic strife continued to divide the Kansas territory, the popular support and power of the proslavery faction began to deteriorate steadily. Despite their defeat at Osawatomie, the Free-State settlers were able to bolster their defenses and secure their hold on most of northern Kansas in the fall of 1856. By 1857, only portions of southeastern Kansas remained embroiled in violence.

As the open hostilities waned, the fight for Kansas turned once more to the political arena. After years of separate voting, the settlers on both sides of the controversy were finally persuaded to participate in a joint election for a single territorial government. This time, however, federal troops were stationed in each precinct to prevent any illegal voting. Casting their ballots on October 6, 1857, the people of Kansas threw their support to the Free-State candidates. Popular sovereignty had succeeded at last.

United under one government, Kansans soon turned their attentions to the matter of statehood. After several drafts, an acceptable state constitution, prohibiting slavery, was finally formulated. Ratified by the electorate in 1859, it was submitted to Congress for final approval.

Since the extension of statehood required the consent of both houses of Congress, the fight for Kansas soon shifted to the national level. While the House of Representatives, with a majority of Northern delegates, welcomed the admission of Kansas as a free state, the Senate, controlled by the Southern bloc, was emphatically opposed to its acceptance on these grounds. For the next year, statehood still remained out of reach. It was not until the secession of the South in 1861 that Senate approval was finally forthcoming.

For Kansas, January 29, 1861, was a red-letter day. As President James Buchanan affixed his signature to the bill granting statehood, the celebrations began. The news spread like wildfire across that state. People gathered at every street corner, rejoicing with cheers, songs and dancing. While banner headlines saluted the new state, cannons, fired in exultation, thundered across the prairies. In Topeka, the new state capital, the celebrations continued long into the night.

"The news was carried to Topeka by pony messenger from Leavenworth," wrote Matilda McFarland, "and the rejoicing was universal and sincere. Now there could be no recurrence of the border ruffian warfare, from which the earlier settlers were still suffering.

"Topeka was ablaze that night, not with the gas or electric light, but with a tallow candle in every window. Some people who must have been very rich, put two in the window. It was an illumination that has always stayed with me and has not been effaced by any of greater brilliancy."

When the Civil War finally erupted a few months later, Kansas threw its wholehearted support to the Northern cause. Military companies were hastily organized in small towns across the state, recruiting nearly two thirds of all the adult men in Kansas. In all, the state furnished over twenty thousand men for the Union Army. Divided into twenty-three regiments and four artillery batteries, the Kansas troops even included five black units and three regiments of Indian soldiers.

"In 1861 the Civil War broke out," recalled Lillian Smith, "and the horror of that stared my Mother in the face, she with those little children on a lone farm, and Father liable to have to go away and leave us all, possibly never to return.

"The day came for Father to go. He went to Emporia and was under the command of Colonel Marsh Murdock, and was sent to Westport Landing, where they were stationed at the time of the Battle of Westport.

"When he was mounted upon the fine bay mare that he was riding away to war, we all stood in the yard by our little home. Father took me, his baby girl, up on the horn of the saddle, and lovingly kissed me goodbye. I could hardly understand what it was all about, but Mother stood there with tears streaming from her big blue eyes and smiling through her tears at Father to cheer him, for he too was weeping, but at last he rode away, and we all huddled together like lost sheep, and went on as best we could.

"I can't understand now how my Mother ever stood up under it all, but she was young and a God-trusting woman, wife and mother, and in that hour she was not forsaken. All the other able-bodied men of the neighborhood had gone too, so she was not the only one, and we all worked with and for each other."

Although most of the troops were sent east to fight in the war, several brigades were retained in Kansas to ward off the increased guerrilla activities of the Confederate rebels and their infamous leader, William C. Quantrill. At this time, Quantrill was one of the most fearless and cold-blooded outlaws in the West. Unlike most earlier proslavery fighters, he was not guided by any overriding moral principles or political ideology. Indeed, he was little more than a ruthless, gun-slinging desperado, and his notorious reputation had left him feared and hated throughout Kansas.

Operating under an assumed name, Quantrill had made Lawrence his headquarters throughout most of 1860. In league with several other outlaws, he was involved in a number of horse stealings and burglaries in the area. His devious conduct soon aroused suspicion, and a grand jury subsequently indicted him for grand larceny and robbery. Faced with imprisonment, Quantrill quickly fled the state.

Unable to peacefully return to Kansas, Quantrill sought protection and immunity in the Missouri border towns. Within a year, his sympathies had strongly shifted to the Southern cause, and after joining the Confederate Army he took command of nearly six hundred local guerrilla fighters. For the next several years, Quantrill and his followers waged relentless attacks on the Kansas border communities, terrifying the population, destroying property everywhere and frustrating thousands of Union Troops.

Among his numerous exploits, Quantrill's famous raid on Lawrence in 1863 was certainly the most brutal and devastating. The unfortunate collapse of a federal prison, killing several Confederate sympathizers, was the key event which ignited the wrath of Quantrill and his troops. As the stronghold of Kansas abolitionism and the home of its dauntless leader, Jim Lane,* the town of Lawrence was deliberately chosen as the target for their vengeance. Conveniently,

* James Henry Lane (1814–66) was one of the most influential and flamboyant political leaders of early Kansas. Instrumental in the organization of the Free-State Party, he served as president of the Topeka constitutional convention in 1855. When Kansas became a state in 1861, Lane was elected, as a Republican, to the United States Senate. Although he was reelected to the Senate in 1865, his popularity with his radical Republican constituency plummeted when Lane publicly supported the lenient Reconstruction policy of President Andrew Johnson. In despair, Senator Lane shot himself to death on July 1, 1866.

no federal troops, except for a few unarmed recruits, were stationed there at the time. Furthermore, most of the town's able-bodied men had been sent to the East to fight for the Union cause. Unprotected and unsuspecting, Lawrence was a particularly vulnerable target.

In the early-morning haze of August 21, 1863, Quantrill and a full force of 450 Missouri Bushwhackers quietly approached the slumbering town and rode in a body up to the high ground facing Main Street. Suddenly the order was given to "Rush on to the town!" With wild, bloodcurdling cries, the band swooped down. Cocking their pistols, they dashed throughout the city, shooting at every man they passed and firing through every open window.

Following Quantrill's command to "burn every house and kill every man," the guerrillas began a well-calculated rampage of wholesale murder, pillage and destruction. In every street, helpless men fell dead or wounded, while their wives and children, still in their nightclothes, ran screaming in terror. Fires ripped through every city block, destroying stores and houses alike. It was pandemonium.

When the terrorists finally retreated, more than two hundred buildings were left in smoldering ruins and 143 innocent people lay dead. Every stable had been ransacked, every home stripped and burned. The solemn survivors slowly began the work of gathering the wounded and burying the dead. In the end, only the anguished wails of the many widows and orphans could break the stunned silence of defeat.

The Soule family had settled in Lawrence as early as 1855. Hiding in the underbrush of an island in the river, the family escaped harm during the 1863 raid, but the devastation of the town left a strong imprint on their memories. Ann Julia Soule later described her fearful search for her family in the wake of the Quantrill raid.

"I had attended high school and taught in different places in the primary rooms and at the time of Quantrill's raid was teaching at Kanwaka, six miles west of town, and from there saw the smoke of the burning town. Came to town before noon, found my own folks living but the house where we lived burned and nothing saved but the lives. In the midst of such sorrow we felt we had much to still be thankful for.

"There was a little island in the river east of the town and there my folks had gone when the raiders, finding the door locked in the basement of the house, had gone to a neighbor's for an axe to break the door. Our family—mother, brother, sister-in-law and sister—with a young man, a merchant, and the man who owned the house and was boarding with us, all hurried from the house by a door on the first floor and started for the river but were stopped on the way. My brother was taken to a stable to get a horse which not suiting the rider, he pointed his revolver at my brother, told him he wouldn't have escaped if he had ammunition and let him go. All proceeded to the island, the women going in a hollow log towed across the shore water route by the men walking through the shallow water.

"The news of the Quantrill raid reached me at Kanwaka early; first, the strange looks of the sun seen through the smoke of the burning town, red and unnatural, but soon the refugees telling of the raid, the killing of everyone, men, women and children. Of course, the terror made them wild with fright and they imagined more than the truth, for no women or children were killed.

"I came to town before noon and as soon as the rebels had gone, went to the house of a friend where five men had been shot, only one of whom lived. Four prominent men were shot down in front of the house. The other, a young clerk in the drug store of Dr. Griswold's, one of the victims, was shot on the street after getting the key to the safe for the ruffian, and his body was burned from a fire close by on Massachusetts St. where he fell.

"My second visit that morning was to the Methodist Church, where many bodies had been taken. I met my brother who was city marshall and was already making plans to have the Eldridge House walls torn down as they were brick and unsafe, liable to fall on people passing.

"I went past the house we lived in, the brick walls still standing, a gridiron hanging on the wall behind the stove, the only thing left from our furnishings. I found where my folks were . . . I went to the island in a hollow log, a man rowing me over, and there I found the rest of the family all very thankful that we were all living. We were taken in by friends until we could get out of town."

In her memoirs, Lavina Gates Chapman also recounted the terrifying events of Quantrill's raid. Herself a resident of Baldwin, she was visiting relatives in Lawrence at the time.

"We went to Lawrence to an aunt of mine by the name of Bissell. They lived in the suburbs of Lawrence, in a two-story brick house. They heard the firing and Cousin said, 'Quantrill is in town. We will bury our money and all valuables.' They soon made away with some and awaited the results.

"By and by they saw a squad coming. Cousin Henry went to the door. They said, 'We will trouble you for your money.' Cousin said, 'You will not take all the money a man has?' He was easily persuaded when a revolver was placed at his head and breast. 'Now,' said they, 'we will relieve you of your watch.' Of course he handed it over and then they turned their horses and rode off. Well, he thanked God that he got off so easily, but the town was on fire.

"Behold there came another squad. Aunt had a porch the full length of her house facing town. They rode up on the porch, all that could get on and all around the house, drunk enough—too devilish, too drunk to load their guns. They snapped their guns at my cousin, then took the butt of the revolver and beat him over his head. He had on a heavy chip hat or they would have killed him. He finally got away into a patch of corn in back of the house.

"They then called for matches. Aunty and cousins said they would not give them to them. They said they were going to burn the house. Sophia followed them upstairs. They took clothes from the closets and put them on the beds, set fire to them, opened up the windows to make a draft, went from one room to another and fired every room. Sophia followed right behind and took feather beds and tried to smother the fire. They took hold of her and jerked her around, took her out on the porch and sat her down, then went in and fired the bedrooms down-stairs. They then set fire to the barn.

"Sophia looked at the horses on the porch; their counterpanes, silk dresses and all their valuable goods were strapped on those horses. She got up and tried to pull them off; they were too firmly bound. The cry rung out above the din, 'Forward! March!' and they went as fast as their horses would go. We looked and behold, the barn was on fire. Sophia rushed to get the horses out, but they had taken them all. Men who were hidden in corn patches around came to help and they got out the buggy and harnesses. There were three hundred widows left in Lawrence that day. One of Mr. Bissell's horses came back that night—did not travel fast enough for them.

"I will mention a family—I have forgotten their name. They saw Lawrence was burning. The lady had her husband go down the cellar through the trap door. The guerillas came to burn the house. She begged for them to spare her house. They said, 'No.' 'Oh, my carpet, the only thing my father gave me! Let me take that up. It is all I have that he gave me.' They said they would give her time to take it up and out. She went to work, took it up, gave the signal to her husband to be ready, then she drew it over the trap door and he crawled under the carpet to a place of safety upon a wood-pile. She carried one end over her over her shoulder and he crawled close to her. She sat down to see that no sparks burned her carpet and thanked God for the privilege of saving her husband.

"I will give you another heart-rendering case that is indelibly stamped on my mind. Griswood, I believe was the name. He was a druggist in Lawrence. He had some money coming to him in the East, so he thought he would go and collect it. He and his wife went and were coming around by Iowa to visit some friends before coming home. He made his collection, came to Iowa, made his visit, wanted to stay a few days longer, but his wife was homesick, so they came home. They got home in the evening.

"Quantrill's men came the next morning. Of course they were rebel sympathizers that knew Griswood had come home with several thousand dollars and if he would give it up peaceably they would spare Mr. Griswood's life. They said they knew all about the money. They took him out in the yard and the word was, 'Your money or your life.' He said, 'Life is sweet, get the money, I can earn more.' Mrs. Griswood got it and gave it to her husband. He handed it to them saying, 'Here is all we have.' It was tied up in a bag. They received it and filled him full of bullets."

At the time of the Lawrence massacre, the Ninth Cavalry of the Union Army was stationed in the vicinity of Douglas County. Although they were alerted to Quantrill's plans to attack the Kansas border area, the commanding officers initially assumed that Lawrence—without troops or ammunition reserves—would not be the target of an enemy assault. When they finally realized their error, the town was already a bed of embers. Nevertheless, the frustrated government troops, along with scores of local settlers, pursued the rebels for many miles. Their response came too late, however, and Quantrill's band returned to the safety of Missouri without mishap.

For the horror-stricken residents of surrounding Kansas communities, Quantrill's prompt retreat to Missouri did little to allay their panic and fear. Terrified that the guerrillas would return, the settlers nervously prepared to defend themselves. Alone on a farm in neighboring Franklin County, Aura Viola St. John and her young family kept on the alert.

"One of our ever-to-be-remembered experiences was the day following the Lawrence massacre. We had no telegraph or telephone communication and mail came once a week from Centropolis, six miles away. This mail was carried by a man on horseback from Lawrence to Centropolis; so any news was taken from one point to another by a carrier on horseback.

"Yet by ten o'clock of the same morning a man rode into the field where the men were haying and said, 'Lawrence was burned this morning and all the inhabitants murdered and a large army is scattering in all directions to kill and burn and wipe out this free state of Kansas. Every militia man must rally and try and head them off, one party is headed this way.'

"The horses were unhitched as quickly as possible, a hurried lunch taken, while my sister-in-law and I ran bullets. The men rode away to try to intercept the party at Prairie City.

"We women wondered and planned what we could do and where we could be most safe in case they came. We finally concluded that the corn field, which in August was an impenetrable forest, was our best refuge. They could not ride through it and it would be almost impossible to find any one. So we rolled a barrel out there filled with bedding, clothing and some eatables, so if they burned the house, we would not be entirely destitute.

"Watching and listening for any unusual noise kept us busy through the day. When night came, we dared not go to bed, but spent the night on the porch, with our little girls dressed, so we could catch them up and run for the corn field if we heard anything alarming. But nothing disturbed us; so many rallied in pursuit they fled to Missouri for safety."

In Topeka to the west, the call to arms was also sounded. On the alert for any further depredations, the citizens fortified their defenses in preparation.

"After the sacking of Lawrence by Quantrill's guerillas," explained Matilda McFarland, "we were in constant dread of an attack on Topeka, as they had threatened to come here next. Several times they were thought to be so near that we all slept in our clothing and each child had a little bag containing articles of more or less value, which we were to carry out in case the house was burned, and save if possible.

"My brother, twelve years of age, wore in a belt what money we had, and was to make his escape at the first alarm, over the roof, hiding in a ravine not far from the house. This precaution was taken because my father had no expectation of his life being spared on account of his strong northern principles, as these were the men who had been the first to fall in the Quantrill raid. It is probably hard for the young people of this generation to realize what harrowing and anxious times the pioneers suffered."

All told, the fight over slavery had brought Kansas an inordinate share of hardship and tragedy. For more than a decade its frontier communities had been torn by political turmoil and partisan hostilities. Wracked by violence in its territorial years, Kansas had not found peace with the attainment of statehood in 1861. Instead, the Civil War had only prolonged its troubles for four more years. In the end, more than 8,500 of its troops suffered war casualties, giving Kansas the highest military death rate of any state in the Union. It was not until 1865, with the end of the Civil War, that its weary settlers finally felt the relief of harmony and stability.

"The war closed," wrote Lillian Smith, "and Father with some of the others returned home. I well remember when the news was brought to Mother, how she rejoiced, and we children ran around trying to work at something to let out some of our excess of joy, for Father was to be home that night, and so he came back to Mother and his children."

CHAPTER FIFTEEN

The Woman Crusaders

Temperance and Suffrage

"Abolition! Prohibition! Suffrage! How we struggled for these issues in Kansas. How simple and natural and right these things seem now that the struggle is over. We did our best with our problems. The result is the heritage we leave our children."

—FANNY HOLSINGER

IN THE WANING YEARS of the pioneer period, Kansas women became increasingly active in a variety of local political issues, civic affairs and reform movements. In towns across the state, women took up the cudgels of temperance and prohibition, Populism and suffrage. The call for stricter law enforcement and more honest government led many into town politics; the demand for more schools and supportive financing got some involved in county issues. Party-platform controversies, constitutional-reform measures, and referendum campaigns drew still others into the state political arena.

In most communities, temperance emerged as the first issue to unite large numbers of women. Although legal prohibition was a logical outgrowth of the movement, temperance itself was primarily a moral rather than a political issue. Its adherents stressed abstinence through prayer, education and individual willpower. Convinced that liquor was the destroyer of the home, they worked to promote clean living and family harmony. In turn, their active involvement in this movement was readily accepted and respected by their spouses and communities.

Support for temperance and prohibition had actually been a part of Kansas politics from the beginning. During the territorial period, many Free-State settlers had actively opposed the liquor traffic. As early as 1857 a group of Lawrence women led one of the first campaigns against liquor sales in Kansas. Incensed by the opening of a nearby saloon, they stormed the establishment with axes and hatchets, destroying every bottle and barrel they could find. But when the state constitution was enacted in 1861, it failed to include any prohibition provision. Although communities were able to enforce their own liquor ordinances, saloons operated freely across the state, without interference from local sheriffs or politicians.

It was during the 1870s that the temperance movement first achieved real cohesion in Kansas. Although various prohibition associations had been formed during the previous decade, their size and influence remained limited. The organization of the National Woman's Christian Temperance Union in 1874 was the spark that ignited the so-called "women's crusade." In Kansas, as in other states, temperance societies were quickly established in one community after another. By 1878, twenty-six local WCTU chapters, along with an official state organization, were already in existence.

As increasing numbers of women joined the WCTU, its momentum gained across the state. In 1878 a statewide newspaper, *The Temperance Banner*, was inaugurated to support temperance activities and prohibition legislation. Community organizers held special town picnics and rallies to recruit members and promote their cause. In rural classrooms, teachers lectured youngsters about the dangers of intoxication, and school superintendents sponsored special essay contests. Local literary societies debated the issue at their weekly meetings, while ministers advocated abstinence in Sunday sermons. Many women adopted prayer as a primary means of persuasion. Supported by their congregations, they often organized religious revivals and street-corner prayer meetings. In bursts of fervor, some women activists even invaded local saloons to pray with the dismayed barkeepers and to lecture their wayward patrons.

Although the women's crusade was carried out across the nation, it was in Kansas that it first achieved decisive results. As the women's efforts intensified during the late 1870s, the WCTU became one of the most influential special-interest lobbies at both the state and local levels. In 1878, John P. St. John, an ardent champion of the temperance cause, was elected governor on a strong prohibition platform. Under his administration, a constitutional amendment prohibiting the sale or manufacture of intoxicants was subsequently passed by the state legislature and submitted to Kansas voters in 1880.

Even though women had not yet attained the right to vote, they campaigned vigorously for the amendment's ratification. In statewide gatherings, white-ribbon temperance stalwarts sponsored prohibition rallies, lectures and prayer meetings. Distinguished orators were sent on speaking tours, and town assemblies staged debates between the temperance and liquor forces. In that one year alone, the president of the state WCTU, Drusilla Wilson, traveled nearly three thousand miles and attended more than three hundred public meetings in rural schoolhouses and churches everywhere. On election day itself, women turned out in large numbers at the polls, distributing last-minute literature and persuading wavering voters.

"I well remember the struggle for state-wide prohibition," wrote Julia Robinson. "The temperance rallies held. Some of the noted speakers who came to help us out. The Good Templar's Societies. Amanda Way was then in her prime.* What a power she was for the cause. I well remember her, having entertained her in our home. John P. St. John, too, was fearless and bold for the cause. Many there were who shouted, 'It can't be done, a state-wide prohibition amendment can't be adopted.' " But when the final vote was tallied, the amendment passed by a narrow margin, making Kansas the first state in the Union to adopt constitutional prohibition.

In the years to come, however, the prohibition amendment did not altogether halt the liquor traffic in Kansas. In many communities, local sheriffs and politicians were reluctant to enforce the measure and allowed many establishments to continue operating illegally. Moreover, druggists were still permitted by law to dispense liquor for "medical, scientific and mechanical purposes."

In the town of Lincoln, the frequent abuse of this provision particularly angered Emily Cornell Biggs, president of the local WCTU.

* Amanda M. Way (1828–1914), a Methodist and Quaker preacher, was a well-known temperance and suffrage reformer. In her native state of Indiana she was instrumental in the organization of the first women's rights movement during the 1850s and 1860s. Moving to Kansas in 1872, Amanda Way continued her work for the temperance and suffrage causes. As a founder of the state's first Woman's Christian Temperance Union, she played an important role in the 1880 campaign for prohibition.

As her daughter, Anna Biggs Heaney, explained, "A druggist by the name of Trump had secured a druggist's permit to sell liquor. All any one had to do at that time to buy liquor of any druggist having it for sale was to sign up for it with the reason therefor as cold, stomach trouble, etc. The administration of the law rested with the discretion of the druggist. And if the druggist had no discretion! So [Mother] wrote 'A Modern Chronicle' for a county convention and told in the Scriptural Chronicle style of the liquor history of the county. And when she came to the granting of the permit to Trump she said, 'And the Whiskites said among themselves, "Lo, aew we not the lucky guys, for behold, though we have but one Trump he taketh the trick." ' That was too much for even the Whiskites. They laughed themselves hoarse."

In the years that followed, the women's crusade continued unabated. Distressed by the ongoing sales of liquor, they persisted in their demands for stricter enforcement of the law. Moreover, they renewed their efforts to reform habitual alcoholics and to educate the young.

If the figure of the woman temperance crusader brings to our modern eyes an image of vindictive self-righteousness, Fannie Holsinger's story shows that not all temperance advocates displayed an inflexible brand of zeal. "There was no WCTU in our town until 1887," she wrote. "I joined the organization then and after a time became its president. We had the usual disheartening experiences. The prohibitory law was not enforced. Women came to me to beg to help save their husbands from the saloon. We besought our friends to secure evidence; we brought suits but seldom secured convictions. We went to interview the city council but were told by them 'We are not a smelling committee.'

"One afternoon at a WCTU meeting an officer came with a summons to appear at the court house immediately. I protested that court would be adjourned before I could get there, as it was an hour's ride, but I had to go. When I arrived court was adjourned, as I knew it would be, but a young man, whom I knew, was waiting for me and said he was instructed to take me to his lawyer's office. The lawyer asked me to release the young man, who was under arrest for running a saloon. I told him that I could not do that. He then asked me to go with him to the county attorney.

"The county attorney presented the case and said to me, 'It is for you to say if he shall be released, for you are the principal witness. I

"I helped my father on the farm and learned to do the work pretty well, as I was strong for a girl," wrote Mary Alice Zimmerman.

Two sisters pose in identical dresses.
COURTESY OF JOANNA STRATTON.

A child-sized wagon pulled by turkeys.

A prosperous prairie Christmas.

Kansas schoolgirls.
COURTESY OF JOANNA STRATTON.

A brother and sister pose for the camera in Meade, Kansas, 1896.

A sod schoolhouse. "I think at the time I was teaching not more than three or four schools had floors," wrote Emma Handy.

A new well-equipped schoolroom with a "really truly" blackboard, near Wilson, Kansas.

A Kansas tornado. One former schoolteacher remembered her students' fright as a sudden Kansas twister came spiraling in their direction.

Schooling evolved at an uneven pace throughout Kansas. Children were attending this dugout schoolhouse in Thomas County as late as 1900, a time when many other school districts had built more permanent and spacious structures.

Play time at the Montgomery County schoolhouse, c. 1892.

An Episcopal congregation from Wichita in front of their makeshift log church.

A frontier baptism, possibly in the Washita River.

An unidentified—and unusually opulent—prairie church.

A view of Old North Main Street in Hays, Kansas, 1879.

The aftermath of an afternoon's violence in front of a Hays saloon.

A Kansas hotel of the early 1870s.

A general store in the town of Oakley.

Office of the Hays City Sentinel. *The newspaper business was not entirely a male preserve. Ellen West Downing would often work "far into the night with a Washington hand press" to get the* Ellis County Star *out on schedule.*

A ride down Main Street, Nortonville, Kansas.

Women were not welcome on the long, grueling cattle drives. Here, a group of cowboys prepares for night guard.

Loading Texas cattle at Abilene as illustrated in Leslie's Illustrated News, *August 19, 1871.*

A Dodge City dance hall, c.1878.

Women participate in branding their own cattle on a Scott County ranch.

Kansas was the new home of many different communities of foreign settlers. Here, a group of Swedes in Greeley County, c.1900.

The original depot of Victoria, Kansas.

A tennis club in an English community much like Victoria.

John Brown.

"We were awakened . . . by firing and the sound of horses' feet." Emma Adair, niece of John Brown, remembered the harrowing events of the Battle of Osawatomie.

Here, the Adair cabin. Fred Brown was killed on his way to the cabin on the morning of August 30, 1856.

Quantrill's Raid, as depicted by Lauretta Louise Fox Fisk.

Matilda McFarland of Topeka recalled how the town steeled itself for attack after Quantrill's raid on Lawrence.

A prohibition meeting in Bismark Grove, Kansas, 1878.

"Smash, women, smash!" cried Carry Nation, the leader of the temperance movement. Here, a wrecked saloon in Enterprise, Kansas.

"Pictures taken at that time show my mother barring the doorway while Carry Nation was carrying out her plan of stamping out vice," wrote Daisy Hoffman Johntz.

"Another one shows the town marshal leading Carry Nation away from the scene of action with my mother in the background."

Olympia Brown, the first woman ordained by the Universalist Church and an ardent suffragist.

Though they were still excluded from state and federal elections, the women of Kansas won the right to vote in city elections in 1887. Soon after, women were elected to city offices. Here, Oskaloosa's all-woman government, 1888.

In Kansas, the cry for equal voting rights was sounded in 1859—but suffragists were still campaigning decades later in the era of the motorcar. Here, a parade in Columbus, Kansas.

have evidence enough to send him to jail.' It was one of the most trying moments of my life. There sat the young man, so like my own boy, waiting for me to send him to jail or to release him. When I said aloud, 'What shall I do?' the county attorney repeated, 'Do as you please. You are the principal witness.'

"I closed my eyes and prayed for guidance. I said then, 'Young man, if I thought you would go into that business again, you had better be in jail, but if you will go into some honest business I will ask that the case be dismissed.' The youth answered, 'Mrs. Holsinger, if you will help me this time I will promise, on my word of honor, that I will never go into the saloon business in Rosedale or anywhere else.'

"Now the queer part of the case was that I was not a witness. I knew nothing of the case. I was simply President of the WCTU which was fighting the traffic. My husband and son were very indignant at the spineless officials who put the case up to me. My WCTU friends thought my own action spineless. One woman withdrew and never came back. But I have never regretted the decision made that day, for the young man became a leader in a Catholic total abstinence society and a good reliable citizen."

In some communities, the temperance campaign became increasingly militant as women tried on their own to close down illegal "joints" and destroy the alcoholic contraband. At the turn of the century, Carry Nation earned national notoriety for her hatchet-wielding foray against the "Demon Rum." With her battle cry "Smash, women, smash," she raided saloons across the state, breaking bottles and barrels, shattering windows and demolishing furniture.

In 1911, Carry Nation carried her crusade to the town of Enterprise, Kansas, where she found support among a number of temperance advocates. Recalling her own mother's participation in the affair, Daisy Hoffman Johntz later wrote: "[Mother] never failed to use every opportunity to exert her influence in behalf of temperance. The second town to be visited and severely dealt with by Carrie Nation was Enterprise and upon reaching there, it was to the Hoffman home, and to Catherine Hopkins Hoffman, that Mrs. Nation went for council and assistance. In my mother she found co-operation and I am happy to say that never again has there been a saloon of any kind in Enterprise. My brother, Emmett, was Mayor of the city and hearing of Mrs. Nation's stay in the town, and not knowing she was in his mother's home at the time, went to mother and told her about it.

Mother showed interest but did not divulge the fact that she, too, knew all and more than he did. Pictures taken at that time show my mother barring the doorway while Carrie Nation was carrying out her plan of stamping out vice. Another one shows the town Marshall leading Carrie Nation away from the scene of action with my mother in the background."

Although most people deplored such violence, Carry Nation's much-publicized tactics proved effective in the enforcement of prohibition. One of her contemporaries later wrote: "I recall, too, the struggles for the enforcement of the law. How Wichita, Leavenworth, Atchison and some other places held out for their many saloons, The Carry Nation crusade came about that time, and while many of us hardly approved of her smashing methods, yet we realized that the agitation was paving the way for the 'ousting' of the traffic."

Along with their campaigns for temperance and prohibition, large numbers of women undertook the cause of woman suffrage. In Kansas the cry for equal voting rights was first sounded in 1859 when three early feminists, Clarina Nichols, Mother Armstrong and Mary Tenney Gray, attended the Wyandotte constitutional convention. Appearing on behalf of Shawnee and Douglas County women's groups, the three sought to have equal suffrage included in the new state's constitution. As uninvited observers, however, they were not permitted to address the convention delegates, and their pleas went unheeded. Nevertheless their unexpected presence proved effective. Under the constitution finally adopted, women were granted the unprecedented right to acquire and possess property and to retain the equal custody of their children. Moreover, in 1861, the first state legislature gave women the right to vote in school elections, making Kansas one of the most progressive states for women's rights.

In 1867, equal suffrage became a statewide controversy when the legislature submitted two constitutional amendments to the Kansas electorate. The first amendment proposed to extend full voting rights to black men; the second proposal sought to enfranchise women as well. The state Democratic Party, convening in September at Leavenworth, formally opposed the woman suffrage amendment. The Republican Party, on the other hand, was divided on the issue. Although several prominent Republicans, including Governor Samuel Crawford, actively supported woman suffrage, many Republican abolitionists opposed the radical measure for fear that any agitation over female enfranchisement would hinder the passage of black suffrage.

Since Kansas was the first state in the Union to consider woman suffrage, the ensuing campaign attracted nationwide attention. Anxious to achieve their first victory, national women's rights leaders took a particularly active interest in the amendment. Throughout the summer, Lucy Stone and her husband, Dr. Henry Blackwell, blazed an oratorical trail across Kansas. Traveling by open wagon, they addressed suffrage debates and town meetings everywhere. In September, Susan B. Anthony, Elizabeth Cady Stanton and George Francis Train arrived to continue the campaign. Throughout the fall they toured northeastern Kansas, delivering speeches, recruiting workers and rallying supporters. In the end, however, their exhaustive efforts proved unsuccessful. When the final votes were tallied, the woman suffrage amendment was defeated by a count of 19,857 to 9,070.

Years later, the Reverend Olympia Brown compiled an account of her experiences in the 1867 campaign. In her own lifetime, Reverend Brown, the first woman ordained by the Universalist Church, was widely recognized for her gifted speaking skills and dedicated suffrage work. Her presence in Kansas, like that of the other prominent feminists, did much to bolster support for the women's cause.

"The writer of this article was young in 1867," she wrote, "just entered upon the Christian ministry, just settled a few years previous in my first parish at Weymouth, Mass. One pleasant spring day Lucy Stone came to Weymouth. She had just returned from Kansas, where she had been to inaugurate the campaign for woman's suffrage, and she wished me to go to Kansas to keep the work going during the summer.

"The amendment to the constitution had passed the legislature the previous winter; it was a compromise, or rather a bluff. The Republicans were then deeply interested in the Negro, and they proposed an amendment to the constitution, striking out the word 'white.' Then the Democrats obstructed legislation by proposing one striking out the word 'male'—finally the Republicans adopted both, thus the enfranchisement of the Negro and of women were both before the people. Lucy Stone said the measure was almost sure to pass, it was only necessary to keep it before the people through the summer. The Republicans, she said, would furnish conveyance and conveniences for the speakers. They would make all the appointments and open their meetings to our cause, and she urged me to go out at once to Leavenworth, where I would meet a member of the Central Committee who would start me on the campaign.

"It is needless to say that an earnest advocate of woman's suffrage would be ready to respond to such an appeal. No difficulty was raised concerning remuneration, and no suggestions of possible failure were made. Youth is enthusiastic and hopeful but experience soon comes to warn, if not to disappoint.

"Arrived at Leavenworth, it appeared that the Republican member of the Central Committee had never heard of me and knew nothing of any arrangement with Lucy Stone. However, a meeting was hastily arranged at Leavenworth and another at a small place nearby. On going to Lawrence it was the same; no one knew of any such arrangement with Lucy Stone, but the Rev. Mr. Bronen of the Universalist Church and his family were most kind and cordial, and a really fine meeting was held at the Unitarian Church. Mr. Milton Reynolds, formerly a student at Albion, Michigan, and the editor of the principal Lawrence paper, gave good notices; all through the campaign his paper was most helpful.

"At Topeka I met Sam Wood,* then very prominent in Kansas politics; in fact he appeared to be the wheel horse of the Republican party. He had arranged to open the campaign at Topeka on the Fourth of July with a big meeting at which he and others besides the writer were to be the speakers.

"This began to look like business. Mr. Wood had made appointments for two months, two speeches a day including Sundays; had one of his circulars there, was sure the meetings were advertised. How good! But where was the conveyance? He knew of the arrangement with Lucy Stone, in fact he probably was the man who had made it, but he said it was one of those things that it might seem that we could do, but we could not do. In short the Republicans had no idea of doing any such things. However, Mr. Wood had written to people along the route, he was sure they would entertain me; he thought good men in each place would convey me on; indeed he had

* Samuel Newitt Wood (1825–91), a prominent Kansas politician and newspaperman, was a member of the Kansas Senate at this time. During the territorial years, Wood had been a leader of the Free-State Party in Lawrence and had served in the territorial legislatures of 1860 and 1861. When Kansas became a state in 1861, he was elected to the first state Senate. He also served in the Kansas House of Representatives in 1864, 1866, 1876 and 1877. On June 23, 1891, Wood was killed in the heat of a county-seat fight in Stevens County, Kansas.

a man there with a horse and buggy to take me to the first place. So I set forth, and continued making two speeches a day and later three speeches a day until the election in November.

"Kansas was then just emerging from the great struggles for freedom which culminated in the civil war. Many of her men had been killed in the conflicts with the border ruffians and in the battles of the war. The crops that season had been destroyed by grasshoppers. Many of the pioneers were suffering from malaria and other diseases incident to the settlement of a new country. There were few public conveyances, either by rail or stage route or livery, and few men owned carriages. The outlook was not encouraging. It developed that the appointments had been made without any knowledge of the country, and they were often fifty miles apart, necessitating starting at four in the morning to reach an appointment at two P.M., and after the lecture and a brief half hour for dinner, we would start again to reach an evening appointment.

"In many places there were no roads, only a trail across the prairie and sometimes not even that. Under such circumstances, to lose our way became almost a daily experience and when now and then we chanced to meet a traveler and inquired the distance to a neighboring town we were often met by the reply that it was 'right smart' or possibly 'a good little bit.' But on we went and the most remarkable thing about the campaign was that notwithstanding all these difficulties, the speaker did not, during the whole four months, miss one appointment.

"They were good men in Kansas in those days, and although securing conveyances by chance, sometimes riding with rough men, Indians or Negroes—anybody that would go there—there was not one instance on the part of these men of rudeness or discourtesy or anything but the utmost kindness and apparent interest in the success of the campaign. Often men would leave their work, sorghum boiling in the kettle or the ploughing of the field, and borrow a horse or a wagon and take the speaker on. The interest that these men took in the cause was most encouraging and inspiring.

"It would take more space than would be afforded in this article to tell of all the incidents that occurred—of the true men and faithful women who helped the work along; of how we were robbed in one place and escaped with only the loss of one night's rest and a supper and breakfast; of how Joel Moody and his wife and two children traveled with the speaker for twelve days because the region was considered unsafe for a woman alone; of how the beautiful Hutchinson family came and sang their sweet songs for freedom; of how the Republican Central Committee sent out circulars against us; of how Judge Spear and L. S. Hallock lectured against woman's suffrage; all this would take a book instead of a brief article.

"In the autumn came Miss Anthony and Mrs. Stanton and George Francis Train. Mr. Train came, he said, because he owned property in Kansas, and because he expected to be the next president of the United States. He made speeches that pleased the crowd, and indeed they were most original. He had a parody on 'Excelsior': 'The shades of night were falling fast, and through a Kansas village passed a maiden with a strange device—"Woman Suffrage." ' Some of his epigrams are worth repeating:

Kansas will win the world's applause
As the sole champion of the woman's cause
So light the bonfires, have the flags unfurled
To the banner state of all the world.

And again:

My mission to Kansas breaks the white woman's chains
Three cheers for virtue and beauty and brains.

"Well, the end came and the votes were counted, and Woman's Suffrage got only a little over one-third of all. But disappointment and defeat were softened by a letter from Susan B. Anthony:

> Dear Olympia: Never was defeat so glorious a victory. My dear Olympia, if ever any money gets into my control, you shall have evidence that I appreciate the Herculean work you have done here in Kansas the past four long months.

I would have gone farther and done more for those words of appreciation from Susan; I was a hero worshipper then."

With the defeat of the amendment, woman suffrage became a dormant issue for many years to come. In February of 1869 a women's convention was held at Topeka in the hope of reviving the cause. The effort proved unsuccessful, and the discouraged delegates were unable to galvanize any organized course of action. In fact, twenty-seven years passed before the Kansas electorate again considered giving women full voting privileges.

Although there was no cohesive women's movement during these years, equal suffrage was by no means a dead issue. In many towns, women's temperance groups supported the cause by including it in their educational lectures and literature. In fact, the state's Prohibition Party officially endorsed suffrage in its 1874 platform. Local literary societies also perpetuated the issue through community debates and assemblies. In view of the strong opposition to the enfranchisement of women, these public discussions invariably attracted attention and controversy.

In the town of Rose Hill, one such debate caused considerable excitement. "During the year 1875," explained Stella Haines, "the first Literary Society was formed, the meetings were held once a week in the homes of the members and debated different subjects. One subject which caused the greatest excitement was 'Resolved That Women Should Have Equal Suffrage With Men.' Four women against four men, with three judges, caused so much interest that people came for ten miles around to this debate, most of the folks asserted it was a foolish idea to think women even wanted to vote. Naturally the men judges decided for the negative. At the close of the decision, while the wild cheering was going on, one of the men debaters jumped on top of a bench, flapped his arms up and down and crowed like a rooster. Mrs. Haines, the main woman speaker, arose and said she had often heard roosters crow when they had whipped another rooster, but never when they had whipped a hen."

In 1879, in the town of Lincoln, the state's first woman suffrage organization was inaugurated. In its first years of operation, the Equal Suffrage Association had only three official members. Nevertheless, its very existence signaled an important turn in the tide as more women emerged to voice their support for full and equal suffrage. Anna Biggs Heaney, the daughter of Emily Cornell Biggs, later wrote: "The first K.E.S.A. local in Lincoln county was organized by Mrs. Biggs, Mrs. George [Sarah E.] Lutes and Mrs. Anna C. Wait. It was well among the first in the state as well as in the county. These three kept the agitation going when it was hardly a live question. If you were a woman suffragist you were just something funny. Mrs. Lutes died not many years after this but for many years Mrs. Biggs and Mrs. Wait kept alive interest and awakened intelligent discussion of the [subject] so near their hearts."

In the following years, other suffrage groups were organized around the state as dedicated women joined in the campaign. "I recall, too, the Suffrage Clubs," wrote Julia Robinson, "how hard the women of our State worked for Equal Suffrage. We were living in Valley Falls in those days and I remember our Suffrage Club. How energetically we worked. We had 'Ode Cards' printed, each member contributing an original song to be sung to a familiar tune that we indicated."

When a neighborhood suffrage club was organized in Topeka, Carrie Sain Whittaker was elected its first president. Although only a schoolgirl at the time, she became an earnest supporter of the women's cause. "After we had lived in town for some time," she explained, "Mrs. Col. Ritchie came down one evening and she and mother after talking things over decided to call a meeting of neighbors and organize a Woman's Suffrage Association. It was called to meet at Col. Ritchie's and my mother took me with her for company coming home. There were not many there, it seems to me not more than six or seven.

"I was then going to school to a Mrs. Maybe I think on the corner of Kansas Ave. and Seventh Street. We were having some lessons in Parliamentary Law, so when they were getting organized they would call on me to tell them how. After we had things planned Mrs. Ritchie said, 'Let's put Carrie in as president, she is the only one who can keep us in order.' I said, 'Oh, you can't do that, it will be several years before I am old enough to vote.' They said, 'You'll be old enough long before we have the right.'

"My father had always said his family of girls had just as much right to help about the government as if we were boys, and mother and he had always taught us to expect Women Suffrage in our day.

"That winter the legislature was in session, and we had a number of legislators who were earnest workers for equal suffrage attend our meetings. Lucy Stone, Henry Blackwell, Susan B. Anthony, and some lesser lights visited Topeka and lectured before the legislature on this all-important subject."

In June of 1884, a statewide organization, the Equal Suffrage Association, was founded, with Hetta Mansfield elected president and Anna C. Wait named vice-president. It was largely through the efforts of this group that the Kansas state legislature renewed the suffrage controversy. When a bill was introduced in 1885 to grant women municipal voting rights, the group delivered to the legislature petitions with some seven thousand signatures. Although the measure was subsequently defeated, members of the Equal Suffrage Association pledged to continue their lobbying efforts. In 1887, women finally won the right to vote and run for office in all city elections, although state and federal elections still excluded them.

This advance brought women new opportunities in the political arena. Over the next few years, increasing numbers of women became active in local affairs, joining campaigns, working in party politics and running for elective offices. On April 4, 1887, Susannah Medora Salter was elected mayor in the small town of Argonia, becoming the first woman in the nation ever to hold the office. Following her unprecedented victory, the towns of Baldwin, Cottonwood Falls, Rossville, Elk Falls and Oskaloosa likewise elected women mayors. In fact, by the turn of the century a total of fifteen women had won mayoral elections across the state.* Minnie Morgan, the mayor of Cottonwood Falls, was even accompanied by an all-woman city council. According to her son, "She was elected along with a council composed of women because of the determination of the voters to secure better law enforcement. The success of her administration was hailed as an outstanding argument for woman suffrage, a cause in which she was always a leader, and which was before the people of Kansas for many years. . . . She believed thoroughly in the rights of women, and was never too much occupied with other affairs to refrain from speaking, writing and working for woman's causes, regardless of personal convenience or present popularity."

* In Kansas, the following women served as mayors prior to the turn of the twentieth century (see "Women in Office," *Kansas Historical Collections,* Vol. 12, pp. 396–401).

Annie Austin, Pleasanton, 1894.
Belle Gray, Canton, 1890.
Antoinette L. Haskell, Gaylord, 1895–96.
Mrs. W. H. Kelly, Edgerton, 1890.
Mrs. A. L. King, Elk Falls, 1889.
Mary D. Lowman, Oskaloosa, 1888–89.
Mrs. H. H. Miller, Rossville, 1889.
Wilhelmina D. Morgan, Cottonwood Falls, 1889.
Dr. Rachel S. Packson, Kiowa, 1891.
Susannah Medora Salter, Argonia, 1887.
Anna M. Strain, Jamestown, 1897.
Lucy M. Sullivan, Baldwin, 1889.
Elizabeth Totten, Beattie, 1899.
Elizabeth Vedder, Haddam, 1891.
Mrs. M. A. Wade, Ellis, 1896.

Some women made strides in the thicket of party politics as well. When the Kansas People's Party was organized by agrarian Populists in 1890, Mary Ellen Lease and Annie Diggs emerged at its forefront. Mary Ellen Lease was one of the party's most electrifying orators. In the campaign of 1890 she delivered more than 150 lectures across the state, urging farmers to "raise less corn and more Hell." While Mary Ellen Lease took to the pulpit, Annie Diggs espoused the party platform through the editorial pages of a Lawrence newspaper. For years her Farmer's Alliance column captivated audiences around the state and earned her a reputation as a key Populist spokeswoman.

In addition to their widening involvement in municipal elections and party politics, women continued their fight for the ballot. In 1894 the state legislature yielded to their growing demands and resubmitted the woman suffrage amendment to the voters. Heated opposition to the measure, however, led to a bitter and divisive campaign.

"When Woman's Suffrage became an issue," recalled Fannie Holsinger, "I cast my lot with the suffragists, believing that the world was made for women too and that [God] gave them dominion. [When] the Suffrage Amendment was voted on I spent the day at the polls. One friend to whom I offered a ticket refused to accept it. Noticing my disappointment he said, 'I'll tell you, Mrs. Holsinger, I think too much of women to see them go down into the dirty pool of politics.' 'Perhaps,' I said, 'we can help to clear the pool.' 'Well,' he said, 'I'll promise not to vote against it.'

"I approached a well dressed, fine looking negro and offered him a ticket. 'I am agin it,' he said. 'Why are you against it?' I asked. 'I married a wife to take care of me and a woman's place is at home.' 'Haven't you some business that needs your attention,' I asked courteously. 'I'm here taking care of the polls and helping to make votes. A woman's place is at home.' He went off, but I did not go home till I got ready."

The equal suffrage amendment was once again defeated at the polls. Although similar measures were introduced in later years, it took nearly two decades for the legislature to approve again such constitutional reform. By then, the woman suffrage movement had become an increasingly important force in state politics. When the suffrage amendment was resubmitted to the 1911 legislature, the women's forces presented over one hundred supporting petitions with the signatures of nearly 25,000 men and women around the state. Under such intense lobbying pressure, the measure passed the House by a vote of 94 to 28 and was subsequently approved by two thirds of the Senate. In ratifying the amendment in 1912, Kansas became the eighth state in the Union to grant women full and equal voting rights.

By this time, the pioneer period had long since drawn to a close. With the passing of the years, the endless miles of virgin prairie had been transformed into cultivated fields and enclosed pastures. Paved roads and automobiles had replaced the old dirt trails and horse-drawn wagons, while the once familiar dugouts and soddies had given way to spacious homes of stone and brick. For the housewife, electricity and running water had lightened the household chores. For the farmer, steam-powered threshers and tractors had reduced the rigors of prairie farming. Improved rail service, rural mail delivery and early telephone lines had alleviated the loneliness of farm life and transformed the sleepy frontier towns into bustling business centers. Kansas, once little more than a barren, wind-swept wilderness, had finally come of age.

America's pioneer great-grandmothers will be remembered both for the uniqueness of their lives and for their significant contributions in civilizing the American West. But their accomplishments should not be measured merely in terms of the schools and churches they built, the ideological campaigns they waged or the political victories they may have won. In the long run, it is the strength of their individualism, their faith and their determination which have remained as an important part of our common heritage.

In the words of one pioneer daughter, these were women who "gave their youth, health, courage and the very best of their lives to the civilization of these great western plains, at a cost no one ever will be able to reckon. There were no words of complaint; just a slow but steady advancement in the face of difficulties and obstacles that stagger one who considers them now. Surely not a star in Heaven will be too bright for the crowns of those brave women who, with lonely hearts and the dismal music of coyote calls, often watched the stars from humble homes, 'out where the West begins.' "

APPENDIX

Guide to the Lilla Day Monroe Collection of Pioneer Stories

Explanation of Notations

D	—daughter	GD	—granddaughter
SN	—son	GSN	—grandson
H	—husband	DIL	—daughter-in-law
S	—sister	SNIL	—son-in-law
B	—brother	SIL	—sister-in-law
		N	—niece

SUBJECT	SOURCE	EMIGRATION DATE	AGE AT EMIGRATION
Abrahams, Mrs. G. F.	Ida M. Walker (D)	1873	21
Adair, Mary E. Gardner (Mrs. Charles S.)	Mrs. S. S. White	1865	14
Adams, Adaline Spencer	Martha Priscilla Spencer (S) and Mrs. F. O. Rindom	1860s	
Adams, Harriet E. Clark (Mrs. Franklin G.)	Dr. Harriet E. Adams (D)	1856	19
Agrelius, Inga (Mrs. Isaac)	Mildred Trygg	1872	62
Aich, Anna Gertrude Brubaker (Mrs. Stephen)	autobiography	native (b. 1879)	
Akin, Margaret	unknown	1870	39
Aldrich, Hattie E. Bassett (Mrs. Harry L.)	autobiography	native (b. 1869)	
Alexander, Hester Ann Scott (Mrs. Joseph M.)	Mrs. F. W. Boyd (D)	1872	18
Alexander, Viola C. Downing (Mrs. James H.)	Mrs. Merrel E. Hutchinson (D)	1876	23
Allee, Fannie Johnston (Mrs. Victor)	autobiography		
Allen, Anna Maria Ellis (Mrs. George A.)	George A. Allen, Jr. (SN)	1870	27
Allen, Electra Rathburn (Mrs. John)	Ella Angel	1871	
Allen, Elizabeth Morgan (Mrs. T. N.)	T. G. Allen (S)	1864	43
Allen, Ella Muck (Mrs. William)	Ella Angel	1872	
Allen, Frances Annette Gude (Mrs. M. J.)	unknown	1886	26
Allerton, Ellen Palmer (Mrs. A. B.)	A. G. Allerton (SN)	1865	30
Almon, Hannah L. (Mrs. Clarence)	autobiography		
Alrich, Emma B. Eldridge (Mrs. Levi L.)	Ella Angel	1879	34
Alstatt, Sarah	Esther H. Norstrom (GD) and Mrs. C. Marion Norstrom	1872	
Altemas, Sarah Jane Baker (Mrs. John)	Ella Angel	1873	44
Anderson, Ann E. Wright (Mrs. George W.)	Effie Loetta Anderson Thompson (D)	1869	22
Anderson, Helen Nelson (Mrs. Lars)	Frances Jennings	1870	22
Anderson, Mariah D. Phipps (Mrs. Alexander)	Ella Anderson Scott (D)	1871	35

SUBJECT	SOURCE	EMIGRATION DATE	AGE AT EMIGRATION
Anderson, Sarah Mooney (Mrs. Dave)	Ella Angel	1874	
Andrews, Susanna Critchfield (Mrs. Thomas)	Joanna Reinhardt (D)	1879	55
Anthony, Sarah M. Lindsley (Mrs. E. O.)	Lizzie Anthony Opdyke (D)	1876	29
Aplington, Kate Adele Smith (Mrs. John)	autobiography	1880	21
Armstrong, Mary C. Strieby	Lalla Maloy Brigham and Mrs. J. M. Miller	1864	
Arnold, Sally Ann Pierson (Mrs. Dawson)	Mata Zimmerman	1855	23
Atkinson, Fannie Cooper (Mrs. W. D.)	W. D. Atkinson (H)	1866	1
Atkinson, Sarah F. Parsons (Mrs. Charles)	Etta M. Linde (D)	1871	10
Avery, Eliza G. Edwards (Mrs. Park)	Anna M. Rowland (D)	1870	51
Axline, Almira Stever (Mrs. Andrew)	Mamie Axline Fay (D)	1877	40
Ayres, May Wadsworth (Mrs. Philip S.)	autobiography	native (b. 1874)	
Bailey, Minnie Kieth (Mrs. John R.)	autobiography	native (b. 1869)	
Baish, Mrs. Frederick	Ella Strieby Baish	1862	
Baker, Catherine E. McClain (Mrs. Isaac L.)	Mrs. Lemon C. Baker (DIL)	1857	
Baker, Clara R.	autobiography	1881	
Balcomb, Lydia E. Goodno (Mrs. Francis)	Mary F. Balcomb (D)	1878	40
Banta, Martha Baird	unknown	1879	
Barker, Lucene Allen (Mrs. George J.)	Mrs. C. S. Finch	1867	23
Barr, Mollie E. Boenitz (Mrs. James F.)	autobiography	1859	10
Bartholomew, Hattie L. Brown (Mrs. John)	Cora Belle Smith	1903	48
Bassett, Mrs.	Mrs. J. B. Darrah	1868	
Baxter, Alzada Lamb (Mrs. Charles)	Ada Musgrave	1858	20
Baxter, Mrs. Edson	autobiography	1860	
Bayless, Elizabeth Glenn (Mrs. James N.)	unknown	1870	32
Bayly, Cornelia Buck (Mrs. Obadiah)	Mrs. R. E. Booker (D)	1871	30

SUBJECT	SOURCE	EMIGRATION DATE	AGE AT EMIGRATION
Beam, Jennie Palmer (Mrs. Francis)	autobiography	1871	26
Beardsley, Decima (Mrs. Mark J.)	autobiography	1875	
Beck, Mary Hamilton Scott (Mrs. M. M.)	Martha M. Beck (D)	1869	
Becker, Catherine E. Stryker (Mrs. Erskine)	Mary E. Rasmussen (D)	1871	22
Beedle, Sarah	Ella Angel	1871	
Benton, Lula Blanche Lines (Mrs. Lyman D.)	autobiography		
Berg, Anna Pearson (Mrs. Bengt)	autobiography	1872	22
Berryman, Sarah Cessna (Mrs. Jerome C.)	Jerome Woods Berryman (GSN)	1831	23
Best, Catherine M. Hettler (Mrs. Christian)	Matilda Best Kenyon	1881	60
Biays, Henrietta Miller (Mrs. William H.)	unknown	1872	28
Biggs, Emily Jane Cornell (Mrs. A. T.)	Anna Biggs Heaney (D)	1871	
Bingham, Anne E. Northrop (Mrs. Charles H.)	autobiography	1869	29
Bingham, Florence Case (Mrs. A. J.)	autobiography	1871	
Bissing, Sara Magrane	autobiography	1879	
Blair, Salome A.	autobiography		
Bliss, Mrs. Charles T.	autobiography		
Bogardus, Hester (Mrs. David)	Carrie Gates McClintic	1866	
Bollman, Theresa Lammers (Mrs. Henry J.)	Fred Bollman (SN)	1877	47
Bowen, Mrs. Preston	Pocahontas Bowen Hanway (D)	1857	
Bowen, Amelia Fosket (Mrs. William B.)	W. B. Bowen (SN)	1871	35
Boyd, Eliza Jane	Ella Bradford (D)	1860s	
Boyd, Ines Fallon (Mrs. George)	Mrs. F. W. Boyd (DIL)	1872	17
Boyd, Mary E. Attwater (Mrs. H. N.)	Major H. N. Boyd (H)	1878	36
Boylan, Castella F. Walter (Mrs. Almon B.)	Lenore Boylan Tate (D)	1875	23
Brandley, Elizabeth R. (Mrs. Henry)	Clara Brandley Hildebrand (D)	1857	14
Bratley, Mary E. Hastings (Mrs. Joseph)	Luverna Williamson	1870	28

SUBJECT	SOURCE	EMIGRATION DATE	AGE AT EMIGRATION
Breese, Margaret M. Irwin (Mrs. Sidney A.)	Carrie Breese Chandler (D)	1866	28
Brigham, Lalla Maloy (Mrs. L. H.)	autobiography	1870s	
Brigham, Mary E. Hutchinson (Mrs. Levi)	Lalla Maloy Brigham		
Broadbent, Sarah E. Glaze (Mrs. Thomas A.)	autobiography	1871	
Brokaw, Lucy Van Fossen	Ruby Slaven	1871	
Brooks, Mary Angeline Boughton (Mrs. Paul R.)	C. S. Finch	1857	
Bross, Frances Taylor (Mrs. Harvey E.)	autobiography	native (b. 1900)	
Bross, Marie A.	autobiography	native (b. 1905)	
Brown, Mrs. Charles Cranston	Dennis Madden		
Brown, Elizabeth Stalker (Mrs. Miles W.)	unknown	1861	39
Brown, Elmira Spencer	Martha P. Spencer (S) and Mrs. F. O. Rindom	1857	17
Brown, Emma C. Sargent (Mrs. Charles L.)	autobiography	1869	25
Brown, Rev. Olympia S.	autobiography	1867	
Buffington, Eliza F. Paschal (Mrs. J. Q.)	Mrs. C. P. Thompson (D)	1865	39
Burlingame, Gertrude E. (Mrs. Ward)	autobiography	1858	19
Burnett, Anna Mary Fisk (Mrs. Jonathan C.)	Edward B. Burnett and Carrie Breese Chandler	1857	24
Burnett, Margaret Denny (Mrs. William)	Mrs. O. L. Burnett	1871	28
Burton, Hettie	Helen C. Dallas	1858	
Burton, Rachel Barber	autobiography		
Bush, Dr. Clara Newlon (Mrs. George P.)	autobiography	1867	
Caddick, Thomas	autobiography	1878	
Caldwell, Maggie White (Mrs. D. N.)	Gertrude Swan (D)	1873	
Campbell, Christina Phillips (Mrs. Alexander)	Mrs. Delia E. Brown	1856	25
Campbell, Martha Ann (Mrs. William M.)	Sam W. Campbell (SN)	1872	

SUBJECT	SOURCE	EMIGRATION DATE	AGE AT EMIGRATION
Campbell, Sarah Cornwell (Mrs. William)	Mary Griffee Robinson	1871	27
Campdoras, Eliza Reader (Mrs. M. A.)	Grace Campdoras (D)	1855	
Capper, Isabella McGrew (Mrs. Herbert)	Arthur Capper (SN)	1857	16
Carlton, Anna Evans (Mrs. John W.)	autobiography		
Carpenter, Agnes Elder (Mrs. J. E.)	Cora Belle Smith	1886	30
Carpenter, Elizabeth Fenner (Mrs. James C.)	Mrs. C. M. Loy (D)	1870	30
Caton, Mrs. W. B.	autobiography	1879	
Cave, Virginia Sims (Mrs. John Bart)	Lo Ree Cave Keough (D)		
Cavender, Catherine Zeigler	autobiography	1877	14
Chapman, Lavina Gates (Mrs. Steven B.)	autobiography	1860	25
Chapman, Sarah A.	autobiography	1870	27
Charles, Lydia Evans	Olwen Myfanwy Cameron (D)	1868	33
Chenoweth, Mary Janes (Mrs. John)	unknown	1868	
Childers, Ruth Furgeson (Mrs. Enoch D.)	unknown	1859	
Clark, Allena Ann Clevenger (Mrs. Horace G.)	Esther Clark Hill (D)	1870s	
Clark, Bell Gates (Mrs. Charlie W.)	autobiography	1864	17
Clark, Edward F.	autobiography	1867	
Clark, Ellen Davis	autobiography	1879	23
Clark, Marovia Still (Mrs. E. S.)	unknown	1851	17
Clark, Mrs. Warren B.	Mrs. F. W. Butler (D)	1869	
Clemons, Martha Curtis Butler (Mrs. Emory)	unknown	1876	41
Clemson, Edith A. Hockenbarger	autobiography	1879	3
Cline, Minerva (Mrs. John N.)	Verlie Snyder White	1860	
Coburn, Lou Jenkins (Mrs. Foster D.)	Gertrude Coburn Jessup (D)		
Cochran, Margaret Ann Hyman (Mrs. George)	unknown	1872	20
Cochran, Mary A. Piper (Mrs. William C.)	Ida Cochran Bartleson (D)		

SUBJECT	SOURCE	EMIGRATION DATE	AGE AT EMIGRATION
Coffin, Lillie B. Marcks	autobiography		
Colaw, Mollie Rebecca Powell (Mrs. Joshua)	autobiography	1881	10
Cole, Eliza James (Mrs. Joseph Mortimer)	Katherine Campdoras	1855	
Cole, Frances E.	Velleda Campdoras	1855	9
Cole, Dr. Sarah A.	Sara Wallace	1882	27
Collier, Elizabeth Frank (Mrs. John W.)	Clara Collier Behring	1881	33
Collins, Jeanetta Coffman (Mrs. Levi C.)	Mrs. Bernice Ludwick (D)	1876	21
Collins, Leora M. Filmore (Mrs. William)	Mata Zimmerman	1861	11
Collinson, Amanda Heaton (Mrs. Simeon D.)	G. W. Collinson (S)		
Colman, Mary Jane Wendell (Mrs. E. A.)	Mrs. J. R. Topping (D) and C. T. Colman (SN)	1854	37
Combs, Millie Fielder (Mrs. Wallace W.)	Cora Belle Smith	1885	30
Comstock, Harriet Woodin	autobiography	1867	
Conrad, Wilma Flora (Mrs. Henry)	Ida St. Helens	native (b. 1860)	
Converse, Mrs. Nathan P.	Mrs. J. E. Johntz	1874	
Cook, Martha Brown (Mrs. John)	Mrs. James M. Robinson (D)		
Copeland, Josephine Ackerman (Mrs. Charles)	Leland Stanford Copeland (SN)	1874	28
Copeland, Mary Rutledge (Mrs. John M.)	Ivy Copeland Deans (D)	1870	
Cordry, Almira Peckham (Mrs. Tom A.)	Ida Almira Cordry Dodd (D)	1871	8
Cordry, Eliza Jane Lindley (Mrs. Asbury)	Mrs. Tom Cordry (DIL)	1871	39
Coudy, Eliza Breen (Mrs. Patrick)	unknown	1879	41
Counts, Mary A. Wilson (Mrs. S. T.)	Jennie Counts Marcy (D)	1877	
Courtney, Alice Patterson (Mrs. William)	Coral Courtney Carter	1875	12
Cowle, Mary Tatman (Mrs. George)	Harriet Cowle Walter (D)	1873	18
Cowley, Nancy Johnson (Mrs. Mathew)	Ruth Satterthwaite	1857	29
Craig, Mrs. George R.	Julia C. Potter (D)	1874	35

SUBJECT	SOURCE	EMIGRATION DATE	AGE AT EMIGRATION
Cramer, Lucy P. Hodge (Mrs. Grant)	autobiography	1873	8
Crary, Sabra A. Teats (Mrs. A. M.)	Mrs. E. H. Donnelly	1871	
Culp, Elizabeth A. Wagner (Mrs. Chesley)	Minnie Culp (D)	1869	26
Currie, Elizabeth Harding (Mrs. Robert L.)	autobiography	1871	
Curtis, Permelia Hubbard	Charles Curtis (GSN)	1860	53
Cutherbertson, Mrs. F. T.	Blanche M. West	1870	
Dallas, Nancy B.	Helen C. Dallas	1859	
Daratt, Ida R. Bastain (Mrs. Oscar R.)	Mrs. E. A. Tufts	1872	21
Darling, Katherine Hyman Calder (Mrs. Ben)	Mrs. J. S. Calder (DIL)	1872	30
Darrah, Hannah Nelson (Mrs. Thomas J.)	autobiography	1868	5
Darrah, Mary Ferguson (Mrs. James B.)	autobiography	1855	4
Darrow, Mary E. McCracken (Mrs. Russell)	autobiography	1870	
Daugherty, Lucy T. Longfellow (Mrs. George)	Lizzie K. Robinson	1857	20
Daugherty, Rosalie V. Cunningham (Mrs. W. J.)	Carrie Breese Chandler	1865	25
Davis, Catherine Hudson (Mrs. Thomas B.)	Anna Boyd Davis Fisher (D)	1855	30
Davis, Elizabeth C. Rich (Mrs. W. D.)	autobiography	1871	21
Davis, Jane Hale (Mrs. Warner)	unknown	1860	48
Davis, Margaret G. Brown (Mrs. Nathan)	Elizabeth Davis Staley (D)	1860	16
Day, Mary Florence Pinkham (Mrs. Charles)	unknown	1851	19
Dean, Martha M. Shipley (Mrs. George)	Cora Belle Smith	1886	32
Dearborn, Sarah Ann Briggs (Mrs. George S.)	Mrs. R. A. Rearwin	1865	40
Deardorff, Ophelia Ingalls (Mrs. Thomas C.)	Mrs. M. F. Creveling	1868	44
Decker, Margaret (Mrs. John A.)	autobiography	native (b. 1873)	
DePoy, Rachel Harshburger (Mrs. Samuel)	Ella Angel	1866	29
Dever, Louisa Meek (Mrs. Thomas)	Della Dever Nix (D)	1865	
DeWald, Anna Elizabeth Streck (Mrs. George)	autobiography	1878	22

SUBJECT	SOURCE	EMIGRATION DATE	AGE AT EMIGRATION
DeWald, Katherine Lohman (Mrs. Jacob G.)	Bertha DeWald (N)	1877	13
Dexter, John, Alonzo and Aaron	Mrs. Frank Oberg	1862	
Dickinson, Lydia Ann (Mrs. James M.)	autobiography	1855	
Dillon, Sarah E. Strieby	Mary Dillon Miller (D) and Lalla Maloy Brigham	1867	
Dix, Susan Mendenhall (Mrs. Isaac H.)	Mabel W. Leonard (D)	1880	39
Dixon, Anna Holmes (Mrs. James T.)	Edith Lawson	1873	43
Donovan, Mary Jane Turner (Mrs. Albert)	Clara Harrington	1859	9
Dornblaser, Sarah M. Foster (Mrs. Benjamin)	Ida Heacock Baker	1875	43
Downing, Ella West (Mrs. Jack H.)	Jack H. Downing (H)	1869	
Drake, Marrietta Barker (Mrs. Erwin)	Una M. Kesler	1877	30
Duncan, Sarah Johns Miller (Mrs. M. L.)	autobiography	1857	18
Dunlap, Esther Bell (Mrs. James)	unknown	1866	6
Dunlop, Jane Girwin (Mrs. James)	Jessie Dunlop Anderson (D) and Hattie Dunlop Sanquist (D)	1871	23
Dunton, Frances J. G. Pemberton (Mrs. William)	Mrs. P. S. Ayres	1860	5
Durst, Emeline Hanna (Mrs. Henry)	autobiography	1871	9
Dusin, Mary Veeh	Lydia Weinman		
Dutton, Susie T. Craig (Mrs. Henry A.)	Minnie Dutton Craig (D)	1864	16
Eberhardt, Anna C. Lambert (Mrs. Christopher)	Blanche Heustis Dyar	1866	24
Edwards, Martha Jane Lady (Mrs. J. B.)	Mary E. Edwards (D) and A. Blanche Edwards	1874	6
Egy, Sarah Ann	A. L. Egy (SN)		
Ehman, Feddie Persinger (Mrs. David)	autobiography	1867	7
Elder, Catherine Cecilia Sook (Mrs. N. G.)	autobiography	1877	26
Eldred, Sophronia Nye (Mrs. J. A.)	unknown	1859	

SUBJECT	SOURCE	EMIGRATION DATE	AGE AT EMIGRATION
Emery, Frances Roberts	unknown	1855	
Eply, Mary V. Ambrose (Mrs. Samuel J.)	Mrs. George Eply (DIL)	1884	43
Espenlaub, Elvira Gromes (Mrs. G. F.)	autobiography		
Espy, Melora Elizabeth (Mrs. Henry J.)	Rev. Clara H. Hazelrigg (D)	1853	17
Evans, Emma Mason (Mrs. James A.)	Cora Belle Smith	1886	31
Ewing, Myra Hawk (Mrs. George W.)	unknown	1871	16
Fall, Delia	Pearl Donnelley	1857	20
Faris, Emma Pitezel (Mrs. Henry V.)	autobiography	1871	27
Farnsworth, Helen Bowker (Mrs. J. B.)	Mrs. Della Bennett	1880	27
Ferrell, Tarsy Salome Myers (Mrs. Lloyd)	Maude F. Dick	1877	17
Ferris, M. Gennette Whitney (Mrs. John H.)	Nettie Ferris Douglass (D)	1874	37
Fielderling, Frances Matthews (Mrs. George P.)	Della Price	1855	25
Fischer, Frederica Hecker	Nannie L. Gander	1869	28
Fisher, Elizabeth Atcheson	Anna Boyd Davis Fisher (DIL)	1856	
Fleming, Lydia Brown (Mrs. Robert T.)	unknown		
Fletcher, Cassie Freeman (Mrs. W. H.)	Mrs. Frances A. Jennings	1868	26
Fletcher, Martha Hainsworth	autobiography	1870	9
Foltz, Rebecca Heberling (Mrs. Martin L.)	unknown	1856	14
Foote, Sarah Gleason (Mrs. Addison)	Bessie A. Brown (D)	1871	15
Ford, Ada	autobiography	1879	15
Frans, Lottie Irene Taylor (Mrs. Fauntleroy)	Maude Frans Dick (D)	1874	32
Frederickson, Johanna (Mrs. John P.)	Nora Nelson	1872	39
Frink, Laura E. Belts (Mrs. Asa A.)	autobiography	1856	4
Fritz, Phoebe Hurr (Mrs. Henry)	Pauline Jeffcoat (GD)		
Frizzell, L. Dora DuMont (Mrs. Edward)	autobiography	1866	1
Fromm, Augusta	Mrs. W. C. Bocker (DIL)	1868	

SUBJECT	SOURCE	EMIGRATION DATE	AGE AT EMIGRATION
Fuhr, Lulu R. Logdon (Mrs. Frank)	autobiography	1885	19
Furgeson, Hannah J. (Mrs. Abner B.)	Ruth Furgeson Childers (D)	1859	
Galbraith, Catherine P. Biggus (Mrs. Thomas)	Mrs. H. B. Oberholser (D)	1878	42
Gale, Ellen Hall (Mrs. Matthew)	Mrs. Lemon G. Baker (D)	1857	22
Gandy, Nancy E. Williams (Mrs. Asbury)	Carrie Breese Chandler	1859	28
Garretson, Mary A. (Mrs. George G.)	autobiography	1883	
Garrison, Hepshiba Hendricks (Mrs. I. T.)	Mary Fletcher Woodford (GD) and Belle Fletcher Ellis (GD)	1859	51
Garvey, Berta Alexander (Mrs. Harry O.)	Harry O. Garvey (H)	1875	11
Gaston, Catherine McGhee (Mrs. Robert)	Agnes Forester (GD)	1873	49
Gates, Anna Pearson Caldwell (Mrs. Josiah)	Carrie Gates McClintic (D)	1868	18
Geis, Mary Isadore Cantwell (Mrs. William)	Blanche Heustis Dyar	1870	22
Gilbert, Lovina Glendenning (Mrs. Arthur B.)	unknown	1870	24
Giles, Lucinda Junken (Mrs. William B.)	Ethel M. Giles	1869	15
Gilkeson, Annie C. MacIntosh (Mrs. Allan D.)	autobiography	1856	12
Gill, Grace Arnold (Mrs. G. T.)	Susan B. Proffitt	1878	
Gillette, Ida (Mrs. L. A.)	autobiography	1877	26
Gilmore, Susannah Charlotte O'Dell	Marie Abels	1857	20
Gleason, Anna (Mrs. William H.)	autobiography	1877	26
Gleason, Joanna Ladd Ayer (Mrs. James)	Alice Bowman Gleason (D)	1858	
Gleason, Sally A. (Mrs. J. F.)	Ella Angel (D)	1871	44
Glenn, Harriet Ann Duncan (Mrs. Benjamin)	Mrs. George Glenn		
Goodale, Laura A. Logan (Mrs. John C.)	autobiography	1873	
Gordon, Elizabeth Keyes Lemaster (Mrs. A. W.)	Mrs. McKensie (D)	1870	27
Gordon, Julia Muffly (Mrs. William L.)	autobiography	1872	28
Graham, Mary Hicks (Mrs. James B.)	Minnie Graham Michel (D)	1874	

SUBJECT	SOURCE	EMIGRATION DATE	AGE AT EMIGRATION
Gray, Anna M. Riley (Mrs. Joseph)	autobiography	1870	23
Green, Annie Little (Mrs. John)	unknown	1886	28
Green, Ella Tarleton	Mrs. William Kercher		
Groom, Euphemia Street (Mrs. William H.)	autobiography	1861	8
Groves, Mary Richards (Mrs. William A.)	Susan B. Proffitt	1885	27
Gugler, Elizabeth Weber (Mrs. Jacob)	Pearl Donnelley		
Guild, Pamelia Butts	Gladys Guild (GD)	1863	
Gullikson, Bernhardina Benson Johnson (Mrs. O.)	autobiography	1879	29
Guthrie, Mary Catherine Hester (Mrs. John)	autobiography	1866	29
Hadden, Emily Dupuy (Mrs. Newton M.)	autobiography	1872	23
Haines, Lavina Oiler (Mrs. John C.)	Roberta Zimmerman	1873	
Haines, Mary E. Brown (Mrs. John C.)	Stella B. Haines (D)	1873	21
Hainline, Prue Haun Gordon (Mrs. Henry O.)	Mrs. W. S. Kenyon	1878	15
Haise, Martha Jane (Mrs. George A.)	Decima Beardsley (S)	1875	
Hall, Elizabeth Decker (Mrs. William)	unknown	1857	19
Hamilton, Alena O'Leary (Mrs. Joseph)	Lena N. Latimer	1872	18
Hamilton, Mary O'Leary (Mrs. John W.)	Alena O'Leary Hamilton (S)	1871	
Handy, Emma Chandler	autobiography	1876	
Hanley, Carrie E. Pfeiffer (Mrs. George)	George Hanley (H)	1870	18
Hanna, Margaret Philips (Mrs. B. J. F.)	Lucy Hanna Morgan (D)	1866	40
Harbaugh, Sarah Bogart (Mrs. Valentine)	Edith Lawson	1871	39
Hardman, Ellen Wilford (Mrs. Nathaniel)	Leslye Hardman Womer (D)	1871	20
Harlan, Delilah Hendrix (Mrs. Andrew J.)	Ida Blackburn (GD)	1885	53
Harms, Hannah Aschman (Mrs. B.)	autobiography	1874	1
Harris, Jane Hill (Mrs. Amos Matthews)	India Harris Simmons (D)	1887	52
Haseltine, Louisa Merrick (Mrs. John H.)	Ella Angel	1873	41

SUBJECT	SOURCE	EMIGRATION DATE	AGE AT EMIGRATION
Haseltine, Mary E. Thomas (Mrs. John A.)	autobiography	1878	19
Hatch, Dorathy Hammond (Mrs. Albert O.)	Mrs. W. E. Mort (D)	1872	28
Haun, Elizabeth Best (Mrs. Thomas S.)	Mrs. W. S. Kenyon and Margaret Haun Raser (D)	1878	15
Haun, Notely Ann Blackburn (Mrs. William)	Mrs. W. S. Kenyon	1878	57
Havemann, Mary Carrick (Mrs. Gus)	autobiography	1859	17
Hay, Elizabeth Walton Benedict (Mrs. William)	autobiography	1858	17
Hays, Caroline Pinney (Mrs. George)	Grace Hays Blackburn (D)	1868	35
Heacock, Anna	Ida Heacock Baker (D)	1869	
Healey, Florence I. Curtis (Mrs. Thomas)	autobiography	1887	29
Hedin, Anna Rosander	Mildred Trygg	1869	29
Hedlund, Maria Vaver (Mrs. Pete)	Mildred Trygg	1872	37
Heinselman, Eliza Reynolds (Mrs. Robert)	autobiography	1880	
Hemphill, Mary Jane Carnine (Mrs. James B.)	Cora F. Curry (D)	1868	33
Henshaw, Leah Ellen (Mrs. Barney C.)	unknown	1885	41
Hentschel, Rose Fertemes (Mrs. Cornelius)	Cora Belle Smith	1886	22
Herington, Jane Waters Parkins (Mrs. M. D.)	unknown		
Hiatt, Mary Eleanor Maris (Mrs. Oliver S.)	Effie Hiatt Van Tuyl (D)	1866	26
Hiatt, Sarah Wattles	Helen C. Dallas	1856	
Hildebrand, Louise P. (Mrs. Christian)	Louise P. Lowry	1873	
Hildreth, Mrs. O. B.	Elizabeth Prentis Mack	1871	
Hill, Addie Burrow (Mrs. John)	Hattie Watson Kirkendall	1871	
Hill, Emma G.	autobiography	1873	
Hill, Sarah Prosser (Mrs. John W.)	Jessie Hill Rowland (D)	1872	47
Hills, Alice Dutton (Mrs. Silas Norman)	Frances Hills and Nellie Shepard Waynick	1857	14

SUBJECT	SOURCE	EMIGRATION DATE	AGE AT EMIGRATION
Hinckley, Eliza Hays (Mrs. L. D.)	Grace Hays Blackburn (N)	1860	34
Hinshaw, Sarah Ann Hiatt (Mrs. Andrew)	John E. Hinshaw (SN)	1855	17
Hitchcock, Ellen Simmons (Mrs. Sidney L.)	Mrs. R. J. Truscott	1856	1
Hoag, Ellen D. McConnell (Mrs. Edward)	Elizabeth Prentis Mack	1871	
Hodges, Lydia Ann Hartshorn (Mrs. William)	Mrs. Walter Mason	1869	
Hoffman, Agatha Gantenbein (Mrs. Michael)	unknown	1867	18
Hoffman, Catherine A. Hopkins (Mrs. Christian)	Daisy Hoffman Johntz (D)	1869	11
Hoffman, Mary Frances Welsh (Mrs. L. A.)	autobiography	1857	6
Hoisington, Hannah C. Miller	S. N. Hoisington (SN)	1872	48
Hoisington, S. N.	autobiography	1871	17
Hokanson, Mrs. C. J.	Esther Hawkinson Norstrom (D)	1869	30
Hokanson, Christine	autobiography		
Hollingsworth, Margaret Spencer	Martha Priscilla Spencer (S) and Mrs. F. O. Rindom	1857	11
Holsinger, Fannie	autobiography		
Holsinger, Flora May Gandy (Mrs. William)	Carrie Breese Chandler	1859	2
Holt, Phoebe Jane King (Mrs. Servetus S.)	Elizabeth Holt Mercer (D)	1885	47
Hook, Mary Elizabeth Shuch (Mrs. Rezin H.)	Mata Zimmerman	1857	3
Hoopman, Mary Corbett (Mrs. I. C.)	Edith Lawson	1880	
Horton, Mary Ann Sawyer Prescott (Mrs. Albert)	autobiography	1873	32
Howard, Acasta Roe (Mrs. Porter L.)	unknown	1879	35
Howard, Hannah	Vera A. Pearson (GD)	1866	
Huffman, Della Shaw (Mrs. Joseph T.)	autobiography	1872	6
Huffman, Mattie A. Gilbert	autobiography	1856	1
Hughes, Clara L. Strieby (Mrs. A. J.)	Mary Dillon Miller (D) and Lalla Maloy Brigham	1862	44

SUBJECT	SOURCE	EMIGRATION DATE	AGE AT EMIGRATION
Humphrey, Lydia Betts (Mrs. Eugene)	autobiography	1880	15
Humphrey, Martha Merritt (Mrs. W. Howard)	autobiography	1879	23
Humphrey, Mary Annie Vance (Mrs. James)	Adele Humphrey (D)	1861	23
Hunn, Elizabeth Rebman (Mrs. Joseph J.)	Idella Alderman Anderson	1857	32
Hunt, Clara M. Barber	autobiography	1877	8
Hurst, Anna Galvin (Mrs. Nathaniel)	Florence Lemon (GD)	1873	41
Husband, Ella Williams (Mrs. E. J.)	autobiography	1869	8
Hutchison, Martha Ann Ward Lytle	autobiography	1870	12
Huyler, Mrs. J. W.	Mrs. W. C. Owen	native (b. 1864)	
Idol, Jane Hobbs (Mrs. J. M.)	Mrs. F. M. Pearl	1856	20
Inman, Mrs. Henry	autobiography	1868	
Jackson, Almeda Myers Mullin (Mrs. Mortimer)	Mrs. Harry C. Smith	1873	24
Jackson, Mary	Minnie Jackson Sutton (D) and Izil Polson (GD)	1862	28
Jay, Phoebe Patty (Mrs. Levi)	Mary Alice Jones	1871	41
Jeffcoat, Emily Harrington (Mrs. Amasa)	Pauline Jeffcoat (GD)	1870	32
Jennings, Frances A. (Mrs. W. L.)	Earl W. Jennings (SN) and Ethel Jennings Gebhart (D)	1879	
Jessee, Nancy Weaver (Mrs. William)	unknown	1853	44
John, Nancy J. Woodrum (Mrs. Nathan M.)	Mrs. W. T. John	1870	23
Johnson, Annie Williams (Mrs. S. C.)	Lizzie Johnson Haney	1866	36
Johnson, Ary Phoebus Selsor (Mrs. John J.)	a daughter	1877	37
Johnson, Carolina Erickson Larson (Mrs. Francis)	Carolina, Ida, Otilia and Hanna Johnson (D)	1869	33
Johnson, Eliza Williams (Mrs. Merit)	A. H. Ryon	1860	10
Johnson, Emily Hiddleson (Mrs. W. A.)	autobiography	1871	12

SUBJECT	SOURCE	EMIGRATION DATE	AGE AT EMIGRATION
Johnson, Mariah E. Straight (Mrs. Samuel)	Laura Wells (D)	1870	28
Johnson, Rhoda Newlin (Mrs. William P.)	Lalla Maloy Brigham	1869	23
Jones, Charlotte Wheeler (Mrs. Horace)	Mrs. H. W. Jones (DIL)	1856	26
Jones, Emma M. Davis (Mrs. Joseph R.)	Mabel Gray McNeice	1870	14
Jones, Margaret McClure (Mrs. Mortimer A.)	autobiography	1873	17
Jones, Mary Callahan (Mrs. Benjamin L.)	Ida St. Helens	1870	22
Jones, Melvina Rhoades (Mrs. Ora)	Mrs. Harry C. Smith	1873	32
Justice, Mrs. B. S.	autobiography	1880	
Kackley, Olive	Mrs. F. W. Boyd	1886	5
Kandt, Dorothea Bradow (Mrs. John)	Pearl Donnelley	1859	
Kandt, Fannie Cook (Mrs. A. F.)	Pearl Donnelley	1873	
Kandt, Minnie Brehmer (Mrs. Henry W.)	Pearl Donnelley	1859	8
Keith, Mary Frances Grossman (Mrs. Uri S.)	Minnie Keith Bailey (D)	1863	18
Keller, Mary L. Dickerson (Mrs. L. F.)	autobiography	1871	
Kelley, Josephine Abigail Bates	Mata Zimmerman	1865	19
Kellogg, Florence Shaw (Mrs. Charles H.)	R. S. Kellogg (SN)	1882	31
Kellogg, Susan V. Ames (Mrs. Findley M.)	Mrs. J. C. McArthur	1886	45
Kendrew, Anna Schoonover (Mrs. John)	Ina Myrtle Smith	1878	30
Kenyon, Matilda Best (Mrs. Walton S.)	Mrs. W. S. Kenyon	1882	26
Kenyon, Sarah Burdick (Mrs. Randal J.)	Mrs. W. S. Kenyon	1881	
Kessler, Elizabeth Snyder (Mrs. Michael)	Edith Lawson	1872	
Kimpton, Josephine C. Butler (Mrs. Joseph H.)	Cora Kimpton Hinchman (D)	1858	20
Kindblade, Cinderella M. Soles (Mrs. John F.)	autobiography	1873	30
King, Lydia E. White (Mrs. A. L.)	Agnes King Barry (D)	1875	36
King, Mary Frances Hottle (Mrs. Richard M.)	unknown	1855	12
Kinney, Lurelda Saunders (Mrs. John)	Mrs. L. M. Hart (D)	1860	22

SUBJECT	SOURCE	EMIGRATION DATE	AGE AT EMIGRATION
Kisner, Emma Seever (Mrs. J.)	unknown	1870	16
Kline, Dr. Sarah Miller (Mrs. John B.)	autobiography	1881	30
Knuth, Annie Koepke (Mrs. John)	Pearl Donnelley	1860	7
Kramer, Mary Parnham (Mrs. David Edward)	autobiography	1871	
Krebs, Elizabeth Oelder (Mrs. John)	Maude Griffis	1870	22
Kretuer, Emma B. Weaver (Mrs. Peter F.)	autobiography	1871	4
Ladd, Mina Bailey	autobiography	1875	
Lamb, Martha Carr (Mrs. John W.)	Mrs. George Smith (D)	1859	18
Lane, Ida Koch	autobiography	native (b. 1863)	
Lanning, Sarah Emma Preston (Mrs. Aaron L.)	A. L. Lanning (H)	1857	9
Lape, Fannie Bump (Mrs. William)	Mabel Gray McNeice	1870	11
Lassell, Celia Taylor (Mrs. William H.)	Carrie Lassell Detrick (D)	1878	
Lawless, Minnie A. Taylor (Mrs. George)	autobiography	1885	13
Layne, Clara Hurst (Mrs. O. O.)	autobiography	1885	26
Leahy, Mary Moore (Mrs. James G.)	Elizabeth Leahy (D) and Mrs. J. S. Bird	1879	
Lecleve, Mrs. A. S.	Annette Lecleve Botkin (D)	1873	
Lee, Anna Jane Seece (Mrs. John)	unknown	1870	32
Leidigh, Catherine Anne Myers (Mrs. Jacob)	Mrs. I. V. Stewart (D)	1870	30
Leonard, Juliette Lane (Mrs. Lot)	Mary Leonard Chandler (D)	1859	18
Leonard, Kate Adeline Withers (Mrs. Thomas)	Eva Morley Murphy	1885	32
Leonard, Martha Walton (Mrs. Morgan R.)	unknown	1857	23
Lewis, Martha Jane Baird (Mrs. H. M.)	unknown	1867	21
Lewis, Mary Kinney (Mrs. Cary M.)	Frances Lewis Dawson (D)	1873	22
Lindberg, Carolina Carlson (Mrs. Carl)	C. O. Lindberg	1869	
Lindsay, Fannie Batchelor (Mrs. Joseph M.)	William Allen White	1877	27

SUBJECT	SOURCE	EMIGRATION DATE	AGE AT EMIGRATION
Little, Harriet Z. Adams (Mrs. William E.)	O. W. Little (SN)	1866	
Littler, Susan Free Satchel (Mrs. Nation)	Ella Littler Vale (D)		
Lloyd, Ellen Jones (Mrs. Thomas S.)	autobiography	1872	29
Lobdell, Roxanna Godding (Mrs. Darius J.)	Myrtle Lobdell Fogelburg (D)	1857	22
Lockard, Mary Isabel Gettys (Mrs. R. M.)	autobiography	1870	13
Logan, Belle McNair	autobiography	1872	14
Logan, Eliza A. Martin	autobiography	1872	14
Logan, Mary Elizabeth Beck (Mrs. Jeremiah)	Mary Ann Logan Norris (D)	1859	19
Lohman, Katherine Dumler (Mrs. John)	Berta DeWald		
Long, Harriet Marie Sage (Mrs. David B.)	Cora Belle Long Roth (D)	1866	26
Long, Lou May Beall (Mrs. Arthur)	Cora Belle Smith		
Lorry, Marie E. Roland (Mrs. Claude)	Lily Bowers Crampton	1870	48
Loucks, Amy M. Sturtevant (Mrs. William P.)	C. A. Loucks (SN)	1879	36
Loughstreth, Alice M. Hand (Mrs. Charles)	Mrs. W. D. O'Loughlin	1869	27
Lundstrom, Greta J. Larson (Mrs. Fred)	Mrs. Frank Lindberg	1868	
Lyon, Mary M. Cornell (Mrs. Daniel)	autobiography	1872	32
Lyons, Lydia Edwina Smith (Mrs. William D.)	autobiography	1857	1
Lyons, Sarah A. Gray Bush (Mrs. Horace G.)	autobiography	1857	13
Macredie, Janet Jameson (Mrs. Thomas L.)	unknown	1870	16
Mahoney, Margaret Howard (Mrs. Jeremiah)	Edith Lawson		
Maichel, Mary Cresence Berhalter (Mrs. Joseph)	Mrs. A. E. Topping	1856	21
Mallows, Sarah Scott (Mrs. Samuel)	Mrs. Fred Massey	1865	16
Malone, Carrie Murphy (Mrs. Frank)	autobiography	1866	3
Malone, Emily (Mrs. Andrew J.)	Mrs. L. J. Morris	1878	41
Maloy, Paralee Ray (Mrs. John)	Lalla Maloy Brigham (D)	1861	20
Mann, Adelaide Louise Dunham (Mrs. Stillman)	Florence Lemmons (GD)	1878	36

SUBJECT	SOURCE	EMIGRATION DATE	AGE AT EMIGRATION
Marcks, Sarah Ann Hittell (Mrs. Willoughby M.)	Lillie Marcks Coffin (D)	1869	29
Marcy, Jennie Counts	autobiography	1877	
Margreiter, Katherine Springer (Mrs. Jacob)	Ella Angel	1870	
Marsh, Caroline Coberly (Mrs. John W.)	autobiography	1856	7
Marsh, Rebecca Rocky (Mrs. William A.)	Clara May Marsh Hawes (D)	1878	
Marshall, Adelaide L. (Mrs. Samuel)	Mae Marshall Topping (D)	1856	20
Marshall, Emma Sells (Mrs. Charles J.)	autobiography		
Martin, Caroline Martin (Mrs. William J.)	autobiography	1857	3
Martin, Mary Elizabeth Hill (Mrs. W. W.)	Cora Belle Smith	1887	29
Matthews, Charles T.	Mrs. H. L. Hart (S)	1874	23
Mauk, Eliza F. (Mrs. George)	Sarah Steele (D)	1868	
McAdam, Isabell Buzzi (Mrs. Thomas)	Ema Parker Redd	1872	5
McAllister, Mary E. (Mrs. Silas)	H. M. Fletcher (SNIL)	1878	27
McAtee, Etta Clyde Kelley (Mrs. Charles W.)	autobiography	native (b. 1868)	
McCabe, Mrs. Bernard	autobiography	1866	16
McCarthy, Minerva Reed (Mrs. Eugene)	unknown	1871	
McClanahan, Mrs. Charles	Mrs. G. L. Glenn	1850s	
McComb, Elizabeth Anne Simmon (Mrs. Samuel)	autobiography	1875	13
McConnell, Rosella Levett (Mrs. Oscar)	Mary McConnell Graham (D)	1862	32
McCord, Priscilla F. Davis (Mrs. R. D.)	Eula McCord Fletcher (D)	1872	25
McCulloch, Sarah Wilkerson (Mrs. J. P.)	Mrs. H. W. Andrews (D)	1870	35
McDowell, Cordelia Niles (Mrs. John S.)	autobiography	1874	27
McFarland, Matilda Steele (Mrs. James D.)	autobiography	1860	8
McGee, Katie R. Hammond	autobiography	1871	4
Mrs. W. J. McGeorge	Lalla Maloy Brigham	1870	
McIntosh, James	autobiography	1879	

SUBJECT	SOURCE	EMIGRATION DATE	AGE AT EMIGRATION
McKitrick, Clara Moorhead (Mrs. Noah A.)	autobiography	1870	23
McKune, Kate Miller (Mrs. Silas)	autobiography	1878	22
McNeice, Mabel Gray (Mrs. William R.)	autobiography	native (b. 1885)	
McTaggart, Maggie Annis Beigle (Mrs. Daniel)	Mabel Gray McNeice	1869	29
Meall, Eliza Waples (Mrs. Dewar)	Mrs. John Kyle	1871	40
Middlekauf, Josephine (Mrs. Joseph H.)	autobiography	1867	
Milburn, Emma Jane Whaley (Mrs. Hosea M.)	Cora Belle Smith	1871	15
Miller, Catherine Boone (Mrs. Charles H.)	autobiography	1872	17
Miller, Clarinda Dawson (Mrs. Alexander R.)	Eva Miller Hill (D)	1859	24
Miller, Della Huff (Mrs. Fred)	Ella Angel	1872	15
Miller, Mary McNee (Mrs. Arch)	Pearle Miller	1865	28
Miller, Ninnie B. Newby (Mrs. John J.)	autobiography	1884	
Miner, Eliza Smith (Mrs. Selden)	unknown	1880	41
Missimer, Mary Jones (Mrs. Samuel)	Edith Lawson	1873	
Mitchell, Addie Parsons (Mrs. M. L.)	autobiography	native (b. 1868)	
Mitchell, Amanda Fitzland Moore (Mrs. John D.)	Elizabeth Mitchell Petro (D)	1870	
Moden, Maja Anderson (Mrs. Daniel)	unknown	1868	32
Moore, Kate Dunsworth (Mrs. Nathan)	autobiography	1885	
Moore, Malvina Utt (Mrs. Wiley)	Emma Tennat (S)	1859	16
Morgan, Anna Brewster (Mrs. James)	autobiography		
Morgan, Mabel Dean (Mrs. Jesse C.)	Cora Belle Smith	1886	15
Morgan, Mary Turley (Mrs. Levi G.)	Cora Belle Smith		
Morgan, Minnie D. Yoast (Mrs. William H.)	W. Y. Morgan (SN)	1869	29
Morrison, Mary Belle Metcalf (Mrs. Henry R.)	autobiography	1884	27
Morse, Emma Wattles	Helen C. Dallas	1856	
Moser, Ida Saxton	autobiography	native (b. 1861)	

SUBJECT	SOURCE	EMIGRATION DATE	AGE AT EMIGRATION
Muck, Melina Heft (Mrs. John)	unknown	1872	43
Murphy, Eva Maria Morely (Mrs. Eugene F.)	autobiography	1887	29
Murphy, Jane Black (Mrs. Aidan)	Florence Lemmons (GD)	1878	36
Murphy, Mrs. Thomas	Carrie Lassell Detrick	1872	
Myers, Catherine Younkin (Mrs. Daniel H.)	Ada L. Miller (D)	1860	23
Myers, Harriet Beebe (Mrs. William B.)	Laura M. French	1885	51
Myers, Kathryn Elizabeth Wynn	autobiography	1871	15
Myers, Mary Guthrie (Mrs. Lewis K.)	Mrs. W. M. Martin (D)	1871	31
Neibling, Elizabeth Jane Swartz (Mrs. Jeremiah)	Mata Zimmerman	1863	31
Neifert, Mary E. Gants (Mrs. I. F.)	unknown	1871	15
Neifert, Melina Jane Reed (Mrs. Jake)	unknown	1871	
Neil, Catherine Jane Heberling (Mrs. George)	unknown	1856	9
Nelson, Carolina Peterson (Mrs. Johannes)	autobiography	1869	25
Nelon, Stina Maria Graberg (Mrs. John)	Mrs. Frank Lindberg	1868	
New, Emma Mitchell (Mrs. J. Homer)	autobiography	1877	26
Nichols, Hannah M. Scott (Mrs. James R.)	Guilford Scott Nichols (SN)	1872	23
Nichols, Sarah Milmine (Mrs. John L.)	unknown	1871	34
Nincehelser, Minnie Wendorff (Mrs. William)	May Ellen Nincehelser (D)	native (b. 1860)	
Nixon, Almon C.	autobiography		
Norstrom, Anna Swenson (Mrs. C. F.)	Marie Norstrom Linneer (D) and Anna Norstrom Helberg (D)	1868	22
Norton, Elizabeth Coughlan (Mrs. William)	Minnie Norton and Carrie Breese Chandler	1854	
Norton, Hannah Oliver (Mrs. H. S.)	unknown	1871	
Norton, Rhoda Rolfe (Mrs. Alexandra H.)	Mrs. John S. Morrell (GD)	1871	28
Noyes, Caroline	autobiography	1866	15

SUBJECT	SOURCE	EMIGRATION DATE	AGE AT EMIGRATION
Nuzum, Sarah Sifers (Mrs. Edgar)	Mata Zimmerman	1857	33
Oberholser, Harriet Galbraith (Mrs. Harlan)	Rose M. Coffin	1878	13
O'Brien, Jennie Broughton (Mrs. John)	Mabel Gray McNeice	1870	17
Oliver, Josephine Gustafson (Mrs. Carl A.)	unknown	1885	35
Oliver, Sarah Jayne (Mrs. George B.)	Katherine Elspeth Oliver (D)	1868	32
O'Loughlin, Mrs. John H.	autobiography	1879	9
O'Loughlin, Mary V. Farrell (Mrs. John)	Mrs. W. D. O'Loughlin	1871	11
Olson, Anna (Mrs. Anders M.)	Christine Olson Johnson (D)	1869	32
Olson, Margaret Williamson (Mrs. W. C.)	autobiography	1879	35
Olsson, Anna L. Johnson (Mrs. Olof)	Mrs. Frank Lindberg and Mrs. F. O. Johnson	1869	28
Osborn, Mrs. Stephen J.	autobiography	1879	
Ostlund, Susan Ida Moss (Mrs. J. H.)	autobiography	1878	12
Ott, Justina Schieve (Mrs. Christian M.)	Mrs. Walter Mason	1856	18
Overfield, Margaret Fergusson (Mrs. Thomas)	Mabel Gray McNeice	1854	23
Owen, Mary Tedstone (Mrs. Charles)	Dora Kingman	1866	23
Owen, Olive Packard (Mrs. William)	autobiography	1857	15
Owen, Sarah Ann Howe (Mrs. William)	Lucille Owen (D)	native (b. 1860)	
Pagenkopf, Mrs. Gotlop	Pearl Donnelley		
Painter, Bettie C. Robbins (Mrs. D. H.)	Lalla Maloy Brigham	native (b. 1850s)	
Painter, Emily Hackworth (Mrs. R. M.)	Mrs. E. E. Pinnick (D)	1884	39
Palmer, Olive (Mrs. Arthur T.)	Carlotta Palmer Detwiler	1876	
Palmer, Rebecca	Helen C. Dallas	1858	
Palmquist, Brita Lisa	C. Palmquist	1870	49
Pappan, Julie Gonvil (Mrs. Louis)	Charles Curtis	native (b. 1800)	
Parent, Eliza Jennie Dobson (Mrs. Ephraim)	autobiography	1870	20

SUBJECT	SOURCE	EMIGRATION DATE	AGE AT EMIGRATION
Park, Phoebe Ann Lowrey (Mrs. Fernando)	autobiography	1870	31
Parker, Celestia Gregg Melvin	Nellie Zimmerman (GD)	1869	
Parker, Emma Woodward (Mrs. M. V. B.)	Mrs. Walter Mason	1868	
Parker, Katherine Mills (Mrs. Roswell)	Lydia Gardner Willard	1858	20
Parnham, Margaret (Mrs. Charles)	Delbert Parnham (SN)	1871	
Parrott, Mrs. Fred	Mrs. George T. Drake and	1871	
	Mrs. C. F. Mulvane		
Parsons, Catherine A. Houston (Mrs. Luke)	Addie Parsons Mitchell (D)	1854	11
Paulen, Lucy B. Johnson (Mrs. Jacob)	Ben S. Paulen		
Pearl, Margaret C. White (Mrs. Thomas J.)	Mrs. T. C. Nelson (D)	1873	16
	Mrs. J. C. Hart (D)		
Pearson, Carrie (Mrs. Andrew)	Vera A. Pearson (GD)	1868	
Pearson, Elsie A. Howard (Mrs. John)	Vera A. Pearson (D)	1866	
Peaslee, Elizabeth Smith (Mrs. Don A.)	autobiography	1870	
Pennel, Bithia Yoxall (Mrs. W. M.)	autobiography	1872	20
Perigo, Lannie Frost (Mrs. J. G.)	autobiography		
Perring, Mary E. Whaley (Mrs. Charles C.)	Bertha Perring Taylor (D)	1872	20
Peterson, Hattie E. Moon (Mrs. Frank A.)	autobiography	1873	1
Philip, Jane Hardie (Mrs. George)	autobiography	1873	
Phillippy, Minnie S. M. Nelson (Mrs. Isaac)	autobiography	native (b. 1871)	
Phillips, Lucretia Spencer	Martha Priscilla Spencer (S) and	1861	17
	Mrs. F. O. Rindom		
Pickering, Rosanna Done Ferguson	Mary Ferguson Sibbitt (D)	1869	
Pierson, Nancy Annette Shaw (Mrs. George)	Salome A. Blair (D)	1876	52
Pinkston, Sarah A. Lyon Mack (Mrs. Ephraim)	Carrie Breese Chandler	1854	17
Platt, Mrs. John W.	Lucy Platt Stants (D)	native (b. 1857)	

SUBJECT	SOURCE	EMIGRATION DATE	AGE AT EMIGRATION
Plumb, Martha Jane Yates (Mrs. John B.)	Carrie Louise Plumb Talbot (D) and Lily Powers Crampton	1870s	30s
Plummer, Theoline (Mrs. L. N.)	autobiography	1869	21
Poff, Mary Ellen Medearis (Mrs. Joseph A.)	Grace E. Poff (D)	1870	34
Polley, Mary Akins Flinn (Mrs. J. H.)	Mrs. Ransom Mundell (D)	1854	
Poor, Frances Jordon	autobiography	1870	
Porter, Emily Wingfield (Mrs. Elmer)	Sylvia M. Porter Haucke (D)	1872	12
Potts, Elizabeth A. G. Brander (Mrs. William)	Issie B. Potts (D)	1866	23
Pracht, Marinda F. Pratt (Mrs. Frederick)	Rella Pracht Stotts (D)	1860	11
Prenninger, Mrs. M.	Mrs. James Humes (D)	1871	
Prentis, Caroline Edwards Cambell (Mrs. Noble)	autobiography		
Prentiss, Anna Julia Soule (Mrs. Selvester B.)	autobiography	1855	13
Preston, Margaret J. Robinson (Mrs. Thomas)	A. L. Lanning (SNIL)	1857	35
Pringle, Louise Gear (Mrs. Robert)	Berenice Wilson		
Pritchard, Annie Pierce (Mrs. Levi)	autobiography	1879	33
Proffitt, Susan Burcham (Mrs. Evert J.)	autobiography		
Prouty, Mrs. H. W.	H. W. Prouty (H)	1871	
Pruitt, Mary J.	Luverna Williamson	1869	21
Rarick, Lavina H. Harper (Mrs. Orin S.)	unknown	1870s	30s
Ray, Marietta Drocon (Mrs. Luke E.)	Lalla Maloy Brigham	1862	42
Reader, Elizabeth Smith (Mrs. Samuel James)	Elizabeth Reader (D)	1867	
Reader, Samuel James	Elizabeth Reader (D)	1855	19
Reckards, Martha S. Murphy (Mrs. Marshall)	Edwin Morris Reckards (SN)	1865	21
Records, Lucinda Cadwell	Fannie A. Hunter (GD)	1868	
Rector, Mary Elizabeth DuVal (Mrs. Nathan)	Vonnie Rector Griffith (D)	1872	30
Rees, Nancy Goodwin (Mrs. John)	Mrs. Sherman G. Rees (DIL)	1866	

SUBJECT	SOURCE	EMIGRATION DATE	AGE AT EMIGRATION
Reese, Mrs. G. A.	autobiography	1870	17
Reinhardt, Henrietta Buettner (Mrs. Herman)	unknown	1871	
Remington, Emma Adair (Mrs. J. B.)	autobiography	1854	7
Render, family	Mrs. Leo Gibbens		
Ricards, Harriet Louise Jones (Mrs. Benjamin)	Maude Ricards Riddle	1874	28
Rice, Alazinia (Mrs. Perry)	Ella Angel	1870	31
Rice, Roxana E. Miller Crowe (Mrs. Martin)	autobiography	1880	47
Rich, Hannah Hinshaw (Mrs. Richard)	Stephen H. Rich (SN)	1860	55
Richmond, Florence (Mrs. R. A.)	autobiography	1879	
Rickart, Hattie Brown (Mrs. Curtis H.)	Cora Belle Smith	1887	15
Ridings, Lucy Jane Manly (Mrs. Isaac)	Georgie N. Howard	1884	
Right, Eliza Rathburn (Mrs. R. M.)	Ella Strieby Right	1860	50s
Ringberg, Mary Lundquist	autobiography	1870	13
Ringeisen, Katherine Bonard (Mrs. William)	autobiography	1872	24
Ringle, Jane Morris (Mrs. Daniel)	Ida St. Helens	1860	24
Robbins, Mrs. James A.	Lalla Maloy Brigham	1850s	
Roberts, Huldah E. Fairholm (Mrs. John W.)	Mary M. Roberts (D)	1859	37
Robinson, Julia G. (Mrs. A. W.)	autobiography	1876	
Robinson, Sara T. D. Lawrence	C. S. Finch	1854	27
Robinson, Sarah	Alice Boyd	1879	
Rockwell, Julia Snyder (Mrs. Bertrand)	autobiography	1867	17
Rockwood, Martha J. Hunt (Mrs. William W.)	Mrs. W. M. Keyser (D)	1867	28
Rodocker, Mattie E.	autobiography	1876	
Rogers, Anna Wood (Mrs. John G.)	autobiography		
Rorabaugh, Mrs. Everett	autobiography	1872	
Rouse, Hazel Macdonald (Mrs. Benjamin A.)	autobiography	native (b. 1886)	

SUBJECT	SOURCE	EMIGRATION DATE	AGE AT EMIGRATION
Rouse, Mary Amelia Rarick (Mrs. Mayo)	autobiography	1871	10
Rouse, Mary Saunders (Mrs. Wallace T.)	autobiography	1876	17
Rowe, Margaret E. Smith	autobiography	1868	
Royal, Minnie Miller (Mrs. James P.)	autobiography	1869	13
Royston, Margaret E. Timmerman (Mrs. Amos C.)	Luverna Williamson	1876	26
Rucker, Katie E. Austin	autobiography	1872	
Ruggles, Susanna Spencer	Martha Priscilla Spencer (S) and Mrs. F. O. Rindom	1857	25
Rugh, Caroline Heim (Mrs. Christian)	C. E. Rugh (SN)	1878	47
Ruppenthal, Anna Barbara Immendorf (Mrs. Jacob)	J. C. Ruppenthal (SN)	1877	37
Ryon, Mary Bush (Mrs. A. H.)	A. H. Ryon (H)	1872	25
Sain, Betsy Anne Griffin (Mrs. L. G.)	Carrie Sain Whittaker (D)	1859	38
St. Denis, Caroline Burlon (Mrs. Gideon)	Una M. Kessler	1871	40
St. John, Aura Viola Stanton (Mrs. Marsena)	autobiography	1858	25
St. John, Susan Parker (Mrs. John P.)	Mrs. Walter Mason	1869	
Salathiel, Jemima Corel (Mrs. John)	Ida St. Helens	1855	13
Sands, Isabel (Mrs. Charles A.)	Harriet Davis	1865	
Sands, Isabella (Mrs. Charles)	Lem A. Woods	1856	31
Sanner, Hattie	autobiography	1872	
Sapp, Jasper S.	unknown	1884	
Satterfield, Elizabeth Baysinger Craig	Margaret Frost (D)	1866	
Savage, Amanda Crandall (Mrs. Joseph)	Susan Daphne Savage Alford (D)	1855	29
Savage, Mary Burgess (Mrs. Joseph)	Susan Daphne Savage Alford		
Sawyer, Elvira L. Putnam (Mrs. Thomas G.)	Mary Sawyer Monroe (D)	1888	27
Sayre, Martha Adaline Piles (Mrs. Richard)	Charles A. Sayre (SN)	1865	27
Schmidt, Lucy Ann Thompson (Mrs. John F.)	Mrs. W. B. Clark	1855	19

SUBJECT	SOURCE	EMIGRATION DATE	AGE AT EMIGRATION
Scholl, Rebecca Gansil (Mrs. George)	Ella Angel	1874	28
Scott, Lilian	Jennie C. Marcy	1870s	
Segreves, Louise Lee (Mrs. P. H.)	Mrs. J. A. Decher		
Selder, Augusta Noyes (Mrs. J. W.)	Caroline L. Noyes	1866	
Sellers, Anna	Berenice Wilson		
Severson, Anne (Mrs. Ole)	unknown	1879	
Shafer, Mattie Jane Jessee (Mrs. Leonard)	unknown	1854	11
Shaffer, Sarah Ann Stoke (Mrs. Charles)	Edith Lawson	1872	27
Shaft, Jane Parker (Mrs. William G.)	Jessie Shaft Cope (D)	1857	37
Sharp, Nancy Landrum (Mrs. John)	Mary Leonard Chandler	1860	
Shaw, Grace Eva Hilliker (Mrs. Thomas J.)	Lenore Shaw Bland (D)	1873	15
Shaw, Prudence Tyler	Bertha B. Moore (N)	1877	
Shean, Anstress Dudley	Mrs. C. S. Finch	1857	
Shearer, Matilda Netz (Mrs. George)	Minnie N. Campbell (D)	1878	41
Shelden, Mary Lamb (Mrs. Alvah)	autobiography	1869	13
Shellenbarger, Amanda Spencer	Martha Priscilla Spencer (S) and Mrs. F. O. Rindom	1857	
Shepard, Daphne Dutton (Mrs. H. D.)	Nellie Shepard Waynick (D)	1857	9
Shepherd, Millie Birdsall (Mrs. Augustus)	Jessie F. Taylor (D)	1879	
Shreves, Vesta Westgate (Mrs. John G.)	autobiography	1879	
Sibbit, Mary Ferguson	autobiography	1869	11
Silver, Mrs. William	Mrs. H. J. Merten (D)	1850s	
Simmons, India Harris (Mrs. H. E.)	autobiography	1887	
Simmons, Mary Adeline Garrett (Mrs. H. N.)	Carrie Breese Chandler	1867	27
Simons, Jennie B. Gowdy (Mrs. Adolphus E.)	W. C. Simons	1878	42

SUBJECT	SOURCE	EMIGRATION DATE	AGE AT EMIGRATION
Simpson, Flora Lord (Mrs. John P.)	autobiography	1874	
Simpson, Sarah	Helen C. Dallas		
Skelton, Anne Holtby (Mrs. Joseph)	Edith Skelton Spaulding (D)	1879	30
Skelton, Jessie (Mrs. John)	autobiography	1879	
Slaven, Emily Candace Williams (Mrs. James)	autobiography	1871	16
Slocum, Elizabeth King (Mrs. George W.)	Florence Slocum Mayrath (D)	1873	24
Smalley, Ellen Rice (Mrs. Joseph)	Verlie Snyder White (GD)	1854	1
Smith, Alice M. Stewart (Mrs. Harry C.)	autobiography	1883	
Smith, Mrs. Alvin	Minnie Smith (D)	1871	
Smith, Caroline Abbott (Mrs. I. S.)	autobiography	1855	
Smith, Carrie Stearns	autobiography	1867	
Smith, Catherine (Mrs. Benjamin)	Mrs. R. D. Hunter (D)	1876	
Smith, Emma Brumfield (Mrs. Coleman)	Mrs. George Bolton (D)	1864	29
Smith, Emma Louisa Leonard (Mrs. E. T.)	autobiography	1879	30
Smith, Luna Collins (Mrs. Edward C.)	Mata Zimmerman	native (b. 1868)	
Smith, Mary Loque Brighton (Mrs. W. F.)	Ida St. Helens	1868	25
Smith, Sarah Elizabeth Reed Conn (Mrs. B. E.)	George L. Conn (SN)	1874	37
Smith, Susan Currier (Mrs. John M.)	autobiography	1874	31
Snyder, Frances Charlotte Jillson (Mrs. Elias)	Verlie Snyder White (D)	1858	13
Snyder, Grace L.	unknown		
Southwick, Caroline Curran (Mrs. Albert)	Mrs. Mabel White	1875	30
Sowers, Ann M. A. Rose (Mrs. William)	Mrs. George Sowers (DIL)	1860	26
Spalding, Margaret Wilson (Mrs. E. L.)	J. C. Ruppenthal (SNIL)	1858	14
Sparks, H. A. Brooks (Mrs. Morris E.)	autobiography	1871	15
Speck, Sarah Eleanor Armfield	George Remsbury	1855	25

SUBJECT	SOURCE	EMIGRATION DATE	AGE AT EMIGRATION
Spencer, Martha Priscilla	Margaret Feather (N)	1861	11
Spencer, Mary	Martha Priscilla Spencer (S) and Mrs. F. O. Rindom	1857	
Spencer, Sarah	unknown	1857	
Sponable, Myra Dudley Shean (Mrs. John W.)	unknown	1857	15
Springer, Mary (Mrs. Warren)	unknown		
Staatz, Friederika Oesterreich (Mrs. Charlie)	Pearl Donnelley	1857	19
Staatz, Maria Gantenbein (Mrs. John)	Daisy Hoffman Johntz	1868	21
Staley, Sarah Brown (Mrs. Edwin)	Elizabeth Davis Staley	1855	11
Stearnes, Mary	Helen C. Dallas		
Steele, Hance	Amelia Steele	1876	
Steinberger, Lou Flory (Mrs. George)	Berenice Wilson	1887	
Stevens, Irena R. Babcock (Mrs. Hestor C.)	autobiography	native (b. 1876)	
Stevens, Susan P. (Mrs. J. T.)	Clara Seagondollar	1864	
Stewart, Emma Shearon (Mrs. Will J.)	autobiography	1869	14
Stewart, Margaret Bigger (Mrs. Samuel)	Robert Bigger Stewart (SN)	1887	35
Stilley, Margaret Springs (Mrs. W. T.)	Carrie McClintic	1869	21
Stinson, Julia Ann Beauchemie (Mrs. Thomas N.)	Lenore Monroe Stratton	native (b. 1834)	
Stolp, Ottilie Therese Johannette (Mrs. Paul)	Theodore Stolp, B. D. (SN)	native (b. 1876)	
Stotts, Adeline Howell (Mrs. Ebenezer)	Carrie Breese Chandler		
Stotts, Elizabeth Dorsey (Mrs. Ebenezer)	Carrie Breese Chandler	1857	19
Stotts, Sarah A. Benbow (Mrs. Ebenezer)	Carrie Breese Chandler		
Stoughton, Martha J. Davis (Mrs. A. E.)	Elizabeth Davis Staley	native (b. 1863)	
Stratford, Jennie Long (Mrs. Edward D.)	Jessie Perry Stratford	1870	13
Strieby, Caroline Wright (Mrs. C. H.)	Ella Strieby Bash	1860	11
Strode, Mary L. (Mrs. George W.)	Una M. Kessler	1860s	40s

SUBJECT	SOURCE	EMIGRATION DATE	AGE AT EMIGRATION
Strong, Hannah	Helen C. Dallas	1858	
Stuart, Phoebe Wooton (Mrs. Ivy)	Ella Angel	1871	15
Sudendorf, Lizette W. Lance (Mrs. Herman H.)	Leila Sudendorf Rearwin (GD)	1859	32
Sutton, Mrs. W. R.	Alice Sutton McGeorge	1873	
Swarts, Mary Jane P. Allison (Mrs. Benjamin)	Mildred S. Swarts (GD)	1869	45
Swenson, Ida Charlotte Axelson (Mrs. S. P.)	Mrs. Melvin R. Guard (D)	1876	16
Swenson, Irene Arrabella Dexter (Mrs. Eric)	Geneva S. Oberg, Otis D. Swenson and Wilbur E. Swenson	1863	3
Swenson, Mrs. J. Alfred	autobiography	1869	6
Tacha, Kate Heilman (Mrs. Godfrey)	autobiography	1873	
Tallman, Lillian	autobiography		
Taylor, Lyda Duncan (Mrs. George)	Mabel Gray McNeice	1870	15
Taylor, Minerva Thompson (Mrs. Joseph)	Mata Zimmerman	1858	33
Taylor, Minnie Waters (Mrs. Norton)	Jennie C. Marcy	1869	18
Thomas, Emma Alice Sargent (Mrs. Charles)	Nellie Thomas Goss (D)	1871	27
Thomas, Mary Elizabeth Sparks (Mrs. D. W.)	Olive Thomas (N)	1873	30
Thomas, Olive Elizabeth Gringsby (Mrs. Robert)	Olive Thomas (D)	1873	24
Thompson, Emeline Merriam (Mrs. Henry C.)	Mata Zimmerman	1840s	30s
Thompson, Matilda Ann Thompson (Mrs. William)	Gertrude Myers (D)	1856	14
Tisdale, Betsy Ann Bangs (Mrs. Henry)	Mrs. C. S. Finch	1862	30
Toothaker, Lydia E. Murphy (Mrs. William H.)	autobiography	1859	
Train, Christina Magnuson (Mrs. John)	Otilia Johnson Train	1869	25
Trego, Alice Manington (Mrs. J. H.)	Helen C. Dallas	1857	
Troutman, Marcia Gordon (Mrs. James A.)	unknown	native (b. 1860)	
Turner, Henrietta Stoddard	autobiography	1871	

SUBJECT	SOURCE	EMIGRATION DATE	AGE AT EMIGRATION
Turner, Rebecca Andrew (Mrs. William)	unknown	1874	29
Turner, Sarah Jayne Cook (Mrs. William H.)	Mrs. Edwin A. Tufts	1850s	
Tygart, Ida May Jenkins (Mrs. John M.)	autobiography	1883	22
Underwood, Juliet Planck (Mrs. W. H.)	autobiography	1873	27
Unsell, Martha J. Newby (Mrs. James W.)	Minnie Newby Miller (SN)	1884	
Vallette, Emily Woods (Mrs. H. F.)	unknown	1871	
Van Atta, Rebecca Jane (Mrs. John A.)	John R. Van Atta (SN), Merle Van Atta Gates (D), Mary E. Van Atta (D) and Rebecca Van Atta Allen (D)	1871	
Van Meter, Frances M. (Mrs. B. R.)	Mrs. Lambert (D)	1871	
Van Natta, Emma Arminta Shawhan (Mrs. Jacob)	Lillian S. Smith (D)	1860	20
Van Ness, Eliza Spencer	Martha Priscilla Spencer (S) and Mrs. F. O. Rindom	1857	
Vannoy, Sarah Jane Luster (Mrs. John)	Mrs. Charles Houston	1867	
Van Zile, Mary Louise Pierce (Mrs. Gilbert J.)	autobiography	native (b. 1872)	
Venable, Lina Canfield (Mrs. James)	autobiography	1878	20
Verbeck, Isabelle Walker (Mrs. George I.)	autobiography		
Vickstrand, Maria Carlson (Mrs. Nels)	Hannah Vickstrand	1868	
Viets, Adelheit Grother (Mrs. John)	autobiography	1867	21
Volker, Minnie Sanders (Mrs. Henry)	Mrs. Henry Volker, Jr. (DIL)	1878	48
Von Schriltz, Mrs. B. S.	Ethel M. Bosley (D)	1884	27
Wagaman, Sarah A. Cullum	autobiography	1871	
Wahl, Barbara Graw (Mrs. Jacob)	autobiography	1872	32
Wait, Anna Amelia Churchill (Mrs. Walter S.)	unknown	1871	34
Wallace, Louise Bigham (Mrs. Albert R.)	Myra Wallace Hinshaw (D)	1875	4

SUBJECT	SOURCE	EMIGRATION DATE	AGE AT EMIGRATION
Wallace, Sena Hartzell (Mrs. William W.)	autobiography	1889	41
Walter, Harriet E. Cowle Bockoven (Mrs. W. T.)	autobiography	native (b. 1873)	
Ward, Jennie M. (Mrs. M. L.)	Verlie Snyder White	1870	
Wardell, Carolina Backlund (Mrs. Vivat E.)	Esther Wardell Bengston (D)	1868	29
Warkentin, Mrs. Bernard	Elizabeth Prentis Mack	1875	
Washburn, Alice Jane Hurt (Mrs. William)	Elizabeth H. Webb (D)	1877	27
Waterman, Alma L. (Mrs. J. H.)	autobiography	1880	25
Watkins, Martha Ann Faulconer (Mrs. James)	Haysie Watkins McLoon (D)	1865	20
Watson, Caroline Morehouse (Mrs. James F.)	Carrie M. Watson	1858	
Watson, Eva C. Agrelius	Mildred Trygg	1872	34
Watson, Mary J. Burrow (Mrs. A. J.)	Hattie Watson Kirkendall	1871	
Watson, Saluda B. F. Christian (Mrs. Robert)	Gertrude Millicent Evans Hoad (GD)	1850s	
Watson, Sarah Jane Williams (Mrs. Aaron B.)	Mrs. L. L. Chandler	1859	19
Wattles, Sarah	Helen C. Dallas	1856	
Weaver, Ivy Henderson King	autobiography	native (b. 1872)	
Weidenheimer, Myrtle Hummer (Mrs. George)	Minnie A. Taylor Lawless	1871	8
Weir, Sarah J. M. Coon (Mrs. Frank)	Cora Belle Smith	1879	25
Wells, Katie Hammatt (Mrs. John)	Alena Hamilton	1870	20
Wentworth, Charlotte B. Mills (Mrs. Hiram)	Everett M. Wentworth (SN)	1871	35
White, Genorie B.	autobiography	1886	
White, Mary Ann Hatton (Mrs. Allen)	William Allen White (SN)	1864	34
White, Nancy C. Collins (Mrs. I. M.)	Mata Zimmerman	1855	10
White, Sarah J. Hammond (Mrs. W. H.)	autobiography	1859	8
Whiting, Katherine Amelia Whitney (Mrs. A. B.)	A. B. Whiting	1859	21
Whitney, Anna Eliza Holmes (Mrs. William C.)	Ella Angel	1871	46
Whitney, Fannie Halliday (Mrs. Oliver)	W. C. Whitney (SN)	1869	28

SUBJECT	SOURCE	EMIGRATION DATE	AGE AT EMIGRATION
Whitney, Josephine Parnell (Mrs. Oliver C.)	Edna Whitney Edwards (D)	1857	21
Whitright, Mary Dilla Evans (Mrs. Joseph)	autobiography	1875	14
Wickham, Pauline Floeder (Mrs. C. H.)	autobiography	1862	2
Wickins, Margaret Ray (Mrs. Thomas K.)	Nannie Bingham	1876	33
Williams, Julia Hoisington (Mrs. Milton)	S. N. Hoisington	1872	24
Williams, Mary O'Neil (Mrs. L. D.)	autobiography	1870	
Wilson, Annie Kirkham (Mrs. Aaron M.)	Mata E. Zimmerman	1870s	2
Wilson, Bessie Josephine Felton (Mrs. John W.)	autobiography	native (b. 1873)	
Wilson, Hattie Monfarte	autobiography	1869	12
Winslow, Anna J. Frazer (Mrs. Josiah W.)	unknown	1873	25
Witham, Lucy Cooly (Mrs. Jonathan)	Mrs. C. E. Barger (D)	1870	45
Wolcott, Arabella Geer (Mrs. Charles K.)	Grace G. Wolcott (D)	1872	24
Wolverton, Nancy Reed Root	unknown	1871	
Womer, Margaret Mitchell (Mrs. Sylvester)	autobiography	1874	18
Wood, Caroline Breese (Mrs. Stephen M.)	Carrie Breese Chandler (N)	1866	33
Wood, Elizabeth Hobart (Mrs. Sylvester)	Mabel Gray McNeice	1872	38
Wood, Margaret Lyon (Mrs. Samuel N.)	Bessie Wood (GD)	1854	24
Wood, Margaret Wilson (Mrs. William)	Mrs. Alvin Gates (D)	1871	37
Woodburn, Mary Roberts (Mrs. John A.)	Mrs. A. E. Crane (D)	1860	22
Wooden, Martha Elizabeth Lick (Mrs. William)	Martha Wooden King (D)	1878	45
Woods, Anne Cline	Idella Alderman Anderson	1855	1
Woodward, Elvira M. (Mrs. Addison A.)	autobiography		
Wooton, Sarah Hixon (Mrs. Andrew)	Ella Angel	1864	
Wright, Annie L. Norton (Mrs. George E.)	unknown		
Yeager, Catherine Rogler (Mrs. George W.)	Charles D. Yeager (SN)	1860	16
Young, Mary J. (Mrs. I. D.)	Grace G. Young (D)	1874	

SUBJECT	SOURCE	EMIGRATION DATE	AGE AT EMIGRATION
Zimmerman, Arabella C. Thomas (Mrs. Isiah)	Roberta Zimmerman (D)		
Zimmerman, Helen Stevens (Mrs. Will J.)	Mrs. George Marty (D) and Mary Alice Zimmerman (D)	1872	20
Zimmerman, Mary Alice Mallows (Mrs. Mark E.)	autobiography	native (b. 1868)	
Zimmerman, Mary Elizabeth Maynard (Mrs. John)	Mrs. R. H. Merrick	1855	4
Zimmerman, Phoebe Higgs Smiley (Mrs. B. F. G.)	Warren Zimmerman (SN)	1872	25

Bibliography

Adams, Ramon F. *Western Words: A Dictionary of the American West.* Norman, Okla.: University of Oklahoma Press, 1968.

Andreas, A. T. *History of the State of Kansas.* Chicago: A. T. Andreas, 1883.

Baughman, Robert W. *Kansas Post Offices.* Topeka, Kan.: The Kansas State Historical Society, 1961.

Billington, Ray Allen. *Westward Expansion: A History of the American Frontier*, 4th ed. New York: Macmillan Publishing Company, Inc., 1974.

Blackmar, Frank W., ed. *Kansas*, 2 vols. Chicago: Standard Publishing Company, 1912.

Brown, Dee. *The Gentle Tamers: Women of the Old Wild West.* New York: Putnam, 1958.

Brownlee, W. Elliot, and Brownlee, Mary M. *Women in the American Economy.* New Haven: Yale University Press, 1976.

Clark, Carroll D., and Roberts, Roy L. *People of Kansas.* Topeka, Kan.: The Kansas State Planning Board, 1936.

Clark, Thomas B. *Frontier America: The Story of the Westward Movement.* New York: Charles Scribner's Sons, 1959.

Connelley, William E. *A Standard History of Kansas and Kansans*, 5 vols. Chicago: Lewis Publishing Company, 1918.

Custer, George A. *My Life on the Plains*, edited by Milo Milton Quaife. New York: The Citadel Press, 1962.

Davis, Kenneth S. *Kansas: A Bicentennial History.* New York: W. W. Norton and Company, Inc., 1976.

Debo, Angie. *A History of the Indians of the United States.* Norman, Okla.: University of Oklahoma Press, 1970.

Dick, Everett. *The Sod House Frontier.* Lincoln, Neb.: Johnsen Publishing Company, 1954.

———. *Vanguards of the Frontier.* New York: D. Appleton-Century Company, Inc., 1941.

Drago, Harry Sinclair. *Great American Cattle Trails.* New York: Dodd, Mead and Company, 1965.

———. *Wild, Woolly and Wicked.* New York: Bramhall House, 1960.

Dykstra, Robert R. *The Cattle Towns.* New York: Alfred A. Knopf, Inc., 1968.

Foreman, Grant. *Indian Removal.* Norman, Okla.: University of Oklahoma Press, 1932.

Fowler, William W. *Woman on the American Frontier.* Hartford: S. S. Scranton and Company, 1882.

Hays Daily News, Centennial Edition, June 25, 1967.

Henry, Stuart. *Conquering Our Great American Plains.* New York: E. P. Dutton and Company, Inc., 1930.

Howes, Charles C. *This Place Called Kansas.* Norman, Okla.: University of Oklahoma Press, 1952.

Jones, Evan. *The Plains States.* New York: Time-Life Books, 1968.

Kansas Facts: A Year Book of the State. Topeka, Kan.: Charles P. Beebe, 1929.

Kansas Historical Collections, 17 vols. Topeka, Kan.: The Kansas State Historical Society, 1881–1928.

The Kansas Historical Quarterly, 43 vols. Topeka, Kan.: The Kansas State Historical Society, 1931–77.

Lamar, Howard R. *The Reader's Encyclopedia of the American West.* New York: Thomas Y. Crowell Company, 1977.

Larson, T. A. "Dolls, Vassals and Drudges—Pioneer Women in the West," *The Western Historical Quarterly,* Vol. 3, No 1 (January, 1972).

Lowie, Robert H. *Indians of the Plains.* New York; McGraw-Hill Book Company, Inc., 1954.

Miller, Nyle; Langsdorf, Edgar; and Richmond, Robert W. *Kansas in Newspapers.* Topeka, Kan.: The Kansas State Historical Society, 1963.

Miller, Raymond Curtis. "The Background of Populism in Kansas," *The Mississippi Valley of Historical Review,* Vol. 11 (1925), pp. 469–89.

Monaghan, Jay. *Civil War on the Western Border, 1854–1865.* Boston: Little, Brown and Company, 1955.

Muilenburg, Grace, and Swineford, Ada. *Land of the Post Rock.* Lawrence, Kan.: The University Press of Kansas, 1975.

Oringderff, Barbara. *True Sod.* North Newton, Kan.: Mennonite Press, Inc., 1976.

Paulson, Ross Evans, *Woman's Suffrage and Prohibition: A Comparative Study of Equality and Social Control.* Glenview, Ill.: Scott, Foresman and Company, 1973.

Richmond, Robert W. *Kansas: A Land of Contrasts.* St. Charles, Mo.: Forum Press, 1974.

Robinson, Sara T. L. *Kansas: Its Exterior and Interior Life.* Boston: Crosby, Nichols and Company, 1856.

Ross, Nancy Wilson. *Westward the Women.* New York: Random House, 1944.

Schmitt, Martin E., and Brown, Dee. *The Settlers' West.* New York: Ballantine Books, 1955.

Scott, Anne Firor. *The American Woman: Who Was She?* Englewood Cliffs, N.J.: Prentice-Hall, Inc., 1971.

Socolofsky, Homer E., and Self, Huber. *Historical Atlas of Kansas*. Norman, Okla.: University of Oklahoma Press, 1972.

Stanton, Elizabeth Cady; Anthony, Susan B.; and Gage, Matilda Joslyn. *History of Woman Suffrage*, Vol. 2. New York: Fowler and Wells Publishers, 1882.

Stevenson, Anna B. *A Sunflower Sheaf*. New York: The Exposition Press, 1946.

Tinkle, Lon, and Maxwell, Allen, editors. *The Cowboy Reader*. New York: David McKay Company, Inc., 1959.

Washburn, Wilcomb E. *The Indian in America*. New York: Harper and Row, Inc., 1975.

Webb, Walter Prescott. *The Great Plains*. New York: Grosset and Dunlap, 1931.

Whittemore, Margaret. *Historic Kansas: A Centenary Sketchbook*. Lawrence, Kan.: University of Kansas Press, 1954.

Wright, Louis B. *Life on the American Frontier*. New York: G. P. Putnam's Sons, 1971.

Zornow, William Frank. *Kansas: A History of the Jayhawk State*. Norman, Okla.: University of Oklahoma Press, 1957.

Index

About the Author

Joanna L. Stratton was born and raised in Washington, D.C., but considers Kansas and her family there as her second home. She began her work on *Pioneer Women* while attending Harvard College, from which she graduated with honors in 1976. She is currently pursuing graduate studies at Stanford University.

FRONTI

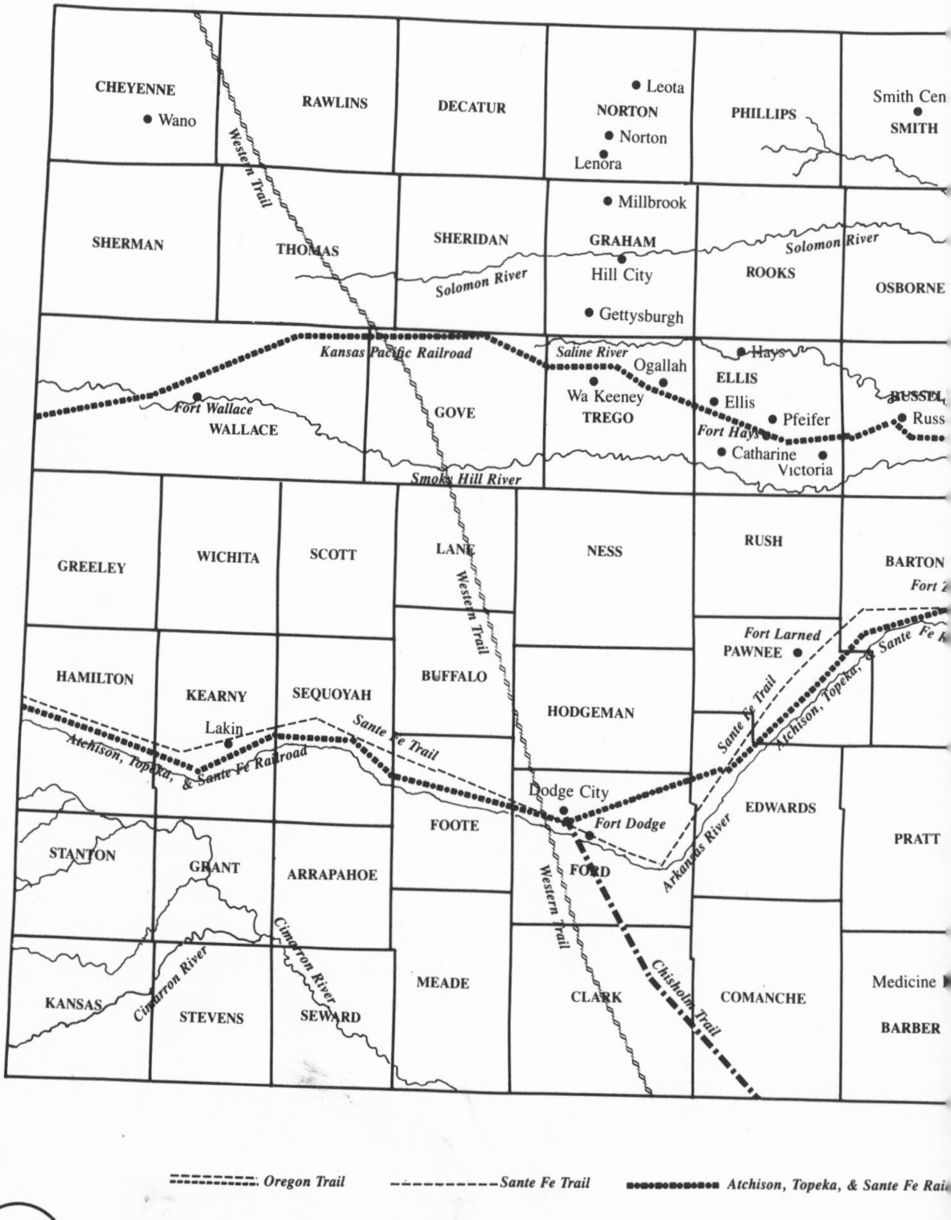

CHEYENNE
Wano
RAWLINS
DECATUR
Leota
NORTON
Norton
Lenora
PHILLIPS
Smith Cen
SMITH
Western Trail
SHERMAN
THOMAS
SHERIDAN
Millbrook
GRAHAM
Hill City
Gettysburgh
ROOKS
OSBORNE
Solomon River
Solomon River
Kansas Pacific Railroad
Saline River
Hays
Ogallah
ELLIS
Fort Wallace
WALLACE
GOVE
Wa Keeney
TREGO
Ellis
Pfeifer
RUSSELL
Russ
Fort Hays
Catharine
Victoria
Smoky Hill River
GREELEY
WICHITA
SCOTT
LANE
NESS
RUSH
BARTON
Fort
Western Trail
Fort Larned
PAWNEE
HAMILTON
KEARNY
SEQUOYAH
BUFFALO
HODGEMAN
Sante Fe Trail
Atchison, Topeka, & Sante Fe R
Lakin
Sante Fe Trail
Atchison, Topeka, & Sante Fe Railroad
Dodge City
Fort Dodge
EDWARDS
FOOTE
PRATT
STANTON
GRANT
ARRAPAHOE
FORD
Arkansas River
Western Trail
Cimarron River
KANSAS
Cimarron River
STEVENS
SEWARD
MEADE
CLARK
Chisholm Trail
COMANCHE
Medicine
BARBER

Oregon Trail
Sante Fe Trail
Atchison, Topeka, & Sante Fe Rai